WHAT IS WRITTEN REMAINS

What Is Written Remains

Historical Essays on the Libraries of Notre Dame

Edited by

Maureen Gleason and Katharina J. Blackstead

Published for the University Libraries of Notre Dame
by the University of Notre Dame Press

Notre Dame   London

Library of Congress Cataloging-in-Publication Data

What is written remains : historical essays on the libraries of Notre Dame
/ edited by Maureen Gleason and Katharina J. Blackstead.
   p. cm.
   ISBN 0-268-01949-5
   1. University of Notre Dame. Library--History. 2. Academic librar-
ies--Indiana--Notre Dame--History. I. Gleason, Maureen. II. Blackstead,
Katharina J.
   Z733.U865W48 1994
   027.7772'89--dc20   93-40670
                                                         CIP

Contents

Contributors

Charlotte Ames is American Catholic studies bibliographer at the University Libraries of Notre Dame.

Laura Bayard is head of the Catalog and Database Maintenance Section, Cataloging Department, at the University Libraries of Notre Dame.

Katharina J. Blackstead is library advancement officer at the University Libraries of Notre Dame.

Theodore J. Cachey, Jr. is associate professor, Department of Romance Languages and Literatures at the University of Notre Dame.

Christian Dupont is a graduate student in the Department of Theology, University of Notre Dame.

Laura Fuderer is rare books librarian at the University Libraries of Notre Dame.

Maureen Gleason is deputy director of the University Libraries of Notre Dame.

Philip Gleason is professor of history at the University of Notre Dame.

Robert J. Havlik is engineering librarian *emeritus* at the University Libraries of Notre Dame.

Stephen M. Hayes is documents librarian at the University Libraries of Notre Dame.

Louis Jordan is head of the Department of Special Collections at the University Libraries of Notre Dame.

Sophia K. Jordan is head of the Preservation Department at the University Libraries of Notre Dame.

Anne Kearney is assistant professor of history, Jefferson Community College, Louisville, Kentucky.

Alan D. Krieger is theology and philosophy bibliographer at the University Libraries of Notre Dame.

Robert C. Miller is director of libraries at the University of Notre Dame.

Marina Smyth is Medieval Institute librarian at the University Libraries of Notre Dame.

Marsha Stevenson is head of the Reference Department at the University Libraries of Notre Dame.

Rafael E. Tarrago is Latin American studies, government and international studies bibliographer at the University Libraries of Notre Dame.

Acknowledgements

The editors want to express their appreciation to all those who helped to bring this volume into being. Besides the contributors who managed to meet deadlines despite very full schedules, we want to thank the staffs of the University Libraries' Special Collections Department, the University Archives, and the Provincial Archives. These individuals provided knowledgeable guidance to their collections, and were patient with a sudden descent of researchers requiring access to their files. Invaluable assistance was also provided by Melodie Eiteljorge, special assistant to the director of libraries, whose computer expertise and sharp eye for details of grammar and spelling contributed much to the final form of the book.

We are most grateful to the members of the Advisory Council for University Libraries, without whose enthusiasm and support this publication would not have been possible. And finally, to Director of Libraries Robert C. Miller, a special tribute. He not only provided the initial spark for the book, but his confidence and encouragement kept us going to the end.

Abbreviations

The following abbreviations will be used throughout the book for frequently cited sources:

AR, followed by fiscal year: University of Notre Dame Library. "Annual Report."

Bulletin, **UND**, followed by date: University of Notre Dame. *Bulletin of the University of Notre Dame* (Notre Dame, Ind.: University Press, 1905–1946), and University of Notre Dame. *Bulletin of Information.* (Notre Dame, Ind.: The University, 1946–   ).

Catalogue, **UND**, followed by date: University of Notre Dame. *Catalogue of the University of Notre Dame* (Notre Dame, University Press, 1898–1904).

ULND: University Libraries of Notre Dame.

UNDA, accompanied by Archives' code when applicable: University of Notre Dame Archives.

Walter: Frank Keller Walter, "Report of a Survey of the University of Notre Dame Library" (Notre Dame, Ind., 1920).

Wilson/Lundy: Louis R. Wilson and Frank A. Lundy, *Report of a Survey of the Library of the University of Notre Dame for the University of Notre Dame, November 1950–March 1952* (Chicago: American Library Association, 1952).

Introduction

During the academic year 1993-94 the University Libraries of Notre Dame are celebrating the acquisition of their two-millionth volume. It is a fitting time to recall the people, events, and achievements that brought the libraries from a few hundred books in a room in the University's Main Building to the almost two million in the fourteen-story Hesburgh Library, whose thirtieth birthday we are also commemorating.

Those writing the history of universities often neglect their libraries; mistakenly so, since the history of the library contributes to an understanding of its parent institution. The circumstances of the library's founding and subsequent development often reflect the vision and values of the university's leaders. Library collecting practices are affected by curricular and research emphases. The evolution of the campus physical environment can be seen in the location and design of library buildings. The ebb and flow of a university's financial fortunes, as well as its fundraising success, can be traced in its support for the library.

In many such ways the past of the Notre Dame Libraries illuminates the history of the University, but accounts of that past have been scarce and often sketchy. The essays collected here are a start at remedying this deficiency, but the University Libraries' story is of more than local significance. One can see in it indicators of trends in scholarship and in academic library practice. It is a story worth telling and a lasting memorial of the libraries' year of celebration.

This volume does not attempt to present a systematic and comprehensive account of the libraries' history. It is, rather, a collection of essays, each highlighting a significant aspect of the libraries' character and development. Since the Notre Dame Library had only

1

two directors during its first 50 years the spirit and work of these two men established the foundation on which later developments built. Hence, James E. Edwards, the nineteenth-century collector, and the Reverend Paul J. Foik, C.S.C., the twentieth-century organizer, deserve and receive special attention here. The formation of the collection, both by intention and by circumstance, is narrated in another essay. Descriptions of Notre Dame's special collections are of particular interest to book lovers, since these are the treasures that make each library unique. In the case of Notre Dame, the contributions of John A. Zahm, C.S.C., book collector, are striking. American Catholic materials in the libraries and archives are the subject of a chapter which records the growth of a research collection of distinction. Distinguished as well is Notre Dame's collection of medieval sources, and another chapter describes its formation. Sports and Notre Dame have long been associated and we have not ignored the genesis of the libraries' sports research collection.

The account presented here of the two library buildings built at Notre Dame in the twentieth century reveals, of course, beliefs about library architecture that influenced the very different designs of each, but, beyond that, it also uncovers other forces at work within the University at the time of their construction.

In bringing to light forgotten connections of the Notre Dame Libraries with issues in the larger world, the essays deepen our understanding of history. Two examples would be the maneuvering of Father Sorin with Congressman Schuyler Colfax to establish our U.S. documents collection; and the participation of several individuals connected to Notre Dame in the effort to develop a classification system intellectually appropriate for Catholic theology collections. Finally, a narrative of how automation came to the Notre Dame Libraries brings up to date the story that officially began 120 years ago.

A chronology compiled by Robert C. Miller provides a concise guide through those years, citing events which significantly affected or reflected the development of the libraries at Notre Dame. The chronology is divided into four periods based on the changing nature of the libraries as they responded to their environment: Collegiate Years, from 1842 to 1916; University Library era, from 1917 to 1962; Research Library period, from 1963 to 1975; and the present era, beginning in 1976 and labelled Technology and the Research Library. The principal sources for the information presented are listed in a bibliography at the end of the chronology.

The contributors to the volume are all persons with a close relationship to the University Libraries. Most are librarians but among them are also faculty members, former staff, and students. Their enthusiasm has grown as the formerly obscure past of the institution they know has taken shape before their eyes.

In a time when change sometimes seems to overwhelm us, we intend that this attempt to capture the past of the libraries will not only stimulate its further analysis but will also provide the foundation for fruitful reflection on the libraries' future.

———————————————————

Notre Dame Library Collections of the Nineteenth Century: the Legacy of the Fire of 1879

The story of library collection growth at Notre Dame during the nineteenth century is really two stories: one marked by halting beginnings until the late 1860s, followed by steady growth through the next decade; the other, a tale of remarkably rapid recovery and growth following the virtual destruction of the University by fire on April 23, 1879. Accordingly, the narrative of this chapter will naturally divide into two parts, with the second being dominated by the man whose tireless work and devotion to library collection growth was clearly the greatest single factor in rebuilding the collection: Library Director and Professor James F. Edwards.

The earliest libraries at Notre Dame were apparently those of a number of literary and religious societies; for example, the Silver Jubilee history volume of 1869 tells us that the archconfraternity, devoted to the Blessed Virgin Mary and dating back to 1845, "possesses a good religious library."[1] The same source also takes note of libraries associated with the St. Aloysius Philodemic Society (organized in 1851) and the St. Edward's Literary and Historic Society.

As early as the 1865–66 academic year, the *Annual Catalogue* of the University notes that the institution "possesses a valuable library of about seven thousand volumes";[2] this may be the first mention of the College Library, which in the Silver Jubilee volume is described as holding 7,000 volumes and as having been first formed "by bringing

4

together private libraries, obtained through donation or purchase." The account goes on to list among its holdings 17 different encyclopedias, 145 volumes comprising the complete works of the Fathers of the Church, numerous classical authors in a variety of languages, and the *Dublin Review*.[3] The librarian at that time was the Rev. J. C. Carrier, who is listed as such for the first time in the *Annual Catalogue* of 1866–67, and who apparently significantly enhanced the collection through a trip to France in the spring of 1866, where he procured instruments for the cabinet of physics, chemicals for the laboratory, and objects of natural history for the museum, as well as books for the library. The result of his labors was that 20 large boxes were sent from Paris to Notre Dame, which included "a collection of two hundred volumes presented by the French government."[4] This library, which was in the central portion of the pre-fire Main Building,[5] grew principally through donations, as the *Notre Dame Scholastic* of October 2, 1869 frankly notes:

Our Library is far from complete, and at the present rate of increase it will take many years to make it what it ought to be. The authorities of the University can only afford a moderate sum yearly towards its completion; donations will therefore be thankfully received, and the benefactors of our Library may trust that their names will be faithfully recorded in its archives.[6]

By May of 1870, the size of the College Library collection had grown to 10,000 volumes,[7] and the *Scholastic* through the decade contains acknowledgements for such gifts as a collection of Civil War maps and a four-volume *Geological Survey of Indiana*.[8]

Yet there was trouble brewing. The *Scholastic* of November 4, 1876 complains:

Where is the College Library going, or rather where has it gone? Is it approaching its end? It is a real pity and shame that it is reduced to the state in which we now find it. After an existence of many years, notwithstanding that additions are made to it yearly, it remains with the same number of volumes (perhaps a few less), at the end of the year, that were on the shelves in the beginning. Books are carried off, never to be returned...Three years ago, Rev. J. C. Carrier, then Librarian, had the Library in good condition, such as it will not be again for years, if ever, should the books be carried away as they

5

have been. The shelves of the Library then contained somewhere near ten thousand volumes. We certainly can safely say that there are not that number of books now.[9]

The writer then announces that in an attempt to curb this rampant theft problem, henceforth no one will be allowed to enter the library without the librarian present.[10] The scope of the problem might appear surprising in that the first Circulating Library (which will be discussed shortly) had been in operation for several years, but clearly it concerned the administration sufficiently to warrant a major article in the *Scholastic* and a proposed solution.

It seems likely that the problem at least receded in importance since, as we shall see, the College Library survived into the 1880s; indeed, in October 1879, a mere six months after the fire, the *Scholastic* noted that at Notre Dame there were "two distinct libraries—one for the special use of the students, and conducted by them under the name of the Lemonnier Library Association; the other is the Community or College Library, presided over by the Rev. Father Stoffel, C.S.C."[11]

The idea of a special lending library for students was one of the great legacies of the fourth president of the University, the Rev. Augustus Lemonnier, and "with a keen eye for choosing the right man for the right position, Father Lemonnier, before his death, appointed Professor James F. Edwards to take charge."[12] "Jimmie," as he was affectionately called, is perhaps better known as the founder of the Notre Dame Archives and Bishops' Memorial Hall; indeed, he is truly the founder of American Catholic archival activity. But his role as archivist will be covered in another chapter; our immediate task is to examine his role as director of the Lemonnier Library, a position he held until his death in January 1911.

Edwards, a native of Toledo and the son of Irish immigrants, came to Notre Dame at the age of nine as a minim and entered the Senior Department in 1866; it was probably at this point that Lemonnier began to exert a major influence on the young man. He became a candidate for the priesthood in 1871, but his "delicate health could not keep pace with his religious zeal"[13] and he was forced to return home to Toledo. But by September 1872, Edwards was back at Notre Dame as an assistant professor of rhetoric and Latin, while he also continued to pursue his Bachelor of Law degree. Already known as an archival collector and for his ability to make friends,[14] Edwards seemed to be the natural choice for directing the new Circulating Library and Lemonnier "gradually turned over the responsibility of the project to him."[15]

While the Golden Jubilee volume dates Lemonnier's conception of the plan for a students' circulating library to 1873, and Edwards' taking charge of same to 1874,[16] a close examination of the *Scholastic* shows that these dates should probably be established as 1872 and 1873 respectively. The "library movement" proposed by Lemonnier to institute a circulating library is first mentioned in the October 12, 1872 issue of the *Scholastic* [17] and a library of "three hundred volumes of the choicest selections, made by competent hands from amongst the best authors" was in place by November 1872.[18] Although "a merger of various club and society libraries may have assisted in the establishment of this library,"[19] it seems clear that membership fees and donations were driving collection growth from an early date. The $1.00 student fee was specified in the *Scholastic* issue of January 25, 1873; the June 28 issue makes clear that this fee was for a single school session.[20] Meanwhile, during the same school year, the Circulating Library Society thanked its director, Lemonnier, for his "many elegant donations to our Library, including the works of Shakespeare."[21] Edwards had clearly taken charge of the library by the fall of 1873, as the *Scholastic* directs those interested in procuring books from the Circulating Library to him.[22]

While student fees undoubtedly played an important role in the early growth of the library, the fact that Edwards had a talent for "making friends readily" and that the "appreciation of grateful parents and the affection of former students were shown by contributions given to him either in the form of books or money for the library"[23] was a pivotal element in the library's steady growth through the 1870s.

Before turning to that development, let us briefly glimpse the Circulating Library collection as it existed during that first year of 1872–73. Among Edwards' papers in the Notre Dame archives is a printed *Catalogue of the Circulating Library*, 24 pages long, arranged by author and title, and listing approximately 900 volumes. The early circulating collection at Notre Dame was virtually all English-language and emphasized history (especially church history), literature and biography. It featured, for example, a thirteen-volume edition of Gibbon's *History of Rome*; four works by Macaulay, including a two-volume *History of England*; Butler's *Lives of the Saints*; a *Catechism of Scripture History*; an *Ecclesiastical History*, probably that of Eusebius; excellent collections of works by James Fenimore Cooper (31 titles), Washington Irving (17 titles), Sir Walter Scott (16 titles), and William Thackeray (17 titles); and there are over 60 titles beginning with "Life" or "Lives." Interestingly, at this early date there were very few titles in the natural sciences, with the exception of a few volumes featuring coastal and geological surveys.[24]

The library grew steadily through the decade, and the *Scholastic*, particularly in the first few years, proudly chronicled this growth and encouraged the students' use of the library. At the beginning of the 1873–74 school year, there appeared this notice:

> The Circulating Library is now ready for use with its thousand well-selected volumes. It will afford to the students a very fine opportunity of employing usefully their leisure time by perusing books. Catalogues will be given to all subscribers, so that they can choose the books they wish to read. We do not think that any expense or trouble has been spared to give to our Circulating Library its proper place among our other institutions here. All fair-minded persons will easily see that much more good can be accomplished for all by a well-equipped and well-managed concern, than by half a dozen smaller libraries which were doing good only to very few.[25]

The statement then goes on to specify that the $1.00 per session fee remains in force for non-students and "non-members" of literary or religious societies; members of same are to be charged only $.50.[26] The library must have been popular with students from the beginning; a December 1873 *Scholastic* notice chided those who kept books out longer than the apparently official loan period of two weeks.[27] By January of 1874, the library held 1,250 volumes,[28] and by October of that year the total was up to 1,600.[29] Lemonnier died in the summer of 1874 and the November 28, 1874 issue of the *Scholastic* announced that "the name of the Circulating Library has been changed to the 'Lemonnier Circulating Library,' in honor of the late Father Lemonnier, who was its founder."[30] The editorial tone of the *Scholastic* during these years struck a decidedly moral chord in encouraging the use of the library:

In order to furnish good reading cheaply, nothing can be better than a well-conducted circulating library. When the books are well-selected, parents have no fear of their children reading books which would be hurtful to them. Such is the case with the Lemonnier Circulating Library here at Notre Dame. The books have been selected with great care; most of them are standard works. No book is allowed in the library which contains anything injurious to either morals or religion. The consequence is that the collection of books is select and valuable, and all persons who can should become members of the Association.[31]

A semi-annual "report of the Librarian" summarized in the February 6, 1875 issue of the *Scholastic* reports a library volume count of 1,809, with $160.00 received from members; during the previous five months, "181 volumes were purchased for $120.45, besides Zell's *Encyclopedia* (two vols.), $33.75." In that period, 183 volumes were purchased and 36 volumes donated.[32] A similar report issued a year later (for the previous session) reveals similar expenditures, but a marked upturn in donations; 204 books purchased and 158 "presented."[33] In line with these figures, the *Scholastic* of February 26, 1876 was able to boast that the library now contains "about three thousand well-selected volumes. About five hundred dollars are spent annually in the purchase of books, which are for the use of the students of the College. It contains complete sets of the *Edinburgh Review, Blackwood's Magazine,* the *Atlantic Monthly,* the *Catholic World,* besides most of the standard works on history, biography, travels, poetry, etc., etc."[34] This article, incidentally, in listing library resources at Notre Dame, mentions an Ave Maria Library, apparently for the use of the editor of that magazine; it contained standard works in philosophy, theology, and ecclesiastical history, as well as sets of the principal reviews and magazines. There is little mention of this facility elsewhere in the pages of the *Scholastic* either before or after the fire and it seems doubtful that it was intended for widespread student use.

By November of 1877, the Lemonnier Library collection was approaching 5,000 volumes[35] and as the decade drew to a close it seems clear that great progress was being made. There were regular "books received" lists appearing in the *Scholastic* and important titles were being added on a regular basis, including volumes from the *Ante-Nicene Christian Library*[36] and *Sadlier's Catholic Almanac,* as well as the

Works of Charles Dickens in 15 volumes, Charlotte Bronte's *Jane Eyre*,[37] and Ranke's *History of the Popes*.[38]

It is also clear that Edwards' talent for attracting donations, so crucial to collection-building after the fire, was already proving to be a crucial asset for the fledgling library. Grateful acknowledgements for donations received routinely graced the pages of the *Scholastic*. Typical is the following notice:

> The members of the Students' Circulating Library return their sincere thanks to Thos. Ewing, A. M. of Lancaster, Ohio, for a generous donation of fifty volumes of choice reading—consisting of books of fiction, travel and biography.
> J.F. Edwards, Librarian.[39]

If the donations involved particularly important titles, Edwards would often publicly acknowledge both the donor and the work or works; it is noted, for example, that "Rev. Father Oster, of Vincennes, has the thanks of the Librarian of the Lemonnier Library for 'Alberti Magni Paradisus Animae,' Antwerp, 1565, a precious relic of the saintly Bishop Bruté, enriched with his autograph and many marginal notes."[40] Similarly, Edwards acknowledges a "magnificent donation" by the Rev. Arthur P. Haviland of Philadelphia of a "great number of Catholic papers," including the *London Tablet, Catholic Standard, Boston Pilot, Pittsburgh Catholic, Irish-American, New York Tablet, Dublin Nation, Catholic Mirror*, and others [41] not quite a year, we may note poignantly, before the fire. Edwards would even name shelves in the library after particularly generous donors,[42] and it is instructive that several of these, such as W. J. Onahan of Chicago, would be of great importance in rebuilding the collection following the catastrophe to come.

The fire which struck the University on April 23, 1879 virtually wiped out its library resources; yet within weeks both the College Library and the Lemonnier Library were rising from the ashes, mainly through the tremendous generosity shown by a variety of donors. Edwards' industry in attracting important gifts for the Circulating Library would prove crucial in the years to come, but in the immediate aftermath of the fire there seems to have been an explosive outpouring of support for both libraries as their friends became aware of what had happened. Thus, before turning to the collecting methods employed by Edwards from the mid-1880s onward, a chronology of the libraries' rapid growth to the end of the century would seem to be instructive in gaining an understanding of the cumulative effect of both donor generosity and Edwards' efforts.

An appeal for donations to the College Library was issued in the *Scholastic* of July 12, 1879 [43] and, perhaps inspired by "the heroic exertions of devoted students" in saving a number of books from the fire,[44] a number of interested parties responded swiftly. The Rev. Cooney, C.S.C., donated his entire 1,500-volume library, mainly in the areas of Catholic theology and history, while Col. W. Anderson of Circleville, Ohio gave over 100 volumes, including works by Fenelon and Bossuet. Meanwhile, major Catholic publishers of the period were proving helpful as well; John Murphy & Co. of Baltimore contributed 200 bound volumes of their publications and Benziger Brothers of New York sent numerous volumes, including lives of Popes Pius IX and Leo XIII.[45] By the time the *Annual Catalogue* for 1879–80 was issued, there were already 6,000 volumes in the College Library [46] and 1,000 more were added in the next year. As late as 1883, money donations apparently were still being received; in the spring of that year, "a generous friend" sent through the Rev. Daniel Hudson, editor of the *Ave Maria*, a check for $100.[47] At some point around this time, the holdings of the College Library were apparently integrated into the circulating collection; a later issue of the *Scholastic* dates the merger of what by then was known as the Faculty Library into the Lemonnier collection to 1882, although the accuracy of that date, given the local donation just cited, seems to be questionable.[48]

The response to the crisis faced by the Lemonnier Circulating Library was no less stunning. Only one month after the fire it could be said that "scarcely a week passed without the presentation of one or more volumes, and often whole sets of the most elegant and valuable books." Mr. Onahan of Chicago, whom we have already met, had at this point already sent 100 volumes of "choice literature," while the editor of the *Ave Maria* contributed his set of the *Dublin Review* and Edward Flynn, a bookbinder from Kalamazoo, Michigan, sent a complete set of *Scribner's Magazine*.[49] Within two months of the fire, the circulating library numbered 1,000 volumes[50] and donations continued to flow in that summer; one September issue of the *Scholastic* lists 11 donors and over 50 titles.[51] The Rev. Haviland proved to be as valuable a donor after the fire as he was before, presenting "five large packages containing complete volumes of Catholic newspapers and magazines."[52] The *Annual Catalogue* for 1879–80 reports that the Lemonnier Circulating Library, now temporarily located in the Columbian Society Hall, holds over 3,200 "choice English works."[53]

The enthusiastic response of Lemonnier Library donors continued during 1880. The Catholic bookseller Peter F. Cunningham presented over 20 volumes, while the Catholic publisher Sadlier & Co. also contributed significantly,[54] including the four-volume edition of Cardinal Manning's *Select Works.* Among individuals, Cardinal John Henry Newman sent word from the Oratory in England that he would be willing to send "half a dozen of his volumes to the librarian if he would be kind enough to choose them."[55] Edward Forrester presented, through Jacob Wile of Laporte, a complete set of the *Metropolitan*, a monthly magazine "devoted to Religion, Education, Literature, and General Information," while his sister, Miss Lavina Forrester, donated Gibbon's *The History of the Decline and Fall of the Roman Empire*, with notes by the Rev. H. H. Milman.[56]

While much of this giving undoubtedly represented spontaneous acts of generosity, it is also true that in the year after the fire the *Scholastic* published detailed lists of donors on a regular basis and more than once explicitly called for donations; over time, it must be assumed, this effort, too, had an effect. In fact, in May 1880, after listing some of the significant donors of the last year, it issued the following reminder:

> The gentlemen above alluded to have done their duty in their regard...now to a number of others, who could have done a little in this way, what have we to say? Well, the truth is we cannot say much—we only say: contribute a little towards replacing the libraries of Notre Dame, and by it you won't lose anything...Charity covereth a multitude of sins; and since this is the case, why are we so slow in doing a good turn, in assisting a most noble cause—the education of our youth?[57]

It must have been clear to many at the University that the relatively limited income provided by membership fees simply would not allow a library essentially starting from scratch to develop an adequate collection; fortunately donor response continued to be strong in the years ahead.

The University's 1880–81 catalog had noted that a reading room with many of the day's leading periodicals (*Appleton's Journal, Atlantic Monthly, Lippincott's Magazine, Harper's Magazine*, etc.) was connected with the College Library; apparently, University authorities were satisfied with the Lemonnier Library's recovery during the next year because the reading room was connected with the latter facility in the catalog of 1881–82.[58] This development would appear to predate two important milestones occurring in the progress of the Lemonnier Library in the fall of 1882: the University's first budget appropriation for the library ($500) [59] and the move of the library into the University's Main Building and "a large Gothic apartment, 130 feet in length by 50 in width, with a vaulted ceiling, having an average height of 30 feet." The floor is lined with tables and reading desks, and the *Scholastic* describes the workmanship displayed throughout the library as "superb," giving much credit to Edwards, "to whose untiring zeal and activity the happy and perfect completion of the work must be attributed."[60]

By now, the library had passed the 16,000 volume mark, but donor contributions continued to be impressive throughout the decade. In the spring of 1883, noted American Catholic historian John Gilmary Shea presented 24 titles, including a number of works detailing French explorations and missions in the New World and Shea's own *A Bibliographical Account of Catholic Bibles, Testaments, and other Portions of Scripture, Translated from the Latin Vulgate and Printed in the United States*.[61] Two years later, we find Mr. Onahan cited for another fine donation, his fourth since the fire;[62] later he would be acknowledged as the donor of the important five-volume *The National Manuscripts of Ireland*, which featured facsimiles of the most significant early illuminated books, including the *Book of Kells*.[63] In the spring of 1888 Edwards gratefully acknowledges receiving from Vice President Zahm "a large and valuable collection of books relating to the history, religion and topography of Alaska, Mexico, and the Sandwich Islands." By this time, one can sense that the urgency which accompanied early collection-building efforts immediately after the fire has dissipated to some extent; Edwards describes Zahm's contribution as "a valuable addition to our already well furnished library."[64] Even as the library approached mid-decade, the *Scholastic* can proudly state that it holds *An Address to the Roman Catholics of America* by Bishop

Carroll of Baltimore, "the first Catholic book published in America by an American author."[65]

This remarkable progress in the development of the Lemonnier Library's collection is also reflected in the volume counts of the period; from 16,000 volumes in 1881–82, the count jumped to 26,000 by 1886,[66] 40,000 by 1890,[67] and 55,000 by the turn of the century.[68] While these figures certainly lagged behind those of the major private institutions in the East, they represent remarkable progress over a 20-year period.

Even by 1890, it is clear that the tone of urgency which characterized the *Scholastic's* entries on the library in the weeks and months after the fire has given way to a genuine pride in the facility now available to the student body:

> It is doubtful if there is any college west of the Alleghenies with a library more extensive than that of Notre Dame; and, certainly, few colleges have a more complete or better selected assortment of books of reference.
>
> This is particularly noteworthy when one considers that the present library has been collected almost wholly within the past ten years, and that only recently has the librarian had any means of procuring books other than through donation.

This sketch of the library goes on to give the reader a kind of verbal tour of the place, and there is no mistaking the positive tone of the piece:

> As you enter the door and turn to the right, you come first upon the Latin classics of which there are 600 or more; next to this is the Department of Philosophy, containing the complete works of St. Thomas Aquinas and many of the writings of the Fathers of the Church in the original Latin; in this department there are about 5000 volumes. Next in order is the department of biography with 600 volumes; English and American Poetry, 700 volumes; Essays and Treatises, including the complete works of St. Augustine, 500 volumes.
>
> But it is on her historical library that Notre Dame particularly prides herself. This department has received the especial care of the librarian, who is also the Professor of History, and now contains

between 3000 and 4000 volumes, embracing all the standard histories and also a number of supplemental works on historical subjects.

The article also profiles other aspects of the collection at that time; we find out that it featured 3,000 bound magazines, 1,000 volumes of bound newspapers, 1,000 volumes on general and American literature, and about 500 scientific works. In addition, there was a 2,500-volume reference collection containing "all the standard encyclopedias and reference books" and, in terms of language, the library offered 10,000 volumes in the French language, 300 in German, and 200 each in Spanish and Italian.[69]

As the 1880s wore on and the memory of the fire receded, it is understandable that the number of library donations being received by the University (at least as recorded in the pages of the *Scholastic*) was steadily declining. But Edwards seems to have become more aggressive in his collecting approaches during the last decade and a half of the century, both in terms of buying materials and soliciting gifts; we now turn to an examination of some of these strategies.

There can be no doubt that throughout Edwards' long directorship, collection development must have been primarily gift-driven. The amount of the University appropriation begun in 1882 could not possibly address the vast collection needs of the immediate post-fire era. Indeed, we find that the *Bulletin* of the University, in a section entitled "Needs of the University," made annual appeals for a library endowment well into the first decade of the twentieth century by bluntly noting that "there is no Library fund for the purchase of new books."[70] But Edwards did what he could, establishing a close working relationship with a number of mostly Catholic publishers and booksellers. Edwards' papers are replete with publisher notices from such firms as A.C. McClurg, Open Court, and Daniel McKenna; a list of price quotations from McClurg dated October 22, 1903 lists 28 titles in the areas of French and German literature, church history, and philosophy.[71] The librarian also seems to have been able to establish discount arrangements at times. A 1909 invoice from McClurg lists 19 titles with discounts ranging up to 25 percent.[72]

Edwards was also extremely skilled at ferreting out potentially valuable gifts for the library. McAvoy's reproduction of a portion of a diary that Edwards kept during a trip to the East in the summer of 1888,

15

published in *Catholic Historical Review* in 1952, demonstrates this talent repeatedly. The journey took the librarian and his artist friend Paul Wood to New York, Philadelphia, and Baltimore and was chiefly intended to give the pair a chance to copy portraits of prelates of these cities for the Bishops' Memorial Hall. But along the way, Edwards found numerous opportunities to secure important additions to the library. During his stay in New York, he travelled to Jersey City and on July 11 dined with Monsignor Robert Seton. He was shown many rare books and the Monsignor "partly promised to will his books to Notre Dame";[73] years later, the *Scholastic* announced that he had already given his library to the University before moving to Rome.[74] On July 15, he visited Dr. John Gilmary Shea and records that:

> Dr. Shea gave me the manuscript of the second volume of his Hist. of Catholicity in the U.S. Intended to give me the first but could not find it, promised to send it with some books. Wen[t] to the garret of his house to rummage around among his papers, and books.[75]

In Philadelphia, he called on his friend Mrs. Robbins, the sister of Bishop Francis Gartland, who gave him several books and pamphlets, and the next day he received several pictures and pamphlets from the Financial Secretary of the Archdiocese.[76] His trip to Baltimore seems to have been particularly productive. The evening of July 24 found him at the Cardinal's residence, where he found several newspapers and pamphlets to his liking; he reports that the Cardinal had previously given him permission to take anything he could find that would be of use. On the 27th, he went to Loyola College, where he found a number of bound volumes of Catholic newspapers which he hoped to ultimately acquire "in exchange for other books." Finally, on the 31st, he visited the office of the *Mirror*, where the editor referred him to a woman named Mrs. Goldborough for back numbers of that publication; he subsequently received "many complete volumes from her."[77]

The following year, Edwards took a trip to Europe and the *Scholastic* reports that in Rome Pope Leo XIII himself presented Edwards with a special edition of his poems, while the Vatican's Papal Historian offered him a volume described only as an "interesting book on the history of the Papacy."[78]

It seems likely that Edwards' affable nature won him not only friends, but often library additions as well, whenever he travelled.

Among his papers is a letter dated April 20, 1889 from a representative of the firm of Van Antwerp, Bragg & Co. Publishers of Cincinnati, who writes:

My Dear Professor,
I am almost ashamed of myself, but I have actually forgotten all about the promise I made you some months ago when I met you on the train. It has just occurred to me that I have never sent you the promised copies of the New Eclectic Geographies, and I hasten to forward them to you by express prepaid today, via South Bend. Please accept them with my compliments.[79]

In looking at Edwards' diary of his trip to the East, we see that he was open to the idea of establishing exchange agreements; his papers furnish other examples of this collection strategy. An 1890 letter from the librarian of the American Catholic Historical Society of Philadelphia proposed exchanging various numbers of *Brownson's Review*,[80] and 20 years later, less than a year before Edwards' death, the new librarian at the Society reaffirmed his desire for "co-operative relations."[81] It is not difficult to see how, given the ever growing network of Edwards' friends who shared his interests, exchange agreements would have emerged as an important strategy in filling gaps in the library's collection.

As Edwards' tenure as director drew to a close, the Lemonnier Library still contained less than 100,000 volumes[82] and there is no doubt that Notre Dame still lagged behind some of the larger private institutions in the east in sheer collection size. But it is also equally clear that Edwards' dedication to improving the library, coupled with the remarkable response of numerous friends of the University to the losses incurred by the fire of 1879, provided remarkable progress in rebuilding the collection in a relatively short amount of time. When Edwards died in 1911, he not only left a library that featured a solid collection of "standard works" and some important rarities; he had laid the foundation for more dramatic collection improvements to come.

1. Joseph A. Lyons, comp., *Silver Jubilee of the University of Notre Dame, June 23, 1869*, 2d ed. (Chicago: E. B. Myers, 1869), 58.

2. *Twenty-second Annual Catalogue of the Officers and Students of the University of Notre Dame* (Notre Dame, Ind., 1866), 6.

3. *Silver Jubilee*, 71–72.

4. *A Brief History of the University of Notre Dame Du Lac, Indiana, from 1842 to 1892, Prepared For the Golden Jubilee* (Chicago: Werner, n.d.), 120.

5. *Catalogue*, UND, 24th: 10.

6. *Notre Dame Scholastic* 3 (1869–70): 14.

7. Ibid., 4 (1870–71): 142.

8. Ibid., 12 (1878–79): 32, 110.

9. Ibid., 10 (1876–77): 136–137.

10. The Rev. John A. Zahm was apparently College librarian from 1874 to 1876; the Notre Dame *Catalogues* during these two academic years list him as "librarian." The Rev. Francis C. Bigelow replaced him for the 1876–77 year and, shortly thereafter, the Rev. Nicholas J. Stoffel took over.

11. *Notre Dame Scholastic* 13 (1879–80): 74.

12. Arthur J. Hope, *Notre Dame, One Hundred Years*, Rev. ed. (South Bend, Ind.: Icarus Press, 1978), 222.

13. Damien Tambola, *James F. Edwards, Pioneer Archivist of Catholic Church History of America* (Philadelphia: American Catholic Historical Society of Philadelphia, 1961), 4.

14. Ibid., 3.

15. Ibid., 4.

16. *Golden Jubilee*, 199.

17. *Scholastic* 6 (1872–73): 36.

18. Ibid., 70.

19. John Federowicz, "Forces Affecting the Development of Libraries at the University of Notre Dame, 1843–1968" (Master's thesis, Kent State University, 1968), 4.

20. *Scholastic* 6 (1872–73): 158, 341.

21. Ibid., 171.

22. Ibid., 7 (1873–74): 55.

23. Tambola, 5.

24. James F. Edwards, Papers, [CEDW 27/13], UNDA.

25. *Scholastic* 7 (1873–74): 36.

26. Ibid.

27. Ibid., 118.

28. Ibid., 156.

29. Ibid., 29.

30. Ibid., 122.

31. Ibid., 200.

32. Ibid., 8 (1874–75): 283.
33. Ibid., 9 (1875–76): 362.
34. Ibid., 410.
35. Ibid., 11 (1877–78): 154.
36. Ibid., 9 (1875–76): 171.
37. Ibid., 10 (1876–77): 363.
38. Ibid., 219.
39. Ibid., 7 (1873–74): 317.
40. Ibid., 12 (1878–79): 111.
41. Ibid., 11 (1877–78): 635.
42. Ibid., 10 (1876–77): 27.
43. Ibid., 12 (1878–79): 692.
44. Ibid., 13 (1879–80): 43
45. See the following *Scholastic* issues: 13 (1879–80): 409, 505–506, 489–490, 569–570.
46. *Catalogue*, UND, 36th: 45.
47. *Scholastic* 16 (1882–83): 424
48. Ibid., 23 (1889–90): 630.
49. Ibid., 12 (1878–79): 578.
50. Ibid., 641.
51. Ibid., 13 (1879–80): 44.
52. Ibid., 75.
53. *Catalogue*, UND, 36th: 46.
54. *Scholastic* 13 (1879–80): 521–522, 618–619.
55. Edwards, [CEDW 26/18], UNDA. It seems probable that this brief note from the librarian of the Oratory represented an offer of books authored by the Cardinal, and not of volumes from his personal library.
56. *Scholastic* 14 (1880–81): 173.
57. Ibid., 13 (1879–80): 567.
58. *Catalogue*, UND, 38th: 47.
59. *Scholastic* 16 (1882–83): 42.
60. Ibid., 232.
61. Ibid., 604.
62. Ibid., 19 (1885–86): 80.
63. Ibid., 24 (1890–91): 556.
64. Ibid., 20 (1887–88): 413.
65. Ibid., 17 (1883–84): 587.
66. Ibid., 19 (1885–86): 340.
67. Ibid., 23 (1889–90): 631.
68. *Catalogue*, UND, 1899–1900: 12.
69. *Scholastic* 23 (1889–90): 629, 631.
70. *Bulletin*, UND, 1905–06: 230 and earlier issues.

71. Edwards, [CEDW 27/10], UNDA.

72. Ibid., [16/07].

73. Thomas T. McAvoy, "Miscellany: Manuscript Collections Among American Catholics," *Catholic Historical Review* 37 (1952): 287.

74. *Scholastic* 35 (1901–02): 247.

75. McAvoy, 289.

76. Ibid., 290–291.

77. Ibid., 292–294.

78. *Scholastic* 23 (1889–90): 125.

79. Edwards, [CEDW 26/18], UNDA.

80. Ibid.

81. Ibid., [CEDW 16/11].

82. *Bulletin*, UND, 1909–10: 12.

Catholic Americana at Notre Dame

PHILIP GLEASON AND CHARLOTTE AMES

UNLOC, the University Libraries' online catalog, at present lists almost 1,300 entries under the subject heading "Catholic Church—United States." These entries include a small number that refer to manuscript collections which are under the administrative control of the Archives, an organizational unit separate from the Libraries at Notre Dame. Our aim in this chapter is to provide a sketch of the historical process by which these collections have developed. The story falls into four loosely defined periods and covers both archival and library materials since they are closely related. In fact, the administrative separation between library and archives took place for historical reasons and cannot be adequately understood except in that context.

Foundation Years (1870s–1911)

The *fons et origo* of the whole enterprise was James F. Edwards, who demands attention here as well as in Alan Krieger's chapter on his career as librarian.[1] Neither librarianship nor archival work had been professionalized in Edwards's time, and he was by temperament more a collector than a librarian or archivist. Yet his gifts in his chosen line amounted to genius, and his ceaseless activity over four decades made Notre Dame the nation's leading center of Catholic Americana when he died in 1911. To understand his approach and assess his accomplishments, we need to consider both his personal qualities and the influences that shaped his outlook on the world within which he operated.

Edwards's friendliness and personal charm, reinforced by his good looks and fastidiousness about his appearance, no doubt contributed to his success as a collector. His biographer reports that he treated Cardinal Manning's gentleman-in-waiting with such cordiality in the brief time he was in fact waiting to see the cardinal that Manning's servant spontaneously turned over to Edwards several valuable ecclesiastical mementoes he had been keeping for himself.[2] Even his being known in the oral tradition of Notre Dame as "Jimmie Edwards" conveys something of the affection his contemporaries felt for him and suggests a lively, outgoing personality.

His energy in seeking out materials and his enthusiasm for making Notre Dame the great national center for the history of American Catholicism were, to be sure, elements in Edwards's native disposition. But they also reflected the temperament and approach of Notre Dame's founder, Edward F. Sorin, C.S.C., whose ambitions for the University were limitless and who labored prodigiously to bring them to fulfillment. Considering that Edwards came to Notre Dame in 1859 when he was but nine years old, stayed on after his school days as a faculty member, and lived on campus in close personal contact with Sorin until the latter's death in 1893, it seems reasonable to suggest that Edwards's life work was in a very real sense inspired by Sorin's vision and example.[3] In time, a kind of reciprocity developed between Sorin's and Edwards's efforts. That is, the visibility won for Notre Dame by Sorin strengthened Edwards's hand in appealing for books, manuscripts, and episcopal memorabilia, and eventually the collections he brought together became a new feature adding lustre to the University's reputation.

Edwards combined his affability with an intense religious piety. Although he discovered from a brief trial in the Holy Cross community that the priesthood was not for him, he remained throughout his life deeply religious and profoundly attached to the Catholic church. His religiosity affected his work both in the general sense that it animated the whole of his collecting, and in the more particular sense that his concentration on bishops reflected the episcopally-centered ecclesiology of the day. Considered from this viewpoint, the centerpiece of Edwards's endeavors—the "Bishops' Memorial Hall"—was what we might call the artifactual counterpart to John Gilmary Shea's four-volume *History of the Catholic Church in the United States* (1886–92), for

Shea, too, concentrated on bishops and the growth of formally organized ecclesiastical jurisdictions.[4]

The Bishops' Memorial Hall, with its extensive collection of episcopal portraits, mitres, croziers, pectoral crosses, chalices, and personal memorabilia such as eye-glasses and walking sticks, gave Edwards's operation more the appearance of a museum than a library or archive. But his enthusiasm for collecting was undifferentiated rather than undiscriminating, and he was equally keen to build up what he called the "Catholic Reference Library of America" and the "Catholic Archives of America." Thanks to his talent for friendship, he developed an extensive network of informal agents who kept him informed and channeled materials in his direction. These included several bishops from whom he acquired the nucleus of an unrivalled collection of manuscripts dealing with nineteenth-century American Catholicism, especially in the Middle West. The devotional monthly *Ave Maria*, founded by Father Sorin in 1865 and edited by Edwards's close friend, Father Daniel Hudson, C.S.C., publicized his needs. Edwards also kept in touch with the leading American Catholic historians of his generation and enjoyed their confidence. He supplied source materials for Shea, and hoped (vainly, as it turned out) to acquire the historian's library; he also provided materials for publication in Martin I. J. Griffin's *American Catholic Historical Researches*.[5]

The results of all this activity were truly impressive.[6] By the late 1890s, the library's 3,000 bound volumes of periodicals included, besides *Ave Maria*, long runs of other important Catholic magazines such as *American Catholic Quarterly Review, Brownson's Quarterly Review, Catholic World, Dublin Review, Tablet* (London), *Metropolitan* (New York), *New York Catholic Expositor*, and *United States Catholic Magazine*, along with Griffin's *Researches*, Shea's *United States Catholic Historical Magazine*, and the *Records* of the American Catholic Historical Society of Philadelphia. Among the early Catholic newspapers Edwards had acquired (said to number 1,000 bound volumes) were extended runs of the earliest founded, Bishop John England's *United States Catholic Miscellany* of Charleston; the *Pilot* of Boston; the *New York Freeman's Journal*, and the *Truth Teller*, also of New York; the *Catholic Mirror* of Baltimore; the *Pittsburgh Catholic*; and the *Catholic Telegraph* of Cincinnati. Another important source Notre Dame held almost in its entirety was the *Catholic Directory*.[7]

Particularly noteworthy archival holdings included extensive diocesan collections from New Orleans, Cincinnati, and Detroit; the personal papers of Orestes A. Brownson, the leading American Catholic thinker of the nineteenth century, and those of James A. McMaster, who was for many years editor of the *New York Freeman's Journal*. Likewise significant were the papers of two leading lay Catholics of that era: Henry F. Brownson of Detroit (Orestes's son) and William J. Onahan of Chicago, both of whom were prominently involved in the Catholic lay congresses of 1889 and 1893.[8]

Working alone and swamped by his acquisitions, Edwards was not able to do much toward organizing the archival materials. "I could employ five or six people for an indefinite time in assorting the papers," he once observed wistfully. But although his treasures could not yet be opened for use, he consoled himself with the thought that "The archives are for future generations." Many a researcher of those generations would agree with what John Gilmary Shea wrote even before he had seen the full extent of Edwards's collections: "You have in what you have gathered more material for a real history of the Church in this country...than was ever dreamed of."[9] From the viewpoint of Catholic Americana at Notre Dame, Edwards was the foundation of everything that followed.

Transition to Professionalism (1912–1929)

The keynote of the next epoch is professionalization. In respect to the library proper, the coming of Paul J. Foik, C.S.C., as director in 1912 marks a very definite beginning, and the professionalization of library service continued under Paul R. Byrne, who succeeded Foik in 1924. Professionalization in archival management was slower in coming, not only at Notre Dame but also in the larger world of learning, but with the appointment of Thomas T. McAvoy, C.S.C., as archivist in 1929 we have another clear point of demarcation. Although no notable advances were made in the acquisition of Catholic Americana during this transitional period, the most significant development was the administrative separation of library and archives.

Although Foik was not trained as a librarian, he had a thoroughly. professional outlook, as Anne Kearney has shown in her chapter in this volume. Indeed, it was precisely because he understood so well what the new era in higher education demanded in terms of library facilities, collections, and services that he could not afford to devote much of his attention to Catholic Americana as such. In contrast to Edwards the collector, Foik was the organizer and administrator. To borrow a comparison from the history of American business, Foik's relation to Edwards in the history of the Notre Dame Libraries resembles that of Alfred P. Sloan to Billy Durant in the history of General Motors—both took over what had essentially been one-man shows, but which had reached a degree of scope and complexity that required systematic rationalization.[10]

Foik was personally quite interested in Catholic Americana. His doctoral dissertation in history, which he completed at the Catholic University of America shortly before he came to the Notre Dame Library, dealt with the earliest phases of American Catholic journalism. After moving to Texas, he played a leading role in organizing Catholic historical activities there; while at Notre Dame he strove to acquire collections such as that of the Catholic labor leader Frank Duffy. He took note in his first annual report of the value, and special needs, of the manuscript materials Edwards had gathered, but the relative weight Foik gave to Catholic Americana as compared to broader library needs is suggested by something he said in urging the appointment of an archivist:

> The development of the library and the problem connected therewith is of first importance and will continue to be the principal considera- tion as long as the wheels of progress keep turning. On the other hand, the time is now ripe for the complete organization of the archives, the establishment of a staff personnel in this department and the supplying of a modest appropriation for the physical care of all documentary material.[11]

While we should not infer from this that Foik saw no role for "the wheels of progress" in archival affairs, he clearly thought of them in very different terms from the ongoing needs of the library.

About the actual state of the archival affairs during Foik's director- ship and the early years of Byrne's, we have only the most fragmentary information. When the library was still in the Main Building, Foik spoke of manuscripts being kept "in the vault"; after the new library opened in 1917, it seems that they were stored there in metal filing cases. Outside consultant Frank K. Walter speaks of the Reverend William H. Condon, C.S.C., as working with the archives in 1920, but it is not clear what he was doing nor how long he kept it up. What is clear is that the archives were not open to researchers, although Byrne (and presumably Foik before him) tried to respond to specific inquiries if the materials were at all accessible.[12]

Foik's most extended discussion of the archives occurs in his final annual report and may have been written after he learned he was to be transferred to Texas. In it he not only called for the appointment of an archivist, but insisted that the archivist must be a priest. The reason was that since the Notre Dame collections included diocesan materials, he believed the University to be bound by the ecclesiastical legislation that governed the preservation of records by individual dioceses. The relevant regulations were spelled out in the new Code of Canon Law, promulgated in 1918, from which Foik quoted at length and added by way of conclusion: "The ideal choice of archivist should be a specialist in history, preferably American church history, [but] he must be a clergyman—one with a correct judgment and a discernment of the confidential nature of the materials to be examined and arranged."[13]

We can hardly overlook the irony involved in a stipulation that would have seriously hobbled Jimmie Edwards's collecting had it been in effect in his time. But this retrospective consideration pales by comparison with the effect the clergyman-only rule had on future developments, for what it meant in practice was that the archives would be a separate administrative entity from the library. This came about because Foik's successor as library director, Paul Byrne, was a layman, who understood quite clearly that the archives were not under his jurisdiction. Being disqualified from administering the archives himself, he could hardly be considered competent to superintend the activities of the priest who was entrusted with that responsibility. Foik's interpretation of canon law was thus the primary reason for the separation of the archives from the library. But all lay persons were very much junior partners in Catholic colleges and universities in the 1920s, and it is extremely doubtful that the strong-minded priest who ultimately became archivist would have been willing to report to a lay supervisor even in the absence of canonical prescription.

The strong-minded priest in question was Father Thomas McAvoy, who presided for 40 years over the Archives (which, as a separate entity, we will from now on capitalize). He was not, however, the first Holy Cross priest who tried his hand at the work. We have already noted the elusive presence of Father Condon; he was gone by 1925 at the latest, and in 1927 two other Holy Cross priests—Fathers Francis Butler and William McNamara, both historians—were placed in charge of the Archives. Butler seems to have dropped out almost at once, for the next year Byrne speaks of McNamara alone as having the job.[14] Although he found the work congenial, McNamara did not stay long either; he did, however, leave behind a document describing what he had been doing for the benefit of the person who was being groomed to take his place.

Addressing the soon-to-be-ordained young cleric as "Dear Tom," McNamara explained the system he had been following in processing manuscripts, noting that his method had been approved by the Catholic University's Peter Guilday, the leading Catholic historian of the day. Although he had completed work on about 9,000 documents, McNamara conceded that it made no discernible dent in the mass of materials still to be dealt with (which McAvoy later estimated at 300,000 items). Yet McNamara was not at all disheartened; it was wonderful work, and he exhorted his prospective successor, "Well Mr. McAvoy...Keep your courage up and be happy if you land the archives job." In a more practical vein, he passed along two suggestions from J. Franklin Jameson, the great organizer of historical enterprises with whom he had discussed McAvoy's case: learn all the church history you can; keep up your French, and acquire Spanish, too, if possible.[15]

McAvoy, then completing his theological studies in Washington, was ordained in the summer of 1929, took over from McNamara immediately thereafter, and retained the position of University archivist until his death in 1969. Strictly speaking, he had no systematic professional training for archival work since nothing of the sort was available at the time. However, he had taken advantage of being in Washington to confer with persons expert in the handling of historical manuscripts. One such consultant was Leo F. Stock, a member of Jameson's Division of Historical Research at the Carnegie Institution and a part-time faculty member at the Catholic University of America. McAvoy's most important advisor, however, was John C. Fitzpatrick, who had just resigned from the Manuscript Division of the Library of Congress to undertake the immense task of editing the papers of George Washington in 39 volumes.[16]

Both of these highly respected scholars, who served back-to-back terms as president of the American Catholic Historical Association in 1928 and 1929, continued to offer counsel after McAvoy returned to Notre Dame and began setting to rights what he later referred to as the "rummy pile" of documents he found awaiting him.[17] That was perhaps a little unkind to his predecessors, especially McNamara, but there is no doubt that McAvoy brought a new level of professionalism to the job, along with a renewal of collecting energy that had been absent since Edwards's time.

Growth Along Professional Lines (1929–1969)

McAvoy was unquestionably the dominant figure in respect to Catholic Americana during his tenure as archivist; hence that span of time can be considered the next epoch in our story. But since archives and library now operated with no formal (and very little informal) coordination, we really have two independent lines of development. We turn first to the library.

Under Byrne's directorship (1924–1952) and that of his successor, Victor A. Schaefer (1952–1966), the Notre Dame Library continued to develop along professional lines. Like Foik before them, both of these administrators had too many other things on their minds to devote much attention to Catholic Americana as such. Yet they also realized that it was one of their institution's particular strengths, and did what they could to build up the holdings in that area. Byrne's activities are better documented, so we will concentrate here on his tenure, leaving consideration of Schaefer's principal contribution for the next section.

Byrne continued on a more regular basis the practice Foik had initiated of writing annual reports (in itself, a significant step toward professionalization). From these reports we can classify his attention to Catholic Americana under three headings: continued acquisitions; concern for the preservation and accessibility of Catholic newspapers;

and efforts to enhance the value of certain Catholic periodicals by indexing them.

Among the continuing acquisitions was the "Will and Codicils of Charles Carroll of Carrollton," a $62.50 purchase that had to be approved by the President of the University.[18] Byrne also noted with satisfaction the filling in of Notre Dame's set of *Catholic Directories*, and took pride in having acquired 58 volumes of the *Annales de la Propagation de la Foi*, the publication of a French missionary support society established in 1822 which contained a wealth of historical information in the form of begging letters written by American churchmen. Byrne called this his "most valuable purchase" in 1930, and five years later he exclaimed on acquiring a two-volume index to the *Annales*, "These are so rare as to [be] almost unknown." He was pleased at the number of titles Notre Dame held in a listing of "Early Catholic Americana" being circulated by Wilfrid Parsons, S.J., who was preparing a bibliographic study on that topic.[19] Fathers McNamara and Philip S. Moore, C.S.C., offered counsel on acquisitions in American and medieval history, and it seems reasonable to speculate that other faculty members' interest in the history of Catholic education contributed to building up a strong collection in that area.[20]

Byrne was equally alert to add missing volumes to Notre Dame's collection of Catholic newspapers, which "[t]hough small," he remarked in 1937, "continues to attract scholars from other universities." Indeed, it was user demand—along with his concern for their physical maintenance—that accounted for his main effort in connection with the Catholic newspapers, namely, bringing them up from the basement, where they had simply been piled on the floor, and placing them on special shelving on the front mezzanine.[21] And when Byrne lent his early volumes of the *Pilot* to the Archdiocese of Boston for microfilming, it came to light that Notre Dame was the only place in the country holding a full run of the *Emerald Isle,* a publication that appeared for a few months while the *Pilot* was in suspension.[22]

Frank Walter's 1920 report took note of Notre Dame's "unusually rich" collection of Catholic periodicals, adding that since most of them were not included in standard indexes, it would add greatly to their value to index the more important. This may have had something to do with Foik's later initiation of the *Catholic Periodical Index*, but nothing was done immediately at Notre Dame. Paul Byrne later recalled that the Graduate Committee and chair of the English Department approved the idea of compiling an index to *Ave Maria* as a doctoral project. But when the plan was broached to Father Hudson, then in the twilight of his long career as editor of the magazine, he "threw so much cold water" on it that it had to be dropped.[23] But the "library staff" (meaning, of course, Byrne himself) kept the project in mind, and when President Franklin D. Roosevelt's National Youth Administration made funds available to keep students in school by providing employment for them, the work got under way in earnest. As many as 19 students were employed in some years, and besides *Ave Maria*—the completion of which Byrne announced with pride in 1945—the entire run of the *American Catholic Quarterly Review* was indexed along with an indeterminate portion of the London *Tablet*.[24]

Turning now to the Archives, we note that McAvoy also used NYA-supported students (about 50 of them in 1938) to index Catholic periodicals, but he concentrated on the Notre Dame student magazine, the *Scholastic*, and the most important journals of American Catholic history. Taken together, these two types of Archives indexes presently fill upwards of 400 card-catalog drawers; the former is indispensable for local history, and the latter particularly useful for older publications of the historical miscellany type.[25] But valuable as they are, these indexes are as nothing by comparison to the boon McAvoy conferred on researchers by calendaring several of his principal collections.

Calendaring—by which is meant going through a documentary collection piece by piece, writing a precis of each item, and filing the resulting cards, appropriately coded and cross-referenced, in easily accessible form—is an incredibly labor-intensive process, and it demands a high level of skill, especially when, as in this case, virtually all of the documents are handwritten, many in a foreign language. Yet it was accepted at the time as the norm to be attained, and McAvoy launched into it immediately. He did make use of students, having gotten Fitzpatrick's approval of his system as acceptable when one had to depend on inexperienced help, but he checked over their work and no doubt did most of what was done in the early years. As graduate studies developed at Notre Dame (with McAvoy himself building the program in history), graduate assistants became available for the work.[26]

By 1961 McAvoy could report that calendaring had been completed on the Brownson, Edwards, and Cincinnati papers; that the Detroit collection was two-thirds done; the Hudson papers half-done; and the immense New Orleans collection (the special project of McAvoy's longterm assistant, Mercedes Muenz) completed to the end of the Spanish period.[27] Although calendaring was terminated in the 1970s, the finished product—some 270 file drawers with double rows of three-by-five index cards—constitutes a scholarly resource the true value of which can only be fully appreciated by those who have used it.

Use of the Archives was quite limited for the first few years of McAvoy's regime, for he was determined to get things organized before declaring his holdings open to any and all. However, he responded to inquirers on an individual basis, providing assistance when he could. It seems likely that access was freer and use increased after McAvoy returned from his doctoral studies at Columbia in 1938. He of course demanded professional seriousness and responsibility on the part of those who wanted to use the collections, and he took pains to satisfy himself on these points even in the case of the then very young Arthur M. Schlesinger, Jr., one of the earliest researchers to use the Brownson papers.[28]

McAvoy himself exploited the Archives for his Notre Dame master's essay and his doctoral dissertation at Columbia; in the case of the latter, which dealt with early Indiana Catholicism, we may assume that he also added to his collections many documents, or copies of documents, found elsewhere.[29] As graduate work in history expanded at Notre Dame, other local theses and dissertations were based primarily upon materials in the library and archives, and in not a few cases resulted in the incidental acquisition of new materials related to these investigations. To date, more than two dozen doctoral dissertations on American Catholicism have been done by graduate students in history at Notre Dame, along with a smaller number by students in education and sociology. And during McAvoy's 40-year term as archivist no fewer than 55 master's theses in history focussed on American Catholic topics. Perhaps the most interesting used the J. B. Lamy letters in the Archives to sketch the historical reality behind Willa Cather's *Death Comes for the Archbishop*. This 1933 essay was done by Francis J.

O'Malley, who later became a legendarily charismatic professor of English at Notre Dame.[30]

In respect to adding new archival materials, McAvoy's outstanding achievement was in acquiring microfilm copies of important collections, both in this country and in Europe. For example, Notre Dame now possesses on microfilm the contents of the Archives of the Archdiocese of Baltimore up to the era of Cardinal Gibbons, and a similarly extensive collection from the Archives of the Archdiocese of St. Louis. McAvoy's scholarly interest in the controversy over "Americanism" in the late nineteenth century also led to new microfilm acquisitions. His most notable achievement, however, came as a result of two expeditions to Europe. In the early 1950s, he arranged for the microfilming of letters sent from the United States to Catholic mission support societies in Paris, Lyons, Vienna, and Munich. The 58 reels of these manuscript letters constitute a much richer source than the selected and edited versions that appeared in such publications as the *Annales*, whose acquisition by the library we have already noted.

Ten years later, McAvoy scored an even greater triumph by arranging for the microfilming of the letters dealing with the United States held by the Roman archives of the Sacred Congregation *de Propaganda Fide*, which had jurisdiction over the church in this country until 1908. The value of this collection, whose 67 reels cover a time span from 1622 to 1865, is greatly enhanced by the availability of a printed calendar, which guides the researcher to whatever items are of primary interest. By way, perhaps, of reciprocating the benefit Notre Dame had derived from the filming of documents held elsewhere, McAvoy also arranged for four of his major collections to be included in the microfilming project initiated in the 1960s by the National Historical Publications Commission.[31]

This brings us to the fourth phase of our story, in which microfilming continues to figure prominently.

New Personalities, New Institutions, New Technology (1970–Present)

Both library and archives have had new leadership since Father McAvoy's death, but the first person to be considered here overlaps the preceding period since he was brought to Notre Dame by Schaefer in the early 1960s. This was Francis P. Clark, easily the most unusual personality associated with the development of Catholic Americana at the University.[32]

A descendant of one of the pioneer Catholic families of Kentucky, Clark was born in Louisville in 1936. He first became interested in local Catholic history by doing a grade-school project on his home parish, and what began as a hobby grew first into an obsession, then into a life work. Leaving school after the eighth grade, Clark supported himself as a baker while chasing down every book, newspaper, or manuscript to be found in church basement or rectory attic in the area. In his early 20s, by which time he had written dozens of parish histories and established the basis of a personal library of Catholic Americana that ultimately exceeded 5,000 volumes, Clark launched out on his own as a microfilmer, a technique he had learned by observing the process at the University of Kentucky. At about this time, Schaefer, who hoped to build the Catholic newspaper collection into a distinctive resource of the Notre Dame Library, made Clark's acquaintance at a convention of the Catholic Library Association. He gave the young collector a roving commission to film Catholic newspapers for Notre Dame. By 1964, Clark was working full-time for the library; two years later he moved to South Bend and made the University his permanent base of operations.

In his passion for collecting, his network of friends and unofficial agents scattered about the country, and his informal methods, Clark was Jimmie Edwards *redivivus*. Though he had none of Edwards's dandyism, Clark resembled his great predecessor in his good nature and likability. He was officially attached to the library staff as microfilmer, but was essentially a lone operator who paid as little heed as possible to bureaucratic protocol. Acting on his favorite maxim, "today's trash is tomorrow's treasure," Clark gloried in retrieving discarded materials from waste containers. He often muttered darkly that "higher ups" in the library were itching to clean out his accumulated "junk," and he believed it seriously enough to arrange before his death in 1979 for his personal collections, including books, to go to the Archives rather than the Library.

In University Provost James T. Burtchaell, C.S.C., Clark found a higher-up who appreciated his unique gifts; under this favorable aegis, his activities reached their apogee. In 1975–1976, for example, in

Doing what he loved most: Francis P. Clark, ca. 1965.

addition to his normal duties at the University, Clark travelled to Los Angeles to evaluate a major sports collection (which Notre Dame eventually acquired); went to Washington to organize the packing of another collection; supervised the unpacking of still a third collection when it reached Notre Dame; returned to Washington to film the card catalog of the Civil Rights Center; made five trips to Milwaukee to bring Catholic newspapers back for filming, and visited two other locations for the same purpose.[33]

Clark's most important legacy to Catholic Americana at Notre Dame is undoubtedly the library's matchless collection of Catholic newspapers on microfilm. Besides filming the library's original holdings, Clark brought in (or filmed in the field) scores of other papers, and a continuing acquisition program has been maintained since his death. A directory prepared in 1982 revealed that the Notre Dame Libraries then held positive copies of some 230 Catholic newspapers (the negatives of those filmed by Clark are held by the Archives). The great majority are English-language publications, but the leading German Catholic newspapers are also represented, plus one in French, one in Czech, and two in Native American tongues (both designated as "Sioux").[34] In the 1980s, these titles were added to the libraries' online catalog; the records are now electronically accessible through OCLC and Internet, and Catholic newspapers are among the titles most frequently requested through interlibrary loan.

Second only to the newspapers in importance was Clark's contribution to Notre Dame's holdings in Catholic parish histories. His personal collection, numbering over 2,000 parish histories, is housed in the Archives and must be used there. The libraries hold about 1,300 more, some of which are cataloged and available for borrowing; others, uncataloged, are included among the special collections that do not circulate. A revised directory issued in 1988 covers both library and archival holdings.[35] Taken together, the collection constitutes a unique source for research on the grassroots history of American Catholics of many different ethnic backgrounds, as well as for special topics such as parochial schooling, shifts in devotional life, and church architecture.

A third area to which Clark contributed, although its origins are various indeed, is the collection of Catholic pamphlets. It too is shared between Archives and Libraries; about 4,700 titles were recently made accessible on UNLOC, but the total number held is indeterminate. The pamphlets cover a wide range of topics—evolution and other intellectual trends, peace and war, courtship and marriage, the sacraments, devotional life, etc.—and include works by the major twentieth-century masters of the genre such as John A. O'Brien, Daniel Lord, S.J., Fulton J. Sheen, and John F. Noll. Interesting recent acquisitions are works by Mother Angelica of television fame.[36]

A wholly new, and quite important, institution that makes its appearance at this point in our story is the Charles and Margaret Hall Cushwa Center for the Study of American Catholicism, established in 1975 through the efforts of Jay P. Dolan. Professor Dolan, who joined Notre Dame's history faculty in 1971, served as director of the Cushwa Center from its beginning through 1993. In January, 1994, R. Scott Appleby succeeded Dolan as director of the Cushwa Center. Although the Cushwa Center itself does not collect materials, its activities have done a great deal to encourage the use of Notre Dame's collections as

well as to stimulate interest in American Catholic history more generally.

Cushwa travel grants have aided more than 60 researchers to make
use of library and archival materials; it has provided dissertation-year
fellowships for several Notre Dame graduate students, and its semi-annual *American Catholic Studies Newsletter* keeps scholars abreast of
developments in the field. The Cushwa Center has also sponsored a
half-dozen major conferences and scores of seminars and colloquia; its
manuscript competition has resulted in the publication of 13 books in
the series "Notre Dame Studies in American Catholicism"; and thanks
to generous funding from the Lilly Endowment of Indianapolis, it has
mounted major research projects on the history of American Catholic
seminaries, parish history and life, and Hispanic Catholicism in the
United States.[37]

In the libraries, the most important new institutional feature is the
identification of Catholic Americana as one of the areas of special
concern in collection development, an activity that has been more
systematically pursued since the 1970s. Charlotte Ames's appointment
as bibliographer in American Catholic studies is the major landmark
here. Besides serving as library liaison officer to the Cushwa Center,
Ames is responsible for expenditures from the endowment funds
earmarked for Catholic Americana, and has made use of a portion of
an NEH Challenge Grant for humanities acquisitions to expand the
Catholic newspaper collection. She also prepared a finding aid for this
collection, collaborated in the preparation of the parish history directory, and published an article discussing Catholic pamphlet literature
in more general terms.[38]

Since Father McAvoy's death—which occurred, as he would no
doubt have wished, while he was working in the Archives—two persons
have held the position of archivist. Thomas E. Blantz, C.S.C., took
over after McAvoy and continued the acquisitions, calendaring, and
microfilming policies already in place, while adding oral history
materials on "labor priests" and on the introduction of coeducation at
Notre Dame. But Father Blantz's real love is teaching, and in 1978 he
succeeded in shedding the last of his administrative responsibilities (he
had served earlier as vice president for student affairs) to become a
full-time member of the History Department. After his resignation, the

present archivist, Dr. Wendy Clauson Schlereth, was named to the position.

Since Schlereth's appointment shattered the clergyman-only precedent—to say nothing of the more deeply embedded male-only tradition—it should not surprise us that she has struck out in some new directions as archivist. The most notable of these is the discontinuation of calendaring and the introduction of a computerized system of collection control and access. In addition to the system employed in the Archives itself, general descriptions of 546 of its collections have been prepared in the standard format for "Machine-Readable Cataloging of Archives and Manuscript Collections" (MARC-AMC) and loaded onto UNLOC and OCLC, thus making information about these materials available to scholars throughout the country.

Dr. Schlereth has also introduced a more systematic records-management program for University-related materials and has pursued an active policy of seeking out other collections bearing on American Catholic history. For example, the existing base of nineteenth-century collections dealing with Catholic journalism and publishing has been expanded by new acquisitions including collections from *Commonweal*, *National Catholic Reporter*, and the publishing house of Sheed and Ward. But that is only one dimension of the picture; the comprehensive laser-printed *Guide* to the Archives' collections runs to 287 pages. To give some inkling of the extent of these collections, we note that Notre Dame now serves as the continuing archival repository for the Association of Chicago Priests, the Catholic Peace Fellowship, the Center of Concern, the Conference of Major Superiors of Men, the Leadership Conference of Women Religious, the National Assembly of Religious Women, the National Federation of Priests' Councils, the National Marriage Encounter, and a number of other organizations.[39]

The new control system and the growth of the collections required both a larger staff and more space. The Archives now occupy about three quarters of the space on the sixth floor of the Hesburgh Library, where the Cushwa Center is also located. No doubt Jimmie Edwards would marvel at these institutions, and at the libraries themselves with their two million volumes. But while he, along with Foik, Byrne, McAvoy and all the others, would take pride in what has been done, they would also warn us against resting on our laurels. For while

Catholic life continues in this land, so does the work of preserving and recording it.

---

1. Besides Krieger's chapter, see also Sr. Damien Tambola, O.S.B., "James F. Edwards, Pioneer Archivist of Catholic Church History of America" (Master's thesis, University of Notre Dame, [1958]), which was published with minor changes and under the same title in *Records of the American Catholic Historical Society of Philadelphia* 72 (March–June, 1961): 3–32, and Thomas T. McAvoy, C.S.C., "Manuscript Collections Among American Catholics," *Catholic Historical Review* 37 (October 1951): 281–95, which includes the edited text of a diary kept by Edwards on a trip east in 1888. (The first of these journals is hereafter cited as *RACHS*; the second as *CHR*.)

2. Tambola, "Edwards" (thesis version), 118.

3. Unfortunately there is no biography of Sorin; however, his personality and outlook come through clearly in Edward Sorin, C.S.C., *Chronicles of Notre Dame du Lac*, translated by John M. Toohey, C.S.C., edited and annotated by James T. Connelly, C.S.C. (Notre Dame, Ind.: University of Notre Dame Press, 1992).

4. For discussion of Shea's work, see Henry Warner Bowden, "John Gilmary Shea: A Study of Goals and Methods in Historiography," *CHR* 54 (July 1968): 235–60.

5. Other scholarly friends and supporters were Richard H. Clarke and A.A. Lambing. For discussion of this generation of American Catholic historians, see John P. Cadden, *The Historiography of the American Catholic Church: 1785–1943* (New York: Arno Press, 1978 [orig. ed. 1944]), chaps. 1–4.

6. On acquisitions in Edwards's time, see Tambola, "Edwards" (thesis version), 61, 63, 68, 111, 139–41, 147–48.

7. In 1931, Librarian Paul Byrne noted the purchase of two volumes which completed the *Catholic Directory* set from 1822 to date, and added: "Notre Dame is one of the very few places having this title in such complete form." AR, 1930–31, 3.

8. Edwards himself was one of the organizers of the Catholic Columbian Congress of 1893 and acquired the entire "Columbian Library of Catholic Authors" that had been brought together for the occasion. Tambola, "Edwards" (thesis version), 132–34.

9. Edwards is quoted from J.J. Fitzgerald, "Catholic Archives of America" *Notre Dame Scholastic* 27 (June 30, 1894): 681–83; Shea from Tambola, "Edwards" (thesis version), 98.

10. See Alfred P. Sloan, Jr., *My Years With General Motors* (Garden City, N.Y.: Doubleday, 1964), chaps. 1–3.

11. AR, 1923–24, 119.

12. AR, 1911–12, 5; Frank Keller Walter, "Report of a Survey of the University of Notre Dame Library, Dec. 1–14, 1920" (South Bend, Ind.: n.p., 1920), 6 (cited hereafter as Walter); Byrne to Sr. Salesia, O.S.B., March 3, 1926, UNDA-UARC.

13. Concerning the discretion required of the archivist, Foik added: "The same silent service must also be impressed upon those who are to assist him in this work." AR, 1923–24, 119–22.

14. Byrne to Sr. Salesia, O.S.B., January 1, 1928, UNDA-UARC; Byrne to Charles O'Donnell, C.S.C., September 12, 1928, UNDA-UPCO 9/137. University catalogs list Condon as a teacher of ancient languages from 1920 to 1925; indicate that he went to St. Edward's in Texas in 1925, but returned to Notre Dame the following year. In his old age (he died in 1955), he was a familiar figure in the Library, visiting the Cataloging Department almost daily. Unfortunately, he was also given to excising what he considered offensive material from magazines and books.

15. McNamara to "Dear Tom," January 7, 1929, UNDA-UARC. The estimate of 300,000 comes from a description of McAvoy's work that appeared in the *South Bend News-Times*, February 25, 1934, clipping in UNDA-UDIS, Information Services 111/D35.

16. Stock to McAvoy, September 25, 1929, and Fitzpatrick to McAvoy, October 11, 1929, UNDA-UARC. For the careers of these two men see *New Catholic Encyclopedia*, s.v. "Fitzpatrick, John Clement"; s.v. "Stock, Leo Francis."

17. Stock to McAvoy, October 8, 1931; Fitzpatrick to McAvoy, November 6, 1931, UNDA-UARC; McAvoy to John F. O'Hara, C.S.C., February 26, 1936, UNDA, Earliest Archives Records (copy).

18. Charles L. O'Donnell, C.S.C., to Byrne, September 13, 1928, UNDA-UPCO 9/137.

19. For *Annales*, AR 1929–30, 6; AR, 1934–35, 3; for Parsons's listing, AR, 1936–37, [13–14]. Parsons's *Early Catholic Americana* was published in 1939.

20. For the role of McNamara and Moore, see McAvoy to O'Hara, February 26, 1936, UNDA, Earliest Archives Records (copy). Faculty members with strong interests in Catholic education included two Holy Cross priests, James A. Burns and William F. Cunningham, and three lay professors, Bernard J. Kohlbrenner, and (at a later date) Vincent P. Lannie and Philip Gleason.

21. For quotation and adding missing volumes, AR, 1936–37, [7]; for earlier references to Catholic newspapers, AR, 1926–27, 7; AR, 1927–28, 5–6; AR, 1928–29, 10–11; AR, 1929–30, 8; AR, 1930–31, 3.

22. AR, 1938–39, 6.

23. Walter report, 11; AR, 1944–45, 7–8. Byrne speculated that Hudson opposed the idea because an index would reveal that he had re-used without acknowledgement much material from the early volumes of *Ave Maria*.

24. AR, 1934–35, 2; AR, 1935–36, [4]; AR, 1944–45, 7–8. In 1934–35, student assistance came through FERA (Federal Emergency Relief Administration); it was replaced in 1935 by the NYA, which lasted as a program until 1943, but faded in importance as the outbreak of war created a new demand for labor.

25. McAvoy to Leo P. Foley, C.M., September 28, 1938, UNDA-UARC, describes the project. Byrne had earlier noted competition for work space between students working for the Library and those employed by the Archives. AR, 1936–37, [3].

26. Fitzpatrick to McAvoy, November 6, 1931, UNDA-UARC; clipping from *South Bend News-Times*, February 25, 1934, UNDA-UDIS, Information Services 111/D35. McAvoy served as chair of the History Department from 1939 to 1960.

27. Thomas T. McAvoy, "Catholic Archives and Manuscript Collections," *American Archivist* 24 (October 1961): 409–14.

28. Arthur M. Schlesinger, Jr., to McAvoy, May 26, 1938; Robert H. Haynes to McAvoy, June 2, 1938; McAvoy to Haynes, June 10, 1938, UNDA-UARC.

29. The two works are: McAvoy, "The War Letters of Father Peter Paul Cooney of the Congregation of Holy Cross" (Master's thesis, University of Notre Dame, 1930), which was published in *RACHS* 44 (1933): 47–69, 151–69, 220–37; and McAvoy, *The Catholic Church in Indiana, 1789–1834* (New York: Columbia University Press, 1940).

30. Francis J. O'Malley, "A Literary Addendum: Willa Cather's Archbishop Latour in Reality" (Master's thesis, University of Notre Dame, 1933), does not include a director's name on the title page, but it was based on materials under McAvoy's control and one of the present authors can recall McAvoy's referring to it as a project he directed. O'Malley, incidentally, was listed in the Notre Dame catalog for 1933 as a member of the History Department, and as in both history and English for the next three years; from 1937, he is listed in English alone.

31. See Finbar Kenneally, O.F.M., *United States Documents in the Propaganda Fide Archives: A Calendar*, 10 vols. (Washington: Academy of American Franciscan History, 1968–83). The four Notre Dame collections microfilmed (for which printed *Guides* exist) were: Orestes Augustus Brown-

son papers; the Records of the Diocese of Louisiana and the Floridas, 1576–1803; the Thomas Ewing, Sr., papers; and the William Tecumseh Sherman family papers.

32. The following discussion is based on the authors' personal acquaintance with Clark, information provided by Victor A. Schaefer, and materials in UNDA, especially stories about Clark clipped from the *Louisville Times*, December 15, 1959; *Saint Jude* 28 (May 1962): 43–44; and *Notre Dame Scholastic* 117 (October 10, 1975): 13.

33. A report of Clark's activities is included as a sub-section of AR, 1975–76, which is not paginated continuously.

34. Charlotte Ames, comp., *Directory of Roman Catholic Newspapers on Microfilm: United States* (Notre Dame, Ind.: Memorial Library, 1982).

35. Caroline Mankell Sowinski, William Kevin Cawley, and Charlotte Ames, comps., *Parish History Collection: A Directory of Works at the University of Notre Dame*, 2d ed., rev. and enlarged (Notre Dame, Ind.: University Archives, 1988).

36. For orientation to the topic, see Charlotte Ames, "Catholic Pamphlets and Pamphleteers: A Guide to Indexes and Collections," *RACHS* 103 (Spring 1992): 1–16.

37. For a complete report, see Charles and Margaret Hall Cushwa Center for the Study of American Catholicism, *Report of Activities, 1975–1991* (Notre Dame, Ind.: Cushwa Center, 1991).

38. See above, notes 34, 35, and 36.

39. This listing and the information about MARC-AMC is taken from Wm. Kevin Cawley, "University of Notre Dame Archives," *American Catholic Studies Newsletter* 20 (Spring 1993): 12–13.

Government Documents and the Depository: The Notre Dame Contribution

LAURA BAYARD AND STEPHEN M. HAYES

The National Objective

A young U.S. Congress began an American tradition that set a hallmark for one of the highest ideals of a democratic government; it provided for an informed citizenry through distribution of government information at no cost to recipients. The system for distribution that has evolved, now known as the Depository Library Program, serves as a model for emerging democracies.[1]

Today's Depository Library Program is a hybrid of two traditions. The English tradition of the "publick" printer, imported to the American colonies, evolved into a distinctly American institution of centralized public printing, and became the Government Printing Office (GPO) in 1861.[2]

Simultaneously, Congress developed its own tradition for distribution of its information. The initial dissemination of Congressional resolutions, laws, and orders occurred through newspapers in 1789.[3] Later, the responsibilities for distribution shifted to various departments of the U.S. government while the mechanism for printing of this information beginning in 1801 was contracted to private printers such as Gales & Seaton.[4]

The Printing Act of 1895 merged the two separate traditions—centralized public printing and distribution of government information—to create the Depository Library Program. With remarkably little legislative tinkering since then, the program now serves 1,404 depository libraries [5] in the U.S. and its territories.

Obviously, Congress greatly influenced the evolution of the depository library system. The effects of the collective experiences of depository libraries upon the system, however, may not be as easily apparent. Through the story of the government documents collection at the Notre Dame Libraries, these experiences and their influence in the congressional refinement of the system are revealed. The libraries' story includes the technical processing, intellectual content and physical format issues which arise with a government documents collection.

Notre Dame Library's Early Documents Collection

The government documents collection at Notre Dame predates the libraries' depository status. The U.S. Congress had been regularly providing copies of federal statutes, acts, documents, reports, and journals, to state executives, and state and territorial legislatures by special acts in years after 1813, first under the auspices of the Department of State and then in conjunction with the Library of Congress (LC).[6]

The earliest references to government documents at Notre Dame are found in letters dated 1858 and 1859 preserved by the University Archives and the Province Archives Center. These letters from Schuyler Colfax to Fr. Sorin reveal that the two men corresponded about sets of government documents that Colfax, through his position as U.S. Representative, could distribute at his discretion. Government documents then meant publications that had been or would be published by Congress.[7] By this time, too, the responsibility for distribution of government information had transferred to the Department of the Interior, although Congressional representatives remained empowered to make their own distributions;[8] and incorporated universities, colleges, and historical societies [9] were recognized as eligible recipients. Sorin acted promptly to take advantage of this opportunity.

The following excerpts from Colfax's letters chronicle one example of the practice of distribution of documents by a Congressional representative. In the earliest letter marked "private" and dated September 27, 1858, Congressman Colfax had returned home from an election campaign to find Sorin's letter of inquiry about the first set. He responded from South Bend:

> There is an entire set of them ["Public Documents"] for the last Congress & the present one, embracing many valuable & interesting works, & I do not wonder that you feel an interest in obtaining them for the Library of your College. I have felt inclined to yield to your suggestion, as I have informed one or two mutual friends of us both; but as it is not necessary to make the designation till the 15th of October, which will be after the canvass is over, & when I will have more time to think over the various claims that are made by friends in other parts of the District, I shall defer it till then. My time is so engrossed now with the canvass, & with the refutation of the falsehoods & perversions & personalities to which I have been subjected, that I feel it a duty to defer every thing I can possibly, till after election.[10]

From South Bend on October 21, 1858, Colfax confidentially replied to a letter from Sorin that he had received the day before. He informed Sorin that he had carried out his intention to award the documents after the election. He then stated his reasons for selecting a library other than Notre Dame's to receive the government publications:

> My inclination was to select your Institution, being located in my own County; but I confess that I did not then dream of the heavy vote which your Institution intended to cast against me, & in favor of a candidate, not of their own County. I have no complaint to make of this at all; for I believe every one should vote as they think is best; & if your brethren preferred Col. Walker to myself, neither I nor my friends have any right to object to it. But when the McClure Working Man's Library of LaPorte pressed their application upon me & I learned that nearly every one of their numerous membership, with scarcely an exception, had voted for me against their own townsman, my competitor, I felt that they had claims upon me which I could not resist; & not hearing from you after the election, I accordingly designated that Library on the 16th inst, waiting one day after the time I stated to you. I shall not fail however to remember your Institution in the general distribution of Public Documents; but a gift of this kind under consideration, is expected to be given to a member's friends; & it would look strange & inexplicable if I were to pass over those who manifested their wish that I should have the

right to confer it by voting for me, to confer it when those who had declared by their votes against me that I ought not to have the power of making this selection. I think if you had been in my place, you would not have felt justified in acting differently.

The explanation of 'the votes of Notre Dame,' which you suggest giving to me, if we have the pleasure of meeting, I should like equally well to know, for I acknowledge I was surprised at them, especially as they mostly voted for two other Home candidates on the Republican ticket...[11]

He concluded his letter by recounting that on the day following the election, his political opponent had cited as a reason for Notre Dame's vote against Colfax, statements attributed to Sorin about an article on the Pope that had been published in Colfax's newspaper more than six years previously. Based on other statements in Colfax's letter, Sorin's letter apparently had included an explanation that the voting result was not an intended consequence of his remarks about the newspaper article about the Pope.[12]

Again from South Bend on October 25, 1858, Colfax penned a "private" letter in response to one received from Sorin which, for Colfax, had evidently cleared the misunderstanding about the election results:

If you had only written as plainly before election as in your last letter, there would have been no trouble & no misunderstanding whatever in regard to either the voting or the books...This will answer your inquiry as to what would have been my course if I had to decide between you & LaPorte, & both had voted for me. Indeed, leading friends there knew that my intention was to present the books to you; but after your vote was cast so unanimously & unexpectedly against me, they claimed then that they were certainly entitled to preference, as they unquestionally [sic] were under the circumstances...As to the article about the Pope, I have not the slightest recollection either of it, nor of your speaking to me about it in 1852. But it is no matter now. Your memory is better than mine on this point; & I will not controvert it, though, I have no recollection of what was in the article...[13]

In his letter from Washington, D.C. dated March 2, 1859 the future U.S. vice president, Colfax, wrote another "private" letter to Sorin,

Private.

U.S.R. Washington, Mch 2. 1859.

Dear Sir,

I have instructed the Secretary of the Interior to forward to your Institution, the set of the Annals of Congress which are at my disposal for our part of the District. They are ~~enclosed~~ contained in forty two volumes, and ~~are~~ worth $210. They will reach you as soon after the adjournment of Congress as the Secretary can box up the various sets.

This will prove to you the sincerity of my reply to your last letter; and I think under all the circumstances, considering the vote of your Institution last October, that you cannot charge me with selfishness or ill will. Under the circumstances, I prefer no acknowledgment of it in the papers; as many Associations in the Dist. whose members voted for me, would accuse me of lack of gratitude to them for not embracing the opportunity of sending this valuable collection to the Library.

In haste, Yours Resp'y & Truly

Schuyler Colfax

Letter from Schuyler Colfax to the Rev. Edward Sorin, 2 March 1859.

apparently to follow up on his promise to remember the Notre Dame Library at the time of the general distribution of government documents. He informed Sorin that he had instructed the Secretary of the Interior to forward to Notre Dame a set of 42 volumes of the *Annals of Congress* valued at $210.00. Interestingly, he did not wish public thanks because any notoriety might engender political fallout from other district libraries that had actually supported his election. But he hoped that his action, despite the voting at Notre Dame, would prove that he was not "selfish" or "ill will[ed]."[14]

These lengthy excerpts from Colfax's letters illustrate the political implications that most libraries experienced during that era. Politically motivated usage of the deposit of government information was perceived to be a widespread problem. Congress first addressed this concern in 1860, along with that of private printers' exorbitant charges. It was addressed once again in 1895 when the Printing Act centralized government printing.[15] Political motivations, however, would become an issue again in the 1990s when electronic information was introduced.

In 1883, the library at the University of Notre Dame du Lac was named a depository by Congressman William H. Calkins, Representative from the 13th District. Within the State of Indiana, Notre Dame's designation was the third, after De Pauw University (1879) in Greencastle and Indiana University (1881) in Bloomington.[16] The State Library, considered to be the oldest depository in Indiana despite its "unknown" designation date, serves the Indiana legislature. At the time of Colfax's letters, there were 12 depository libraries in the United States; by the time of the 1895 Printing Act, the number had increased to 419.[17] Although Notre Dame's designation occurred during a time of significant increase in the number of depositories, it, nevertheless, was a relatively early designee, predating, for example, the University of Pennsylvania.

The library's eligibility to receive those government publications available "on deposit" was assured. It was also a mixed blessing. Libraries were not permitted to select which titles were useful at the local level, but were required to receive and permanently retain all publications. The designation, however, lessened the library's dependence upon favors from Indiana Congressmen for securing documents. At this time, "public document" denoted all publications printed by order of Congress or of either House.[18] Because depository publications represented only a portion of the materials considered to be government documents, however, the library continued to rely upon political goodwill for those publications outside of the depository program until the 1895 Printing Act further reduced this dependency.

Actually, the 1895 Act dealt comprehensively with problems associated with the printing and distribution of documents. Under this Act, the responsibilities for both printing and distribution were brought together administratively and organizationally under the new Superintendent of Documents in the GPO, where these responsibilities have remained. In trying to streamline the printing and distribution processes, the Congress empowered the Superintendent to print and sell additional copies of documents as demand required, even when these were not regarded as part of the depository program.[19] Although members of Congress could still designate recipients of government documents, the intention was that the documents would be easily available outside of the Congressional designations. The Act also stabilized the depository status of libraries by tying the status to a Congressional District and therefore reducing dependence upon Representative whim. Publications, then, became available through purchase from the Superintendent of Documents; from other federal agencies, bureaus and offices; by exchange from other entities such as the U.S. Book Exchange; and through jobbers and other direct suppliers.

Knowing the nature of these acquisitions is germane to understanding their value to the Notre Dame Library. Government information is interdisciplinary. When the University widened its academic sphere by establishing new "departments in commerce (1861), science (1865), law (1869) and engineering (1873),"[20] the information in government publications supported the studies in each of the new departments. The titles and their producing agencies shown on an early shipping list verify that the diversity of topics in the publications sent on deposit fitted the new academic departments.

Less than two weeks before the Great Fire of 1879, the *Notre Dame Scholastic* reported a list of *Executive* and *Miscellaneous Documents* and *Reports of Committees* that had been sent by the Department of the Interior to the College Library which at that time was distinct from the Circulating Library.[21] Wilson and Lundy, in their 1950 *Survey* of the Library, asserted that all of the government documents collection had

No. 35.

Department of the Interior,

Washington, D. C., June 27, 1893

The Librarian of *Lemonnier Library of Univ. of Notre Dame du Lac*
Notre Dame, Ind.

SIR:

I have the honor to send, by registered mail, to the above-named library, as a depository of public documents, one sack containing a copy of each of the following-named publications of the Government:

51st Congress—First Session.

SENATE EXECUTIVE DOCUMENTS:
Vol. 3, No. 17. California, Oregon, and Nevada war claims.
Vol. 8, Nos. 54 to 59.
SENATE MISCELLANEOUS DOCUMENTS:
Vol. 1, Nos. 1 to 13.
Vol. 2, Nos. 14 to 163, except No. 78.
Vol. 4, Nos. 164 to 245, except No. 178.
HOUSE EXECUTIVE DOCUMENTS:
Vol. 10, No. 1, part 4. Report of the Postmaster-General. 1889.
Vol. 18, { No. 1, part 8. Report of the Civil Service Commission. 1889.
{ No. 4. Report of the Commissioner of Internal Revenue. 1889.
{ No. 7. Report of the Attorney-General. 1889.
Vol. 19, No. 2. Report on the Finances. 1889.
Vol. 20, No. 3, parts 1 and 2. Report of the Comptroller of the Currency. 1889. Vols. 1 and 2.
Vol. 22, No. 6. Foreign Commerce and Navigation. 1889.
Vol. 28, Nos. 106 to 140, except No. 113.
Vol. 38, No. 410, part 1. Paris Exposition. 1889. Vol. 1.
HOUSE MISCELLANEOUS DOCUMENTS:
Vol. 1, Nos. 1 to 76, except Nos, 4, 5, 6, 41, 44, and 45.
Vol. 9, Nos. 77 to 175, except Nos. 105, 106, 146, 147, and 148.
Vol. 15, No. 176. Tariff Hearings before Committee of Ways and Means.
Vol. 16, Nos. 177 to 260, except Nos. 194, 211, 223, 224, 228, 229, 231 to 234, 237, 238 to 241, 243, 244 to 249, and 257.
Vol. 24, No. 231. Consular Reports. Vol. 30, Nos 105 to 107½.
Vol. 25, { No. 232. Consular Reports. Vol. 31, Nos. 108 to 111.
{ No. 233. Index to Consular Reports. Vols. 18 to 31, Nos. 60 to 111.
Vol. 26, No. 234. Consular Reports. Vol. 32, Nos. 112 to 115.

51st Congress—Second Session.

HOUSE EXECUTIVE DOCUMENTS:
Vol. 9, No. 1, part 3. Report of the Secretary of the Navy. 1890.

52d Congress—First Session.

HOUSE JOURNAL.
HOUSE MISCELLANEOUS DOCUMENTS:
Vol. 41, No. 295. Eighth Annual Report of Bureau of Ethnology. 1886–87.
Vol. 53, No. 343. Monograph of Geological Survey. Vol. 20. Geology of the Eureka District, Hague.

52d Congress—Second Session.

SENATE JOURNAL.
SENATE MISCELLANEOUS DOCUMENTS:
Vol. 8, No. 70. Appropriations, New offices, etc.

Very respectfully,

First Assistant Secretary.

11672 b—450

U.S. Department of the Interior shipping list, 27 June 1893.

been destroyed by the fire.[22] The likelihood that some documents did survive the fire is strengthened by the fact that government documents were located in more than one of the collections that ultimately merged. Regardless, the collection today includes documents that pre-date the fire. James Edwards and his successors have completed gaps and the evidence is replete with statements about the intrinsic value of the information in government documents.

The monetary value of the collection can be understood only when compared to the financial realities of the time. "In 1859, the basic charge, including board, bed, and tuition, laundry, mending, and doctor's care, was $270.00 a year."[23] Schuyler Colfax's allocation to Notre Dame of 42 volumes nearly equaled one student's tuition expenses for a full year. The significance of the free acquisitions must have been readily apparent to the priests and brothers.

In later years, continuing efforts were made to build on this foundation. No history of government documents at Notre Dame would be complete without reference to Marie Lawrence, a librarian whose long career in both public and technical services contributed significantly to identifying and acquiring missing documents. As the library director said in 1941: "Special attention should be called to the work accomplished by [her]...in completing the broken sets in our document section. By a careful check of duplicate lists of documents sent out by other universities, she has been able to complete many broken files."[24]

When Lawrence became the law librarian in November 1945, she began her new job by inventorying and identifying gaps in the law collection, which was then part of the University Library. Many of the gaps occurred within runs of such documents as *Statutes-at-Large, United States Reports, Federal Trade Commission Reports, Interstate Commerce Commission Reports*.[25] Lawrence's efforts to create a core collection of documents for the Law Library are significant. Many of the depository titles that had been received by the University Library became part of the Law Library's collection when it separated from the University Library in 1957. Hesburgh Library's government documents law collection now lacks the earlier years of these titles.

At the behest of the Law Library's then new director, Dr. Roger F. Jacobs, the Law School chose depository status in 1985, seven years after Congress had provided eligibility for law schools.[26] The two depositories on campus are organized differently and administered separately. Other than the patent documents which remain under the purview of the Law Library, the two depository collections overlap in the field of law.

Documents In The Collection: Problems

In exchange for the free documents, the library accepted legal responsibility for providing custody of, service for and free access to depository materials.[27] The library, in other words, was charged with treating government documents as it would any purchased acquisition. The benefit the library would receive was a steady stream of free and valuable current information on many topics. The penalty for failure to fulfill the obligations was termination of depository status. On the surface, the requirements seemed reasonable and achievable. But the nature and proliferation of government documents hampered their incorporation into traditional processes within libraries. In reality, many of these resources often were treated as second-class materials.[28]

The proliferation of government documents was the most obvious problem. As the functions of government expanded, the numbers of documents produced correspondingly increased. That a library was required to receive and permanently house all publications distributed as depository items raised issues of space, physical access, and staffing. The proliferation caused documents to be accumulated and warehoused in separate areas of a library.[29] And proliferation exacerbated the other difficulties associated with the documents' inherent nature, which will be discussed later.

That documents were sometimes stored in separate areas of the library is evident from the earliest annual report (1911/12). Fr. Paul Foik planned to assemble all scattered documents in the basement of Sorin Hall and alluded to their neglect.[30] A reference in the 1964/65 Annual Report of the Social Sciences/Business Administration Department proves that warehousing measures were still resorted to more than 50 years later.

Part of the library's inability to deal with this proliferation of documents is linked with the legal responsibility to provide for permanent custody. From 1913 to 1923, depository libraries returned to the GPO some 1,226,558 publications for lack of storage space or interest to their clientele.[31] Notre Dame Library used this disposal method at least once. "In the process of reorganization there has been withdrawn for return to Washington a total of 1,293 pieces. This has given much needed space in the documents collection."[32]

Congress recognized that it bore the cost not only of production of the documents and the postage for initial distribution, but also of the return of unwanted documents to Washington. Congress's 1922 attempt to reduce costs while satisfying libraries' requests to select only items wanted, created another level of status, the partial depository.[33] Notre Dame, however, did not become a partial depository until 1932 [34] and had to cope with an ever-increasing volume of documents in the meantime.

The enormity of this proliferation can be illustrated by comparing the number of document "pieces" received in 1923/24 and in 1992/93. The Reference Department reported to Foik 3,110 pieces [35] received in 1923/24, while the current documents librarian, Stephen M. Hayes, reported 77,254 pieces received in 1992/93.[36] Roughly, the numbers substantiate the equivalent of a 4.05 percent increase in receipts per annum over 81 years. Today's documents collection numbers approximately three-quarters of a million pieces.

While proliferation creates continual problems because of the sheer numbers, documents' inherent nature indisputably complicates their treatment within libraries. They are free; frequently physically insubstantial; likely to be paperbound; subject to government procurement procedures; often change formats; and are defined more by their issuing agencies than by their subjects. Libraries' traditions of processing and providing access are defined by the nature of their dominant collection. The atypical nature of documents challenges these established traditions.

First of all, documents usually are free. Especially after libraries acquired budgets to purchase materials, they tended to devalue publications received through free acquisitions methods. Also, the size of some of the government documents reinforces the notion that they are ephemeral. Many documents are only single sheets or less than 20 pages. They frequently are routed to gift collections which can result in delays in processing, classification, and access. For years 1956/57 through 1964/65, the annual reports reflect that documents' statistics were included with "gifts."

In addition, after the leather bound *Serial Set* ceased to be the primary distribution edition, paperbound documents became prevalent. For libraries, the question becomes whether or not the responsibility for binding paperbound documents resides with them. One answer, found in the early annual reports, is "a beginning has been made in binding for permanent reference some of the important government publications. This is absolutely necessary if the library is to hold on to its depository privilege and give the best service to its readers."[37] To the present day, no ongoing binding program has been instituted for the paperbound government documents found in the Documents Center.

Another factor complicating routine processing for documents is the government's unique ordering, claiming, and invoicing requirements, different from standard library practices for procurement and receipt. No other characteristic has engendered as many moves from unit to unit within the Notre Dame Libraries as the responsibilities for receipt and ordering. A chronicle of the units that have held these responsibilities began with the Reference Department in 1911/12; shifted to Cataloging; was re-placed in Reference; transferred to the Serials Record Unit; exported to the Social Sciences Department; accepted by the Business and Economics Department; and returned to the Documents Center within Reference in 1974. "Until further notice documentary serials received on the library's partial federal depository status are handled in the..." [fill in favorite library unit here][38]

The Acquisitions Department's report for 1961/62 describes the level of activity engendered by government requirements. The department noted an increase in orders placed with government agencies. These requests, probably for non-GPO imprints, required preliminary letters concerning proper forms and methods of payment. The department decried the high volume of paperwork.[39]

Changes in the formats in which documents are issued have often strained the libraries' ability to accommodate those formats. Increasingly, opportunities to select the paper format over another format have been reduced. When significant portions of the 1990 census data were available only on 200 CD-ROM disks, for example, complaints of inadequate equipment for utilizing this electronic data surfaced in the 1990 Annual Report of the Reference Department. Not to select the title at all, however, was to forego important data in the libraries forever.

The Dilemma of Access

The last and most critical problem relating to the inherent nature of government documents is the difficulty of providing bibliographic and intellectual access to them. The *Report of a Survey of the Library of the University of Notre Dame* (1950) suggests an organizational concept for a documents collection which explicitly provides for the nature of documents:

> 'Documents,' it should be borne in mind, is a collective term applied by librarians to all publications issued by governmental agencies, whether local, state, regional, federal, foreign, or international. It is an imprint concept, applied without regard to physical format or subject content. The concept reflects a convenience in library organization and practice reinforced by the existence of special indices to these publications and by other factors of quantity and complexity.[40]

It was, however, a concept essentially different from that reflected in the typical subject and format arrangement of library collections, as expressed in the classification scheme by which the books are arranged. Employing an archival concept for arranging documents might be more useful, because documents are written for the internal uses of government and shared with the public only to provide for an informed citizenry. Libraries have agreed to act as "keepers" of the documents so that the public's access is convenient. If GPO's classification scheme which reflects the changing nature of agency provenance is retained, the historical record may well be preserved as well as access provided.

A vivid manifestation of the opposing principles of organization, as described above, can be witnessed in the Notre Dame Library's attempts to arrange and rearrange its documents into a collection. Through the voices of Notre Dame librarians past, the problems of organizing, maintaining and providing intellectual access to government documents can be heard.

Little is known about the actual arrangement and physical location of the depository materials for the period between 1859 and 1908, beyond a brief reference in *The Scholastic*. "College Library" was named as the destination of the documents listed in the April 12, 1879 article.[41] The 1895 Annual Report of the Public Printer, however, notes that only 50 of the 419 depository libraries had an intelligent arrangement of documents so they could be easily accessible.[42] This *Report* does not mention into which group Notre Dame Library fell.

In 1909, Notre Dame's eminently quotable first cataloger, Florence (Flo) M. Espy, wrote in one of a series of notes to her boss, Librarian James Edwards:

> I was trying to get all the Smithsonian Publications in one place in the little closet—I find some of them taken away & I find some of the "ethnology" upstairs. There is $11 worth of printed cards for these books & the contents is [sic] valuable for the school.[43]

While *The Scholastic's* April, 1879 list of government titles and volumes received conceivably could be considered a point of access to the government documents collection, Espy was the first to express concern for bibliographic access in a more conventional sense. As a cataloger hired to convert the library's collection to Dewey classification, she perceived the documents collection to be a candidate for her "to do" list. Her assessment of her chances to ever have the time to catalog the collection proved to be accurate. Espy wrote, "To tell you the truth, I do not expect to be here when the government documents are cataloged,"[44] or, in today's vernacular, "not in my lifetime." Additionally, her notes reveal the early purchase of printed cards to facilitate bibliographic access to the collection. Her voice heralded the issues that the Notre Dame Library would attempt to address for the next sixty-odd years.

Father Paul Foik, only a few months into his new job as librarian in 1912, presented his state of the documents collection report and his plan for the operations of the collection. His report corroborates Espy's earlier statement about the scattered storage locations of documents. By outlining his own plan to provide bibliographic access to the collection, he also corroborates that purchased printed cards exist in the library:

> In this department Library of Congress printed cards shall be used as they can be supplied at a cheaper rate than we can write them. For instance, the Department of Agriculture will furnish a complete cataloge [sic] of their publications (author, title, subject, analytical and cross reference headings) for $110. Three or four other bureaus have their own printed card catalogues, copies of which may be

obtained at the same rate as Library of Congress cards. Where department and bureaus do not furnish their own cards the Library of Congress will supply them. Then there is the added advantage of a printed card catalogue. Another case equal in size to that in the main library will therefore be necessary as soon as cataloguing is commenced in the depository. This case shall contain nothin [sic] but government documents cards and shall be situated in Lemonnier Library where it may be readily consulted.[45]

Bibliographic and intellectual access to the library's collection were accomplished through a union card catalog. The idea to include government documents' representation in the card catalog seemed obvious. Foik's plan for a separate catalog for documents was replaced at some time with the cards' integration into the main catalog, although a separate shelflist for documents has always been maintained. Inclusion in the card catalog, however, meant that the documents had to be cataloged.

Foik's extensive comments allude to the recurring problems that would plague the Notre Dame Library's documents collection:

...government documents although nearly all shelved are as yet not arranged. Here the attention of a careful supervisor is constantly necessary since the complications of arrangement are rather puzzling to the inexperienced assistant. Sufficient attention has not been paid to the government checklists and government invoices up to the present time. The sacks of documents as they arrive should be promptly checked off, shortages indicated, and the Supt. of Documents notified. Until such time as these books are perfectly arranged, the cataloguing of them is out of the question.[46]

Cataloging in Foik's time meant using the Dewey Decimal Classification scheme to arrange the collection. During 1928/29, a decision was made to switch to the Library of Congress' scheme.[47] But the premise of cataloging parts of the documents collection persisted as the director's comment in 1932 makes clear: "several important runs in the government documents have been fully cataloged and have had considerable use since being made available."[48]

The trend at the Notre Dame Library to catalog and classify selected portions of the collection continued until the mid-1960s. The 1949/50 Annual Report tells of the removal of specific portions of the documents collection that have been integrated into the stacks. "...a number of the better known and more frequently asked for documents have been bound..., classified and cataloged, and shelved in the regular stacks. This makes them much more easily available to our readers."[49] This quote typifies the classic assumptions about a documents collection. It suggests that "unusually valuable" documents could be cataloged and classified easily, thereby implying that the remainder of the collection is not as valuable.

Increased use of the collection in 1942/43 prompted additional documents to be cataloged fully which in turn resulted in "greater use than ever before of this valuable material. Long runs of certain sets are awaiting binding..."[50] despite being recognized as highly useful and desirable.

Another large documents cataloging project occurred in 1964/65. As before, the documents were retrieved from the basement, but this time it was Memorial Library's basement.[51]

Alternative Arrangements: The *Serial Set* and SuDoc Classification

Throughout, one segment of the documents collection was of particular concern. Espy mentioned titles produced by executive departments that are part of the *Congressional Set*, or, as it is commonly known, the *Serial Set*. The *Serial Set* has always been an important component of the documents collection. It contains Senate and House reports and documents. It also contains some executive documents, issued first as separates ineligible for distribution through depository, then reissued and distributed as part of the *Serial Set* by order of Congress.

The *Serial Set* is fascinating for its historical perspectives. For instance, volumes in *Ethnology*, some about Native American culture, include authentic Native American stories and their English translations. Other volumes, issued by the War Department, include geological surveys with hand-colored maps of the West when the Pacific Railroad was built. And, in a *Joint Committee Report* of over 1,200 pages, three legislators reported to Congress in 1877 on the topic of Chinese immigration and its implications.

The *Serial Set*, however, also illustrates the difficulties of providing bibliographic access to documents. The *Checklist of United States Public Documents* supplied access to the *Serial Set*. Called the *Checklist*, and not the "catalog," for its brief entries, it provided an arrangement for the collection on the shelves [52] and, concurrently, an inventory tool for discerning gaps in the documents collection. Today, CIS's commercially published *U.S. Serial Set Index, 1789–1969* (*CIS*) provides better access to titles within the *Serial Set*. But neither the *Checklist* nor *CIS* provides subject access to a documents collection that has been integrated into a subject classified collection. Much more satisfactory is a classification system designed for government documents.

A classification system for government documents was devised between 1895 and 1903.[53] This scheme contains an important key to addressing successfully the problems arising in documents arrangement. It provides a non-subject-based structure that does not resist the inherent nature of government documents. The Superintendent of Documents Classification (SuDoc) scheme, as it is called, brings together government publications produced by the same agency, department, or bureau. The system depends upon the organization of the government and the agencies' placement therein. Consequently, when government agencies reorganize, a frequent occurrence, the classification numbers for their publications change. Publications from the time of reorganization forward receive new numbers based upon the new position of the producing agency. Often, a reorganized agency's publications are shelved in several different places, even though titles may not have changed; but the agency's administrative position within the government has.

> During the past 2 years many evenings, holidays and other odd moments have been given to straightening out the documents collection. One valuable section—the Congressional Series—of this vast accumulation has at last been systematically arranged according to the government classification and the collection checked in the "Check List."[54]

The reference to the "government classification" system in the quotation from the 1923/24 report of the Notre Dame Library's Reference Department is unclear. Although the SuDoc classification

58

certainly is a possibility, the traditional arrangement of the *Serial Set*, and the way the set is arranged today, is by the serial number. Serial numbers are established consecutive numbers used to arrange Congressional reports or documents, including agency serials reissued in the Congressional edition.[55] A *Checklist* entry for an agency serial such as an annual report, therefore, may contain both a SuDoc number and a serial number. Possibly, Notre Dame's *Serial Set* has been rearranged more than once, an illustration of the difficulties presented by government documents here.

Since 1895, the *Monthly Catalog*, a list of documents produced monthly by GPO with an annual index, and arranged by title under agency and topic, has provided the only regular indexing to government documents. This publication's problems were cited in an argument against a separate documents collection in the Social Sciences Department's annual report of 1967/68:

> If a person needs a publication <u>recently</u> published by the...[GPO], he may not find the *Monthly Catalog* of much assistance. There is often a considerable time lag from the time an item is published until the time it appears...Although there is an index in each of the monthly issues..., there is no cumulation of the index until the December issue. ...[It] can make the search for a recent title both frustrating and time-consuming...It may be necessary to check several volumes...before a title on the required subject is located...The library will not have all of the titles included...so that a library user may find...just the title he wants only to discover that it is not owned by the library.[56]

A New Solution

One of the main tenets of the depository system, of course, is providing access to the collection to people within the Congressional District. The increased use of federal documents by others than the Notre Dame community was noted in 1949/50. This hints also at the increasing demands placed upon the library as a research institution:

> ...more and more use is being made of our Federal Documents than ever before. ...The South Bend Public Library receives only a limited number of federal documents and the Notre Dame Library therefore receives frequent calls from South Bend business men, lawyers and

such industrial organizations as the Bendix Corporation and the Studebaker Corporation.[57]

Two years prior to the Rev. Theodore M. Hesburgh's presidency, the University administration, "requested the American Library Association...to make a survey of the Library."[58] The decision to undertake the survey augurs the era of academic development that characterized the Hesburgh years. The survey's purpose was to assess the library's organization, administration, collections, and operations and to recommend strategies that would allow the library to develop in such a way that it could accommodate the expected demands that would be placed on it as an "agent in the learning, teaching, and research functions."[59]

Wilson and Lundy's mid-century assessment of the government documents collection was:

> Federal and state government publications are less complete than they should be to support the graduate programs in economics, education, history, international relations, political science, and sociology. At present, access to these materials for easy use is limited by reason of lack of space and personnel to service them adequately.[60]

Their recommendation was "that the collection of publications of Federal, state, and foreign governments be built up extensively and administered in such a way as to be easily accessible."[61] To accomplish this, they suggested that "the acquisition, receipt, recording, and processing of government documents...be transferred from the reference department as it now exists to appropriate divisions of the Technical Services...and...an addition to the staff...be made..."[62] Their recommendations would be realized, but not before nearly two decades had intervened.

The Resolutions

Memorial Library's vast space, when it first opened 30 years ago, and its organizational structure were keys to resolving the "documents problem." First, it was acknowledged that LC classified documents should be shelved forever with the "regular" books. Then measures were taken which proved to be interim ones, in retrospect. A clearinghouse was established on the second floor to provide immediate access for documents received until replaced by bound volumes or until LC printed cards arrived. Those documents overseen by the Social Sciences Department were: hearings, reports, bills, slip laws, and the preliminary edition of *U.S. Supreme Court Reports.*[63]

Librarian Michael Abaray offered to the director of the library, the Rev. James W. Simonson on February 29, 1968, a plan for the final solution for the "documents problem." He proposed that government documents become not only a separate collection, but also a collection arranged by the SuDoc classification scheme. "When the Superintendent of Documents classification is employed, both processing and retrieval is greatly simplified."[64] His proposal met opposition from Marie Lawrence who recommended that it "should be reconsidered." She pointed out that his plan "is the same as that used when we first came here to work over forty years ago and which was not satisfactory."[65]

Abaray's proposal, nevertheless, was implemented during the 1968/69 academic year. Lois Cherry, the first documents librarian, held the position which was split between technical services where she cataloged the documents and public services where she rearranged the documents. At the same time, the Social Sciences Department relinquished oversight of the collection to the Business and Economics Department. The new caretakers of the collection stated:

> The establishment of a separate Documents Center was enthusiastically endorsed by this department since the Business Administration and the Economics Faculty rely heavily on government documents for teaching and research.[66]

The last reorganizational milestone is found in the report of the Task Force on Reorganization of Public Services. The thrust of the plan shifted the departments from subject-oriented to function-oriented. Notably, the Reference and Bibliography Department was created on the first floor of Memorial Library. By the end of the 1972/73 academic year, this new department included the Documents Center, where it is today.

With the physical location of the Documents Center established and the SuDoc classified collection on the shelves, focus shifted to providing administrative and reference services. In 1974/75, Stephen M. Hayes was hired as social sciences librarian but within six months received a new position of reference and public documents librarian. Two full-time library assistants were added to the student support staff. In 1989, Michael A. Lutes became assistant documents and night reference librarian.

For the past twenty years, the arrangement for "public documents" has been stable. The processing is centralized within the unit. The collection has been shifted, but not relocated or rearranged. Microtext was moved from the second floor to an area adjacent to the Documents Center to facilitate the use of documents in that format. Reference service to the collection is provided from the Reference Desk. An electronic version of the *Monthly Catalog, GPO on Silverplatter,* now provides access to the collection from a CD-ROM. The problem of access divided between an LC-classified, and a SuDoc-classified collection will be resolved in early 1994, by loading Marcive's electronic bibliographic records into UNLOC, the libraries' online catalog. The efficiency of the organization has been endorsed by GPO inspection reports since 1975, which have reported consistently, "excellent collection, a productive and knowledgeable staff, and a firm commitment to depository public service."[67]

A Changing Collection

GPO introduced microform documents four years before the University Libraries' centenary as a federal depository and changed the face of Notre Dame's documents collection forever. GPO's original intention to issue non-GPO imprinted documents in microfiche format was to augment depository distribution. These undistributed imprints, referred to as "fugitive documents," often result from agencies' failures to fulfill their depository requirements, either purposefully or by accident. Had the augmentation been achieved, the ideal of distributing all government publications through the Depository Library Program would have been realized. But budget cuts during the Reagan years and the cost savings potential of the format, established microfiche as a substitute for paper, rather than as a format for completing collections which would not have the publications otherwise.

Notre Dame Library was one of the first depositories to embrace this new format when given the opportunity in 1979. The library wanted to possess non-GPO imprinted documents and to address space issues. During the 1992/93 academic year, the Documents Center received 82 percent of its documents in microfiche. Requests for budgeting shifted from yearly requests for more shelving for paper documents to yearly requests for more microfiche cabinets.

The current Documents Center contains three particularly noteworthy collections. The STARFICHE, a collection of NASA contractors' reports received initially through the University's NASA contractor status, was transferred from the Engineering Library when the documents were declared to be depository.

The Department of Energy (DOE) produced a limited number of retrospective collections as penance for noncompliance with the depository law. University Libraries' Documents Center is fortunate to be one of the 26 depositories selected to receive this microfiche collection valued at $125,000.

Richard J. O'Melia, a Notre Dame alumnus, donated his personal collection of documents and other materials gathered during his years as General Counsel to the House Un-American Activities Committee.

The 1990s introduction of electronic resources marked the beginning of the electronic era in the Documents Center. Information is now available on CD-ROM, online databases, and other electronic formats. The libraries' collection is expanding to include electronic products such as numeric files and microdata.

Distribution of electronic formats began when a few forward-looking agencies such as the U.S. Bureau of the Census issued its *Test Disc II* and the Environmental Protection Agency issued its *Toxic Release Inventory*. These agencies' independent actions penetrated a barrier prohibiting the distribution of CD-ROM information to depository libraries. Notre Dame Libraries' activity at the national level includes participation in several pilot projects to test the advisability and method of incorporating electronic information into the Depository Library Program. As one of the first test sites, Notre Dame influenced the development of future versions of these and other discs.

Recently the Office of Management and Budget, responding to pressures from the depositories and others, defined government publications to be those of government origination and not to be dependent upon any format in which the information happens to be published. Further, the Congress enacted the GPO Enhancement Bill of 1993 which authorized GPO to publish electronic government information and to distribute it through the depository system. Although the Bill and the regulation are too new yet to have been implemented, electronic government information as depository items routinely received appears to be imminent.

Epilogue or Prologue?

GPO is one of the agencies under scrutiny by the National Performance Review, Vice President Al Gore's effort to reinvent government (RIGO). Among the revisited ideas are that private printers can do a better, more cost-efficient job of publishing than can the GPO; and that a decentralized agency-direct-to-depository distribution program may be better than the current system. This chapter closes literally on the eve of the announcement of the RIGO plan, *From Red Tape to Results: Creating a Government that Works Better and Costs Less*,[68] wherein the GPO and its depository system may be reinvented, and perhaps, returned to that early 1800s model. Whatever happens, Notre Dame's documents collection will feel the effects just as it felt the effects of Schuyler Colfax's political maneuvers.

---

1. Peter Hernon, Charles R. McClure, and Gary R. Purcell, *GPO's Depository Library Program* (Norwood, NJ: Ablex, 1985), vii.

2. Robert E. Kling, Jr., *The Government Printing Office* (New York: Praeger, 1970), 3.

3. Hernon, 3.

4. Kling, 10.

5. United States, Government Printing Office, *Annual Report* (Washington, DC: GPO, 1992), 23.

6. Hernon, 4.

7. Yuri Nakata, *From Press to People* (Chicago: American Library Association, 1979), 1.

8. Hernon, 5.

9. Nakata, 9.

10. Schuyler Colfax to the Rev. Edward Sorin, 27 September 1858, Sorin Period 1858-B Correspondence Collection (hereafter cited as SPCC) 1970-1,

box 4, folder 4 (1858B), Province Archives Center, Notre Dame, IN, (hereafter cited as PA).

11. Schuyler Colfax to the Rev. Edward Sorin, 21 October 1858, SPCC, 1970–1, box 4, folder 4 (1858B), PA.

12. Ibid.

13. Schuyler Colfax to the Rev. Edward Sorin, 25 October 1858, SPCC, 1970–1, box 4, folder 4 (1858B), PA.

14. Schuyler Colfax to the Rev. Edward Sorin, 2 March 1859, University of Notre Dame Early Presidents' Records (hereafter cited as UPEL) 1/2, UNDA.

15. Kling, 17.

16. U.S. Congress, Joint Committee on Printing, *Government Depository Libraries: The Present Law Governing Designated Depository Libraries*, rev. July 1982, 97th Cong., 2d sess., 1982, Committee Print, 102–103.

17. Hernon, 3.

18. U.S. Superintendent of Documents, *Checklist of the United States Public Documents, 1789–1909*, 3rd ed. rev. and enlarged (Washington, DC: GPO, 1911), vii, (hereafter cited as *Checklist*).

19. Kling, 34–35.

20. Thomas J. Schlereth, *The University of Notre Dame: A Portrait of Its History and Campus* (Notre Dame, IN: University of Notre Dame Press, 1976), 37.

21. "Local Items," *The Notre Dame Scholastic* 12 (12 April 1879): 511, (hereafter cited as *Scholastic*).

22. Wilson/Lundy, 30.

23. Arthur J. Hope, *Notre Dame, One Hundred Years*, rev. ed. (Notre Dame, IN: University Press, 1948), 150.

24. AR, 1941–42, 11.

25. AR, Law Librarian, 1945–46, [2].

26. Hernon, 14.

27. 44 USC 1909.

28. Hernon, 7.

29. Ibid., 7.

30. AR, 1911–12, [1-2].

31. *Annual Report of the Public Printer, 1923*, [Bureau ed.] (Washington, DC: GPO, 1924), 13.

32. AR, Reference Department, 1923–24, [2].

33. Nakata, 10.

34. Wilson/Lundy, 30.

35. AR, Reference Department, 1923–24, [2].

36. AR, Documents Center, 1992–93, 4.

37. AR, Reference Department, 1923–24, [2].

38. AR, Acquisitions Department, 1961–62, 8.

39. Ibid.

40. Wilson/Lundy, 116.

41. *Scholastic* 12 (12 April 1879): 511.

42. U.S. Congress, Senate, *Annual Report of the Public Printer*, 54th Cong., 1st sess., 1895, S. Doc. 32 [Congressional ed.] (Washington, DC: GPO, 1895), 25.

43. Florence M. Espy to James Edwards, 1909, Edwards Collection (hereafter cited as CEDW) 27/01, UNDA.

44. Florence M. Espy to James Edwards, 1909, CEDW, 27/01, UNDA.

45. AR, 1911–12, [2].

46. Ibid.

47. AR, 1928–29, 5.

48. AR, 1931–32, 10–11.

49. AR, 1949–50, 3.

50. AR, 1942–43, 6.

51. AR, Social Sciences/Business Administration Department, 1964–65, 8.

52. *Checklist*, xii.

53. Nakata, 69.

54. AR, Reference Department, 1923–24, [1].

55. *Checklist*, xi.

56. AR, Social Sciences Department, 1967–68, 31–32.

57. AR, 1949–50, 3.

58. Wilson/Lundy, vii.

59. Ibid.

60. Ibid., 58.

61. Ibid., 177.

62. Ibid., 124.

63. AR, Social Sciences Department, 1966–67, 5.

64. AR, Social Sciences Department, 1967–68, 30.

65. Ibid.

66. AR, Business and Economics Department, 1968–69, 4.

67. Donald E. Fossedal, Supt. of Documents, to Robert C. Miller, Director of Libraries, 6 December 1988, *U.S. Depository Library Inspection Report, 1988.*

68. "Ending 'Obsolete' Monopolies," *The Washington Post*, 24 August 1993, 1, A15.

Paul J. Foik:
Agent for Change

ANNE KEARNEY

Education and Training

Paul J. Foik came to the Notre Dame Library from Washington, D.C. where he had completed his doctorate in history at the Catholic University writing on the history of journalism.[1] It was during those years that Foik's potential for librarianship was discovered. While a student at CU, Foik lived at Holy Cross College, a house of studies for members of the Congregation of Holy Cross pursuing graduate degrees at Catholic University and/or completing their theological studies before ordination to the priesthood. During Foik's years of residency, Father James A. Burns was the superior, and it was he who first recognized the budding librarian in Foik. In a letter to Provincial Morrissey, Burns commented that he thought Foik would make a good librarian so he had placed him in charge of the seminary library.[2]

Although Foik did not have a degree in library science, he seems to have received some type of training at CU. Whether this was through formal courses or more in the nature of an apprenticeship is not clear.[3] However he obtained his expertise, his appointment as librarian at Notre Dame brought a new era of library professionalism to the University. He did this by lobbying for a new building, developing the collections, hiring professionally trained staff, and by becoming an internationally known and respected librarian.

The Library Building

When Foik began his new duties as librarian in 1912, the library was largely a one-man operation; the only regular employees were student assistants. While Foik would soon seek to change that, his first priority was to consolidate those parts of the collections which had been stored in various buildings all over campus, so that they could be warehoused in the basement of Sorin Hall.[4] Although the University had little capital and no firm fundraising plans, Foik soon began to push for a new library building.

In 1912 the main library collection was inadequately housed in the Administration Building. The quarters were cramped with books two deep on the shelves and piled on the floor; the building was too hot in the summer and too cold in the winter.[5] Foik's success in convincing the administration that a new building was needed soon involved him intimately in its planning and construction. To prepare himself Foik worked closely with the head of the Department of Architecture at Notre Dame. "He studied the Library Building from the Librarians [sic] standpoint, and I studied it from an Architects [sic] standpoint, consequently we both derived a great deal of benefit from this study."[6] Foik also benefitted from consultations with the top academic and public librarians in the country. Mary Eileen Ahern, the editor of *Public Libraries*, gave what remains the best advice possible: "...the library ought to be built from the inside out. The library requirements ought to be planned carefully by library people, and then the problem of encasing this appropriately, substantially and safely ought to be left in the hands of an architect, but an architect ought not to plan the inside of the building except under the direction of a librarian."[7] Ahern was not the only librarian with whom Foik corresponded concerning a new library. He also wrote to William C. Lane, Harvard; William M. Hepburn, Purdue; Walter M. Smith, Wisconsin; William Bishop, Library of Congress; Theodore Koch, University of Michigan; Henry E. Legler, Chicago Public Library; and Earl E. Sperry at Syracuse. Perhaps it was Foik's lack of formal education in librarianship that made him so concerned with doing his homework. Whatever it was, the Notre Dame Library was the better for it.[8]

The selection of an architect soon involved Foik in intra-community politics. The Library Building Committee decided to have a standard competition, allowing architects to submit their drawings and plans for the building. One member of the committee, Father Quinlan, had two brothers-in-law named Kelly who had joined some other architects in founding a firm. Foik described the Kellys as commercial rather than professional architects and their background seems to have been in construction rather than design. Father Quinlan interested his two brothers-in-law in the project and seems to have revealed to them information that should have been confidential. After seven different plans had been submitted Foik asked William Kelly to make a presentation. When Foik asked him questions about his plan, he could not answer even the simple ones. All this activity with the Kellys happened during the summer vacation when Foik and Quinlan were the only committee members on campus. Foik complained to President John Cavanaugh and when the committee members returned, Foik brought the issue before them. They, too, were indignant, but because Father Cavanaugh had left for Ohio, nothing further could be done. At this point Quinlan tried an end run. Claiming that the dispute was a personal one between himself and Foik, Quinlan gave that as the reason the Kellys had withdrawn their plans from the competition. Quinlan went on to request that the Kellys' plans be presented to the executives of the University without further involvement of the committee. Foik was able to prevent this since he had kept the Congregation apprised of the procedures for the competition. When the Kellys' plans were brought before the Library Building Committee, Quinlan was absent and the plans were unanimously rejected. Quinlan, however, was not finished. He had his brothers-in-law show their plans to various professional librarians such as M.E. Ahern, a good friend of Foik. In this way he hoped to further the argument that it was a personal quarrel rather than one based on merit. He did not prevail. The Library Building Committee and the Executive Committee of the University unanimously chose Edward Tilton as the architect for the new library building.[9]

In November of 1915 Foik proudly wrote to Burns, who was still at Holy Cross College, that ground had been broken for the new quarter of a million dollar library and that the architect would be the famous Edward Tilton. Foik also reported that he had checked the plans and the architect with his many friends and contacts among professional librarians:

During the past week, I attended the meeting of the Indiana Library Association and received for Mr. Tilton's plan the hearty approval of experienced librarians. Mr. Utley, permanent Secretary of the American Library Association and Miss M.E. Ahern, another one of the executives of the American Library Association and President of the Illinois Library Association and Editor of "Public Libraries" [sic] think a great deal of the plan as drawn up. Miss Ahern has asked me to give her the first opportunity to discuss the plan in her magazine.

The library, to be built of Bedford stone in a Renaissance style, was to be large enough to hold 618,000 volumes, the Catholic Archives of America, the Art Museum, the Bishops' Memorial Hall, two large reading rooms and sixty carrels. With such a large capacity, Foik was planning a building to last for the next 75 years.[10]

Foik's design problems were over, but his problems regarding construction were only beginning! Once again the reality of community politics caused problems. Brother Irenaeus had received a subcontract for installing the heating system for the library. Problems with the heating system were almost continuous. In one letter to Tilton, evidently having had his fill of Brother Irenaeus, Foik referred to him as the "Enfant Terrible."[11] Because Tilton and Foik corresponded about problems with Irenaeus and other community members, it is no surprise that Foik later wrote Tilton that "much as I esteem the high qualities of both of the higher superiors, yet there is no reason to feel at all dismayed that at some future date the same intimate relations as existed between yourself and several here may be again resumed. The time may not be very long distant when we may not have these men to deal with, but others."[12]

Foik was referring to the 1918 changes in Canon Law which would mean a new president for the University and a new provincial. The appointment of Father James A. Burns as president proved to be fortuitous for the library and Foik for a number of reasons, one of which was the resolution of some of the problems left over from Brother Irenaeus's subcontracting. In January of 1921 Foik wrote Burns about the problem of water from the heating system flooding the basement classrooms. Even in the less formal Notre Dame of 1921, the president was not ordinarily consulted about water problems. Foik was forced to bring this to Burns because those concerned with correcting the work, which had not been done correctly in the first place, had ignored Foik's previous 16 complaints.[13] Burns, however, was a president of action and soon Foik was able to write about the visit of a repairman who solved all of the problems.[14]

Library Collections

In September of 1919 Foik shared with Burns his idea of how the growth of Notre Dame should be measured: in the richness of the collections in the library. Foik optimistically proposed to use the faculty to achieve this goal by asking them to submit recommendations for supplementary materials needed for their courses. Foik was beginning with the most basic level of collecting, course support.[15] The faculty members, as is often their wont today, were not always cooperative. A case in point is Mr. Scheib, dean of the Department of Agriculture. Foik seems to have had a running battle with Scheib for a number of years. The first recorded instance concerned a student who reported to Scheib that he could find nothing in the library on clover. Foik investigated and found that the student had not consulted *The Agricultural Index* as he was instructed but had looked in another reference work. Finding nothing, he did not consult the reference librarian but instead told the circulation librarian that he could find nothing and left. As could be predicted, there was a lot of material in the correct index. In writing this explanation, Foik went on to chide Scheib for his lack of cooperation with the library in regard to student assignments.[16]

Foik's letter seemed to have had little effect, for the very next semester Scheib gave his students five special assignments in such esoteric topics as: Chinese gardens; landscape design in France at the time of Napoleon; Japanese gardens in America; landscape gardening during the Reformation; and landscape design at the time of Caesar! In asking for Scheib's cooperation in building a collection capable of handling such questions, Foik referred to the 1920 survey of the Notre Dame Library in which Frank K. Walter, former dean of the New York Library School, had pointed out the necessity for faculty cooperation in the improvement of reference service. Foik further pointed out that "to send students to the library when a little forethought might have suggested to you that some of these items are lacking is unfair to the students, and unfair and inconsiderate towards ourselves. We are just as anxious as you are to keep up a high appreciation of our efforts."[17]

One of Foik's most noteworthy achievements in collection building was convincing Father John A. Zahm, C.S.C., to donate his personal Dante collection to the University. It formed the basis of what is ranked the third best Dante collection in the United States.[18] Not content with just acquiring it, Foik worked to continue its growth and had much correspondence with a London rare bookdealer and with Baker and Taylor, a major company which helped libraries obtain books and other materials. When donors inquired about what books would be of the most value as gifts, Foik mentioned books by or about Dante.[19]

Foik worked with a variety of people and groups to get donations: judges, businessmen, union leaders. Because of Foik, it was Notre Dame rather than Cornell or Princeton that received the personal library of Frank Duffy, the general secretary of the United Brotherhood of Carpenters and Joiners.[20] Nor did Foik overlook the valuable local materials on Notre Dame. In 1923 he began collecting materials for the Notre Dame Collection and had Paul Byrne, the reference librarian, begin to make a record of all the Notre Dame theses then on file.[21]

Good sources of information for Foik about collections were the Notre Dame alumni who alerted him when potential collections might come on the market. One example is a letter from Paul R. Martin about the Right Reverend T. F. O'Gara's library, one of the best libraries of Irish literature in the country.[22] Another was the Irish collection of Captain Francis O'Neill of Chicago who had been brought to Foik's attention by P. T. O'Sullivan, the father of a Notre Dame student. "I would also like to obtain for future reference the address of Captain O'Neill in order that I might keep him interested in Notre Dame. Do you think that it is about time that you were getting the latter gentleman interested in a visit to the University?"[23] Although it took a number of years Captain O'Neill did eventually donate his collection to the library.

This interest in things Celtic was of some duration. In 1917 the Indiana Ancient Order of Hibernians and Ladies Auxiliary gave the University $2,000 to be used in building up an Irish library and establishing a Celtic museum. Shortly after that Foik established the Irish National Library Foundation as the vehicle for obtaining books and money. The first large addition to that collection was the O'Kelleher philosophical collection which Foik obtained in 1921.[24] But even before that Foik was engaged in fundraising for the Irish National Library Foundation, and it is this activity that brought him to the attention of the Department of Justice. Foik had composed a fundraising form letter for the Foundation which was mailed March 15, 1919. In this letter Foik appealed to Irish nationalism and hatred of England and her censorship as a reason for subscribing to the Foundation. The rhetoric was emotional: "The time has come when Ireland is determined to break forever the chains of English oppression, which have so long bound her...Break up this English censorship of the press; combat English propaganda and opposition to Irish freedom by subscribing or making a donation to the Irish National Library Foundation."[25] A copy of this letter, which was sent to the Rev. Barnard Feeney in County Roscommon, Ireland, came to the attention of the acting chief of the Department of Justice in Washington. He wrote an agent in Fort Wayne, Indiana, that Foik might be involved in Sinn Fein activities. Although the letter was addressed to Mr. Green of Fort Wayne, it was mailed to Mr. Green at Notre Dame, Indiana, who naturally enough brought it to Father Foik![26] There is no evidence that the Department of Justice ever realized its error and Foik, seemingly unperturbed, continued to solicit funds and monies for the Irish collection with his fervor and language undamaged and uncensored. By 1923 the University had received $1,500 for the purchase of Irish books.[27]

Censorship

Foik's attempts to combat censorship and to protect the materials in the library's collections brought him into conflict with Father John O'Hara, later Cardinal O'Hara. Although censoring activities were never part of his official duties at the University, he acted in that capacity on a regular basis. His view of library collections was that they needed frequent and thorough weeding so that the students' minds would remain untouched by anything which he considered immoral, unorthodox or unworthy. O'Hara had no qualms about his ability to determine such materials or about his right to destroy them.

In the fall of 1922 a student named Sachs told Paul Fenlon, then working as a library employee, that his professor had assigned a work of Dumas. Fenlon gave Sachs the book which was on the *Index* with the intent of bringing the case to Father O'Hara who was Prefect of Religion. When the case came to O'Hara's attention he destroyed the book without consulting Foik. Although Foik's letter to O'Hara is couched in almost subservient terms, he still makes clear that books belonging to the library should not be destroyed without his authorization:

I hope you will pardon me in questioning the action which you took in the case of Mr. Sachs, and the work of Dumas. I do not think that the property of the University for which I am responsible should be destroyed without my authorization. I do not wish to make this an issue but am merely questioning the prudence of your action...I question therefore, the right to destroy without at least an interview with the Librarian on the matter in question...Please do not take these remarks in hostile attitude because they are not intended in that way.[28]

Building up collections, however, involved more than simply working with the professors, donors and alumni or defending them against Father O'Hara. From the beginning Foik was handicapped by the mechanics of ordering and paying for library materials. For example, the President of the University approved every order and could also order materials against library funds. It was only after ten years that Foik wrote to President Matthew Walsh asking for some discretionary funds so that he could obtain needed books immediately and purchase second-hand books at good prices.[29]

Even worse problems were encountered in dealing with journals. For some reason the journal subscriptions at times went through the University bookstore which was under the secretary for the University. In 1916 Foik wrote to Father Burke, University secretary, about the problems of subscription renewals. Foik wanted to take the renewals from the bookstore and turn them over to a subscription agency or vendor.[30] Finally in 1922 Foik placed the journal subscriptions with both domestic and international vendors with generally much better results.[31]

Despite having vendors take care of most subscriptions, some periodicals were not available except through direct order to the publisher. One periodical of that nature was the *Extension Magazine*. This was a particularly vexing subscription because the business manager, Mr. Kauffman, sent numerous dunning letters to Foik. "You have received several courteous requests from us asking for payment of your past due account...One of the largest items of expense in modern business, is the cost of carrying outstanding book accounts,..."[32] After Foik had had his staff determine that the account had long since been paid and the check cashed, a pointed letter was sent to Mr. Kauffman. "I am at a loss to know what business methods that you employ, and especially when we have taken the pains which will enable you to check up and set things aright."[33]

Another area of concern was the cost of subscriptions. Immediately after World War I there was a sharp increase in journal prices due to the world economic situation. And, as is true today, publishers charged libraries higher prices for subscriptions than they did individuals. With funds ever short, Foik attempted to partially resolve the situation by having the University pay for professors' subscriptions which were then sent to the library for its collections. Many publishers, although not all, did agree to this arrangement. The American Physical Society wrote that it would be happy to have the University renew Father Irving's membership, but it could send the journal only to the professor.[34]

Personnel

As noted above, when Foik came to Notre Dame his only assistants were students. It was clear to Foik that if Notre Dame was to have a library which matched its intellectual goals for the University, there was a need for full-time clerical help and full-time professional help, too. This situation prevailed until after Frank Walter's report on the library in 1920. The student personnel, who were so desperately needed, were a mixed blessing, and Foik struggled throughout his tenure at Notre Dame to obtain good student workers.

Perhaps it was Foik's previous experiences which caused him to react so strongly to the rumor that Father Burke, director of studies, planned to transfer one of the library student assistants to Father Galligan. Seemingly without any prior investigation, Foik fired a letter of complaint to President Burns. "I would endeavor to overlook the matter if such occurred but once in a long experience, but it is aggravating to have this arbitrary action repeated with such frequency...I cannot perform my work efficiently if this sort of treatment is persisted in."[35]

When Burns asked Burke to respond to Foik's letter, he was incredulous. Burke denied ever removing any students from the library and pointed out that Father O'Hara had given Father Galligan his stenographer. One result of Foik's complaints to Burns was that Foik could hire some staff, but he was told to go slowly on cutting student employment.[36]

75

In 1923 Foik wrote President Walsh on the same subject. This time his complaint was about Mr. Casey who was now in charge of student employment. When disciplinary action resulted in the removal of a student assistant, it took two months to find a replacement. The time would have been even longer if Foik had not been approached by Mr. Gallagher, a student employed in the dining hall, who wished to switch to the library. Foik's woes included losing another student to disciplinary action who was replaced by one with high absenteeism. Another student who had lost his father had to go home for an extended period. To bolster his argument Foik quoted from Walter's "Survey" and his previous reports to President Burns in which he had requested more staff positions. One category of staff position would be for young men who would receive part tuition and part cash for their work.[37] If Walsh answered this request, no written record remains.

Foik had better luck filling his professional positions because they were solely in his hands. As was true in the planning for the new library, Foik often wrote to his colleagues for their advice and to get leads on prospective employees. By 1922 Foik had been able to add both a professionally trained cataloger, Anna Kosek, and a professionally trained reference librarian, Paul Byrne, to his staff. His vision of what the Notre Dame Library could be was shared in a letter to Grace Hill. "I am full of enthusiasm for this work myself and I hope to have a galaxy of enthusiasts and make this the leading Catholic library in the country."[38] Foik believed that the eyes of the library world were on Notre Dame because no other Catholic school had made the advancement that Notre Dame had. "They look to Notre Dame for the initiation of any movement that has its inception in Catholic circles."[39]

Library Instruction

Of course, it is not enough to have a wonderful new building, good collections and the nucleus of a fine staff. What is needed are patrons who will use the collections. Foik was well aware of the Notre Dame students' need for instruction in the use of the library, but to meet this need required the cooperation of their professors. Professorial cooperation was spotty at best. One young professor, George Shuster, later president of Hunter College, but then serving as the head of the Department of Letters, pushed his students to use the library. He gave the library one hour a month for each of the freshman English classes.[40] Foik used these nine classes to acquaint the students with the library. Each class was given a follow-up problem and at the end of the semester, the students had to present their English instructors with a theme covering the important points discussed. Classes began with an orientation visit to the library. The second class was an explanation of the Dewey classification and the arrangement of books on the shelves. Other topics were the card catalog, periodical indexes, the book, reference books in general, reference books for special subjects, government publications and bibliography.[41] At the conclusion of the course, students were asked to respond to a questionnaire which asked, among other things, what books were recommended by the instructors, which ones they had read and which ones were not available in the Notre Dame Library.[42]

Library School [43]

Almost from the time that Foik became librarian, he saw the need for courses in librarianship. The University first listed courses for a School of Library Science in the *General Catalogue, 1916–1917*. The two-year program required that the applicant had completed two years of college and had a reading knowledge of French, German, Spanish and Italian. Students who completed the course work in the three major areas of bibliography, cataloging and administration would receive certificates.[44] By 1917 Foik had expanded the listing of these areas to reflect specific courses. In 1922 Foik hired Miss Gertrude Blanchard from the Carnegie Library of Pittsburgh to teach in the School of Library Science.[45]

Foik's purpose in starting a library school was to obtain needed assistance in running the Notre Dame Library. As he explained to Paul Byrne, "Should I get sufficient students in normal times to take up this work [library science], then I can better claim a couple of assistants to help me in my arduous duties." The first summer session in 1918 seems to have been a great success and Foik soon had numerous Religious writing to inquire about the program.[46] The next session was even better. For many students it was their first opportunity to have formal instruction in librarianship since Notre Dame was the first Catholic institution to offer such courses.[47] A student still exuberant from his course work wrote Foik in 1919, "I have returned to Little Rock filled with enthusiasm over Library work. You confirmed my opinion of the position a library should occupy in our Colleges, and I am determined to build up here one that will reflect honor on you and Notre Dame— sources of the inspiration."[48]

It was such word-of-mouth advertising that kept the students coming. Although Walter in his "Survey" described the courses as suitable for training student assistants and providing preliminary preparation for librarianship, Foik originally envisioned that these first courses would evolve into a Ph.B. in library science.[49] The summer school continued to experience modest growth and Foik wrote to D. Wilson in November of 1923 that "making all due allowances I can truly say, with the students who enjoyed this course, that the work was decidedly a success...Last year we had six students and this year I personally had seventeen taking classification."[50]

Contributions to Librarianship

Foik had been interested for some years in the question of the expansion of the religion section of the Dewey system of classification. When Foik was in charge of the theology library at Holy Cross College, he had devised with Mr. Snyder of the Catholic University a classification system based on Dewey but adjusted to Catholic subjects. Such a system was a necessity in the more specialized theology library of Holy Cross College. In 1915 Foik received a letter from A. Law Voge, a librarian involved in both Dewey and Library of Congress classification systems, announcing a proposed expansion of sections of the Dewey system.[51] Shortly after that Foik wrote to the Executive Board of the American Library Association (ALA) suggesting an expansion of the religion section to provide for the needs of specialized theological libraries.[52] As late as the 1930s theology librarians were still requesting copies of his classification system.

Although Foik had begun his library work without formal training and had to consult with others at the beginning of his career, soon his natural abilities and talents as well as his contributions began to be recognized. As he wrote Paul Byrne:

Men, whose advice I sought a few years ago on a number of things, I now have the satisfaction of advising with me...Another thing that has added considerably to my prestige in the library field was last year when I was asked to speak before the American Library Association, and again this year before the Indiana Library Association; on the latter occasion there being a far larger crowd for my address than for any of the others throughout the convention.[53]

Another way in which Foik's stature was recognized was by his membership on the National Committee of the United States for the Restoration of the University of Louvain. During World War I, the University and its library had been destroyed. In 1918 the National Committee was organized with 50 prominent men such as William Howard Taft and Teddy Roosevelt as members; Herbert Putnam, the Librarian of Congress, was the chair of the Library Committee.[54] Foik was involved in two ways. He was the librarian in charge of selecting books for the Louvain from those collected in the Midwest and sent to Notre Dame.[55] His second involvement was through the address which he presented before the 1919 meeting of the American Library Institute whose membership was limited to 100 and included the most prominent men in librarianship. Foik's paper, "Louvain of the Past," was given as background before further discussion of the activities of the National Committee. Foik reported to H. H. Regnet on the reception of his paper:

Mr. R. R. Bowker, the editor of the *Library Journal*, at the end of my paper rose to his feet and made a resolution expressing to the authorities of Louvain University the mind of the American Library Institute on the subject of cooperation. He insisted that my name should be included with that of...the executive officers and that this resolution should be cabled to Louvain while the conference was still in session.[56]

In addition to the activities already listed, Foik's years at Notre Dame saw him beginning work on a project that lasted almost the entirety of his life: *The Catholic Periodical Index.* Although the complete story of the *CPI* is interesting, only a sketch can be provided here of Foik's role in the founding of the Catholic Library Association and its primary project, the *CPI.*

During the early 1920s there was a widespread movement toward standardization in the field of library education, a typical stage in the development of any profession. As a member of the Catholic Educational Association (CEA), Foik wanted to see the formation of a library section for the improvement of library conditions in Catholic schools. He hoped it would result in stronger libraries and more professionally trained librarians. Although Foik thought the section would eventually join the American Library Association, it evolved into a group separate from both the ALA and its parent organization the CEA; it later became the Catholic Library Association. Three short years after its founding in 1921, the Library Section began the work of determining the ways and means of establishing *The Catholic Periodical Index* which would be a publication comparable to the H.W. Wilson's *Readers' Guide to Periodical Literature*. This was a huge project and the planning for it was barely begun when Foik was sent to Texas.[57]

Exile

In a 1923 letter to Earl Dickens, a member of the Endowment Drive staff who was traveling with Father Burns, Foik sent a message to Burns that he needed to land an endowment for the library. While monies for books and materials were a priority, there was also a need for more personnel. Foik went on to reiterate his long-standing argument of the need for more staff and professional librarians and less or no student assistants. Foik went on, "I wish you to discuss [this]...candidly with Father Burns for I know that he will lend a sympathetic ear, for after all what is my problem is the University's problem." With his next sentence, Foik seems to show some premonition of future events. "Whoever may be destined hereafter to fill my place if such a course is thought to be expedient will face the same situations that I am trying now to solve."[58]

Shortly before the Provincial Council met in 1924 to decide the new obediences, an unusual meeting took place. President Walsh asked Paul Byrne to meet with him to discuss the library. Byrne, who was a Notre Dame alumnus and a professionally trained librarian, had served as a reference librarian since 1922.[59] Within a few days of the meeting, Byrne submitted a letter which detailed what he saw as the problems in the library: 1. lack of supervision in regard to the book and periodical orders; 2. gaps in the bound periodicals; 3. lack of tact with faculty and students; 4. criticisms of the library course; 5. lack of effort in regard to the Dante and Irish collections; 6. inattention to the archives. Byrne softened these criticisms somewhat:

> The desire to have things right had always been present in Father Foik's mind, but the necessary action has often been neglected...I do not think that we should lose sight of the many fine things that Father Foik has to his credit. He has very modern ideas on what an efficient University Library should be...The training received by Father Foik did not fit him particularly to be a librarian. Because of his lack of knowledge of the technical side of library work, he has been greatly handicapped. Until recently he had to run the Library with student help...[which] is not adequate...I do not think this has been fully realized.[60]

On July 7, 1924, the Provincial Council announced the new obediences: Father Foik would be leaving Notre Dame for the post of director of the library at St. Edward's College in Austin, Texas.[61] Fifty years later Paul Byrne opined that Foik had stepped on some toes; "...in those days if you did that, you were sent to Portland or Texas, Austin." Among those at Notre Dame, St. Edward's was known as the Siberia of the Congregation of Holy Cross.[62] Foik's years at Notre Dame were over.

Conclusions

There is no doubt that the criticisms that Byrne wrote Walsh had some validity. However, they were the same problems that Foik had been struggling with since his arrival in 1912 and which he had described to the University administration on a regular basis. In addition, although Foik did not have a library degree, it is doubtful that he was as ignorant of the technical side of library work as Byrne's letter might lead one to conclude. The technical aspects of acquiring material were always hampered by the processes by which the University authorized the expenditure of monies, not by Foik's lack of knowledge. In regard to the other technical aspect of library work, cataloging, a professional cataloger was the first position that Foik had filled. In addition, someone who was able to expand the Dewey Decimal classification system to better reflect the needs of a specialized theological library is not a man who is lacking in technical knowledge, however he may have obtained it. The discussions above on Foik's efforts for the Dante collection and the Irish collections disprove Byrne's charges on that point.

Why, then, was he exiled? There is no doubt that he stepped on people's toes. But another reason for the change may have been that the University administration found it easier to control a lay person than a confrere. Certainly a layman would not be writing all the letters of complaint that Foik did; it would be too dangerous to his continuation in his post. Nor would a lay librarian send letters to Father O'Hara after one of his raids on the collection. And, only a foolish layman would offer unsolicited criticism of the work standards of a member of the congregation like Brother Irenaeus. Foik was reassigned precisely because he was an agent for change who was moving the library too fast into the future with too high standards for the other members of the congregation and faculty to assimilate and support.

During the 12-year period that he was at Notre Dame Foik had many accomplishments. First, there was the new library building which gave Notre Dame the honor of being the first Catholic university in the United States to erect a separate library building.[63] He brought the collections together, worked to strengthen them and make them accessible. He hired the first professionally trained librarians to work at Notre Dame and was constantly seeking to improve his staff. He brought Notre Dame into the larger world of librarianship through his many professional contacts, his work in founding the Catholic Library Association, his founding of the Notre Dame Library School and his work on *The Catholic Periodical Index*. An agent of change, indeed!

---

1. Support for the research for this chapter was received from the University of Louisville in the form of a Graduate Research Grant and the University of Notre Dame in the form of a Research Travel Grant from the Cushwa Center for the Study of American Catholicism.

2. James A. Burns to Andrew Morrissey, October 15, 1906, Morrissey Administration Correspondence, Provincial Archives. Hereafter cited as PA.

3. Paul J. Foik to director of studies, May 19, 1923, Library Correspondence, Archives of the University of Notre Dame. Hereafter cited as LC, UNDA.

4. AR, 1911–12, [1].

5. Paul R. Byrne, "Paul Joseph Foik, C.S.C.," *Catholic Library World* 12 (March 1941): 183.

6. Foik to Lewis R. Wilson, December 13, 1922, LC, UNDA.

7. M.E. Ahern to Foik, May 25, 1915, LC, UNDA.

8. LC, UNDA.

9. Foik to Ahern, November 19, 1915, LC, UNDA.

10. Foik to Burns, November 17, 1915, LC, UNDA; "The New Library," *The Notre Dame Scholastic*, 46 (November 20, 1915): 169. The new library building had to be replaced in 1963 with the Memorial, later Hesburgh, Library which is also experiencing a space problem 30 years later.

11. Foik to Edward Tilton, September 25, 1918, LC, UNDA.

12. Foik to Tilton, December 7, 1918, LC, UNDA.

13. Foik to Burns, January 17, 1921, LC, UNDA.

14. Foik to Burns, March 22, 1921, LC, UNDA.

15. Foik to Burns, September 23, 1919, LC, UNDA.

16. Foik to Dean Scheib, December 11, 1922, LC, UNDA.

17. Foik to Scheib, February 9, 1923, LC, UNDA.

18. Paul R. Byrne, Interview by Thomas Schlereth and Wendy Clauson Schlereth, June 1 and 2, 1974, Oral History, Part One, p. 38, UNDA.

19. Foik to John. P. Bath, November 12, 1923, LC, UNDA.

20. Frank Duffy to John Cavanaugh, August 22, 1922, LC, UNDA.

21. AR, Reference librarian, 1923–24, 3.

22. Paul R. Martin to Foik, June 16, 1924; Foik to Martin, June 30, 1924, LC, UNDA.

23. Foik to P.T. O'Sullivan, October 7, 1918, Foik Papers, PA.

24. Foik to Burns, April 27, 1921, LC, UNDA.

25. Foik form letter, March 15, 1919, LC, UNDA.

26. Allen to Green, May 21, 1919, LC, UNDA; Foik to P.J. Moynihan, September 21, 1920, LC, UNDA.

27. Foik to Sr. M. Fidelis, July 17, 1920, LC, UNDA; Foik to the director of studies, May 19, 1923, LC, UNDA.

28. Foik to John O'Hara, October 28, 1922, LC, UNDA.

29. Foik to Matthew Walsh, October 20, 1922, LC, UNDA.

30. Foik to Burke, November 13, 1916, LC, UNDA.

31. Foik to Buchhandlung Gustav Fock, January 21, 1922, LC, UNDA.

32. J.A. Kauffman to Foik, April 7, 1924, LC, UNDA.

33. Foik to Kauffman, April 9, 1924, LC, UNDA.

34. Foik to American Physical Society, November 14, 1923; Pegram to Foik, December 3, 1923, LC, UNDA.

35. Foik to Burns, November 21, 1919, LC, UNDA.

36. Burke to Burns, December 11, 1919, LC, UNDA.

37. Foik to Walsh, March 20, 1923, LC, UNDA.

38. Foik to Hill, July 13, 1921, LC, UNDA.
39. Foik to Kosek, May 24, 1922, LC, UNDA.
40. Foik to Burns, March 18, 1922, LC, UNDA.
41. "Library Rules and Instruction for Use," n.d., LC, UNDA.
42. "Freshman English Library Questionnaire," n.d., LC, UNDA.
43. The late Marie K. Lawrence provided invaluable assistance in documenting the evolution of the Notre Dame Library School.
44. *General Catalogue of the University of Notre Dame, 1916–1917*, 130.
45. Foik, Department of Library Science (Corrected Copy) n.d., LC, UNDA; *Who's Who in Library Service* ed. by C.C. Williamson and Alice Jewett, (New York: The H.W. Wilson, Co., 1943), 47.
46. Foik to Byrne, October 2, 1918, Foik Papers, PA.
47. John Federowicz, C.S.C., "Forces Affecting the Development of Libraries at the University of Notre Dame 1843–1968" (Master's thesis, Kent State University, 1968), 72.
48. (Signature Illegible) to Foik, July 7, 1919, Foik Correspondence, PA.
49. Walter, 24; Walsh Presidential Papers, UNDA; Foik, "Memorandum Regarding Librarian," June 20, 1916, LC, UNDA.
50. Foik to D. Wilson, November 15, 1923, LC, UNDA.
51. A. Law Voge to co-laborers, November, 1915, LC, UNDA.
52. Foik to executive board of the American Library Association, January 19, 1916, LC, UNDA.
53. Foik to Byrne, January 29, 1920, Foik papers, PA.
54. *New York Times*, November 11, 1918, Sec. ii, 16.
55. Putnam to Foik, November 6, 1919, LC, UNDA.
56. Foik to H.H. Regnet, June 20, 1921, Foik Papers, PA.
57. Foik, "On the Catholic Guide to Periodical Literature," *Proceedings of the Catholic Educational Association*, 21 (November 1924): 317–23; Maryellen Bressie, "Paul J. Foik, C.S.C., Librarian and Historian." (Master's thesis, University of Texas at Austin, 1964), 75–83.
58. Foik to Earl Dickens, April 7, 1923, Endowment Drive Papers, UNDA.
59. Foik to Burns, May 4, 1922, Burns Presidential Papers, UNDA.
60. Byrne to Walsh, June 21, 1924, Walsh Presidential Papers, UNDA.
61. "Provincial Council Minutes," July 7, 1924, PA.
62. Paul R. Byrne, Interview by Thomas Schlereth and Wendy Clauson Schlereth, June 1 and 2, 1974, Oral History, Part 3, p. 12, UNDA; Marie K. Lawrence, "The University Library at Notre Dame in the Twenties and Thirties," paper presented at the Library History Program, Notre Dame, March 13, 1984.
63. Byrne, "The Library of the University of Notre Dame," *Catholic Bookman* 1 (October 1915): 45.

The John A. Zahm
Dante Collection

LOUIS JORDAN, CHRISTIAN DUPONT
AND THEODORE J. CACHEY, JR.

John Augustine Zahm was born on 11 June 1851 in New Lexington, Ohio, where he began his formal education in a one-room log schoolhouse.[1] His mother was a grandniece of Major General Edward Braddock, British officer of French and Indian War fame. With roots struck deep in American soil, Zahm would later distinguish himself in the company of James Cardinal Gibbons and Archbishops John Ireland and John J. Keane as an enthusiast in the cause of Americanizing the Catholic Church in the United States.

Yet Zahm never excluded the Old World from his vision for the New. From an early age he devoted himself to studying the classics. When he came to Notre Dame in 1867, he enrolled in the Classical Course, the standard curriculum for aspiring priests.

At Notre Dame Zahm came under the influence of Joseph Carrier, C.S.C., who was director of the Science Museum, librarian and professor of chemistry and physics. Carrier showed Zahm that scientific research and its promise for progress were not antagonistic to the ideals of intellectual and moral culture endorsed by the Church. Zahm graduated and entered the novitiate of the Congregation of the Holy Cross in 1871. The following year Carrier took Zahm on as his associate and assigned him the duties of curator of the Museum, librarian, and assistant in chemistry, physics and natural sciences. In 1875, at the age of 23, Zahm was ordained to the priesthood. During that year Father

Carrier left Notre Dame and Zahm was appointed professor and co-director of the Science Department.

Zahm, an enthusiastic collector, expanded the Science Department and Museum at Notre Dame. In 1877 he arranged for the University to purchase a zoological and mineral collection containing thousands of specimens. Unfortunately, many of Zahm's acquisitions were lost in the 1879 fire which destroyed the University's Main Building. Nevertheless, Zahm refused to despair. He initiated a fire department and reserve water system, then actively sought to raise funds for the purchase of new items. During the 1880s Zahm assembled a collection of acoustical equipment that was judged one of the best in the world. He spent summers travelling throughout the United States and Europe, recruiting students and taking note of recent inventions. In 1884, thanks largely to Zahm, the University built a state of the art science building (now the LaFortune Hall Student Center). Still greater responsibilities came the following year when, in addition to his other duties, Zahm was named University vice president.

In 1892, Andrew Morrissey, C.S.C., replaced Zahm as vice president, which allowed the latter greater freedom to lecture and to write. That year his first book appeared, *Sound and Music*. It was to be his only work in physics. Zahm thereafter took up a different theme, the relation of science and religion.

It was during this period that Zahm participated in the emerging Catholic Summer School movement, which aimed to introduce Catholic laity to contemporary intellectual issues. Zahm focused his attention on the merits of Darwinism and evolutionary theory, delivering numerous lectures which brought him national recognition. In 1895 because of his achievements in the natural sciences Pope Leo XIII awarded Zahm the degree of doctor of philosophy. The following year Zahm compiled his lecture notes into book form and published them under the title *Evolution and Dogma*.

Early Dante Collecting

In April 1896 the Congregation needed a new Procurator General in Rome and Zahm was the preferred choice. It was during this period, and probably while he was assigned to Italy, that Zahm developed a keen interest in Dante. After Zahm's death in 1921 John Cavanaugh,

C.S.C., who had been President of Notre Dame from 1905-1919, remembered Zahm as: "...an enthusiastic student of Dante, and that for more than thirty years it was one of his daily pieties to read a canto of the Divine Comedy in the original."[2] While in Italy he became known among the antiquarian bookdealers of Rome and Florence as a Dantophile and after his return to America they began sending him listings of the Dante items they had for sale. Zahm's zeal for collecting and his shrewd bargaining instincts were well suited to the task of creating a major collection on the poet. While he was in Italy he made his purchases over the counter rather than through intermediaries so, unfortunately, there is no book-related correspondence from this time extant in the Zahm papers. An anecdotal story about this period was reported by Jim Larrick in *The Notre Dame Scholastic*:

> Father Zahm had asked permission of his superiors to buy some special volumes on Dante which he had found during his travels through Italy. The permission was granted and soon rare books and bills began arriving in what seemed an unending stream. Frantically his superiors cabled Father Zahm to stop purchasing what at the time was construed to be a luxury; he was running the infant university into the red. Strangely, their cables never seemed to reach him, for they always arrived at the place where he had just been.[3]

In January of 1898 Zahm was elected Provincial and returned to Notre Dame. As Provincial, Zahm pursued his dream of transforming Notre Dame into a great Catholic university. He erected buildings and added to the campus art gallery and library. He also continued his Dante acquisitions, purchasing books, engravings, busts and medallions of the poet, through the contacts he had made while in Rome. Zahm's good friend and regular correspondent in Italy, Monsignor Denis O'Connell, frequently acted as his personal agent in Italy. O'Connell had been sent to Rome in 1886 to serve as rector of the North American College. Forced to resign in 1895 during the heat of the Americanist controversy, Cardinal Gibbons retained him in Rome as vicar of his titular church of Santa Maria in Trastevere. In a letter of 5 February 1898, just after returning to Notre Dame from Italy, Zahm wrote to O'Connell reminiscing about the "two delightful years—all too short—we passed together," alluding to what Zahm affectionately referred to as "our Dante" and expressing how much he already missed his friend.[4]

In the following years Zahm would sometimes ask O'Connell to search for particularly rare editions or oversee the shipment of materials. In a letter to Zahm of 27 January 1902 an exasperated O'Connell wrote, "Your Dante can't be found in Rome. I visited several antiquary shops and they know nothing of it. Löscher [a bookdealer] says there were only 100 copies printed. He says he will stay on the track of one, if you want it, but that it will cost certainly not less than 150 lire."[5] In that year alone Zahm collected sculptures from Giovanni Parsanti in Pisa, statues of Dante and Beatrice from Maison de Cluny C. Brunier in Florence, paintings from C. and A. Schwicker in Florence and items from Moscardi, a bronze and metalworker in Florence. According to a 7 July 1902 invoice from Zahm's shipping agent in Italy, the firm French, Lemon and Co., he was being sent items ordered on April 15 and 18 and June 2 which included books from the dealers Franchi, Gonnell, Frangini, Dotti, Olschki, Seeber and Löscher as well as an item from Moscardi. According to the customs invoice of 8 July this shipment included 131 books and pamphlets on Dante and one bronze bust.[6] In a letter of 17 June Zahm remarked to O'Connell, "I am getting so interested in Dante, that I believe, if I were free, I should write a book on him, and another—small one—on Beatrice."[7]

While it is difficult to determine how much material Zahm acquired each year some evidence may be available from an untitled notebook in Zahm's handwriting, listing 173 editions and studies on Dante (consisting of 221 volumes), with the latest date of publication being 1903.[8] The entries are all uniform and with only a very few exceptions were written with the same pen, leading one to suspect they were produced at a single sitting. Also, several important early editions of the *Commedia* which we know Zahm owned by 1903 are not on the list. For instance, Zahm purchased the 1544 and 1578 *Commedia* editions from the bookseller Enrico Vismara of Milan in May of 1901.[9] Since they are not in the notebook it is probable the entries represent Zahm's purchases of new and antiquary materials for a period after 1901, probably 1902 and into the beginning of 1903. We also know that in February 1903 he was billed for a 1716 edition of the *Commedia* from Nardecchia booksellers in Rome,[10] another volume that does not appear in the notebook. Thus it appears this notebook only includes the 1902 and the very beginning of his 1903 purchases. We know he obtained 131 volumes in July of 1902 from orders placed between 15

April and 2 June, so a total of 221 volumes for a period of a little over a year is quite likely. Although a few publications are dated to 1903 most of the items are from the second half of the nineteenth century with a few early editions of the *Commedia*, notably the 1571 Rovillé edition from Lyon, the Verona edition of 1749 and the Venice edition of 1760. In itself this list would represent an exceptional year's work. However, one item in this notebook, acquired early in 1902, was to profoundly affect Zahm's collection. It was a small pamphlet published in Florence in 1901 listed as: G. Acquaticci, *Collezione Dantesca Acquaticci.*

The Acquaticci Purchase

Soon after becoming Provincial, Zahm decided that he could obtain the funds to purchase a major Dante collection, should one become available at the right price. He made several inquiries, and for a time was interested in the famous Leoretti collection.[11] During the spring of 1902 Zahm obtained the above mentioned pamphlet listing the collection assembled by the Italian Dantophile Giulio Acquaticci. The collection consisted of some 594 volumes, including eight incunabula and fine copies of most of the sixteenth century editions of the *Commedia*. On 27 May 1902 Zahm wrote to O'Connell:

Prof. Giulio Acquatici [sic] of Treia near Macerate has a fine Dante Collection of 594 vols. which I should like to become the possessor of, if I can get them at a reasonable price—at a price, for instance, like that which you paid for your splendid collections of minerals. Would you kindly write to him and find out if the collection is for sale and at what price? Tell him the books are for a Dantophile, at a university, and that the collection will be kept intact. This may be a gratification to him to know that his life-work will not be scattered to the four winds immediately after his death. If I can secure this library I shall, with what I now have, possess one of the rarest and most valuable libraries in the world. I know you will do all in your power to help me secure it, if possible. I would write the man myself, but if I did so, I fear he would immediately think he was dealing with an American millionaire, and ask an extravagant price for his books. If you write he will think he is dealing with one of his own countrymen. Bartolini ought to know Acquatici [sic], as he—Acquatici [sic]—has brought out an edition of the *Divina Commedia*.

Probably it would be policy to have Bartolini or some other "Dago" write for you, and if he succeeds in securing the library at a price I can afford to pay, I shall send you—for him—a little check for his trouble. If Bartolini were to know that there is a *mancia* [consideration] in the transaction for himself, he would make a special effort to succeed in the purchase. The owner may not wish to sell at all, but I think he will, if he can get back the money he paid for his books.[12]

Taking Zahm's advice, O'Connell enlisted the assistance of an Italian, Domenico Cardinal Frascarelli who contacted Acquaticci. On 22 June 1902 Acquaticci sent a postcard reply to Frascarelli in Italian, translated as follows:

I am forwarding the catalog of the Dante Collection which I am prepared to sell because I am changing residence. Therein you will find the *final price* that I am asking. Do not be shocked at what I am asking, for I do not intend to make a killing but only to recover the money which I have spent over the last twenty years until now.

You will evaluate the bibliographic importance of the collection for yourself, since I believe you are familiar with the *Bibliografia dantesca*; and if this were not the case it would be necessary to inform you about the search that has been going on for some years *throughout the world* for ancient editions of Dante, such that today those few that can be found authentic, complete and in good condition are *all spoken for*. For this reason, my collection offers precisely that which is no longer available on the European book market. You can come when you will in the coming month, at least until the 27th.[13]

On 28 June O'Connell sent this postcard and a letter from Frascarelli along with the sale catalog to Zahm. Zahm perused the catalog and elected to purchase Acquaticci's extensive collection of early editions of the *Commedia*. Zahm crossed out the editions of 1507, 1544, both 1568 editions and the 1578 edition as items he already owned. The other listings were noted with red checkmarks beside the entries; they totaled 40 titles in 48 volumes covering the years 1477–1739. On 28 July he sent the following reply to O'Connell:

I will give Prof. Acquatici [sic] four thousand lire for the forty-eight vols. marked in red in the accompanying pages taken from his catalogue. These are about one twelfth of the vols. in his collection, although they are the most rare. This is a very high price to pay for 48 vols., but I am willing to pay this amount in order speedily to complete my *Collezione Dantesca*. I know Olschki [an antiquarian book dealer] would ask more than L4,000 for this collection if he had it for sale, but he would not pay more for it, and I do not think he would pay anything approaching the sum I offer. I am quite sure Prof. Acquatici [sic] will wait a very long time until he gets another offer as good as mine, if indeed he ever receives so good a one. I do not want the other works in his collection, as I have most of them already. As to those I have not, I can, I am sure, get them cheaper elsewhere. If you can secure the collection at the price offered, I shall ask you kindly to go to Treia to take charge of the packing of the books, and to see that it corresponds to the description in the Catalogue. I know I am asking a great favor of you, but you like to do favors for your friends. Besides you are the only one in Italy I would trust with such an important commission, for, if the books are not exactly as described in the Catalogue, I do not want them. You can probably stop at Treia on your way from the North, examine and pack the books while there, and take them with you to Rome where you can have them shipped by Lemon & Co. If you will kindly pay for them, I will send you a draft at once—as soon as I hear they are in your possession. Do not trust them with anyone, after you have packed them until you have delivered them to Lemon & Co. It would be so easy to substitute a bad vol. for a good one or to purloin a few of the earlier and rarer ones and then the greater part of the value of the collection would be gone at once. I am sorry I have so little confidence in your *compaesani* but you know how it is yourself. They are not paragons of honesty, and have not been for some time, at least in money matters. I shall, of course, depend on your friend to induce Acquatici [sic] to accept my offer, and shall give him *una buona mancia* if he succeeds, but the acceptance of the offer will be subject to your examination of the books, and finding them as represented.

Kindly let me know at your earliest convenience if Acquatici [sic] accepts my offer, and what you have done in the premises. Let me also know your own expenses in looking after the matter, and I will send you a draft to cover the price of the books, *mancia* for your friend, and your own expenses, etc. If you are successful in securing this collection for me, I hope you will be, I shall have one that any Dantophile might be proud of.[14]

At the time the offer of L4,000 converted to about $775, which in 1991 dollars was equivalent to about $12,300 or almost $255 per volume.[15] Acquaticci accepted the offer, but then Zahm became apprehensive and proposed to pay cash on delivery. Acquaticci did not understand the American practice of C.O.D.; the idea that his most precious volumes would be sent to America before he received payment made him mistrustful and he nearly called off the deal. Eventually, after some tactful humoring by Frascarelli, O'Connell arranged to pick up the books at Acquaticci's home in Treia sometime in November and make payment in full on the spot. O'Connell examined each volume carefully, comparing it with its description in the catalog. A few disputes arose, but Acquaticci settled them all to his advantage—except one. The bottom two-thirds of the title page was missing from the 1545, *Al Segno della Speranza*, Venetian edition, so O'Connell bargained with Acquaticci to throw in an extra unspecified volume for compensation.

In a letter of 25 November O'Connell recounted the episode to Zahm stating, "At last after months of haggling and suspense, the difficult affair of the collection is ended...between an old shylock like yourself and a wild crank like Acquaticci it was no fun being the middle man...[then in closing] I am tired and worn out after the summer."[16] Although there is no record of the shipment, a typewritten listing of the volumes appears among Zahm's book receipts from 1903. Presumably the materials were sent out in December and reached Zahm the next year.

Later Collecting

With the accession of the rarest Renaissance editions from the Acquaticci collection Zahm realized he had taken a significant step toward creating one of the most important Dante collections in America. This spurred him on to seek further materials. The extant book receipts for 1903 are as numerous as those for 1902 and they continue though at a somewhat more moderate rate through 1906.[17] In 1906 Father Morrissey campaigned against Zahm's renewal as Provincial arguing that Zahm had tried to expand Notre Dame too quickly and had run the order into serious debt. On 20 August 1906 Morrissey was elected Provincial. Zahm was deeply disappointed by the course of events and left Notre Dame for Holy Cross College in Washington D.C., which became his new home. During this phase of his life Zahm travelled throughout the U.S. and South America.

His devotion to Dante and the Dante collection continued, but growth in the collection proceeded at a slower pace than previously. On 6 October 1917, just before taking a trip to Europe during the First World War, Zahm secretly wrote a will which he deposited in a steel safe at Holy Cross College, leaving the bulk of his estate to endow the Notre Dame Dante collection.

The year 1921 marked the sixth centenary of Dante's death and was also the year of Zahm's death. He died of pneumonia in Munich on 10 November 1921. But even in his final months he continued to collect. In fact, he was able to acquire a major Dante library of an unnamed private Italian collector consisting of 2,171 books and pamphlets, most of which were autographed by the authors. He also continued ordering antiquary items, witnessed by several receipts and requests from Hiersmann Booksellers dated to April and July of 1921. He continued to purchase material right up to the end: the final invoice, from Hiersmann for five Dante volumes totaling 855 marks, is dated 6 December 1921, almost a month after his death.[18]

Earlier that year Zahm drafted a brief article on the Dante collection that was scheduled to appear in the April 1921 *Notre Dame Scholastic*, which was a special issue devoted to Dante's sexcentenary. Unfortunately, this valuable personal retrospective account of the collection, written under the pseudonym *Dantofilo*, was never published. It is included here as an appendix for it is Zahm's most complete as well as his final thoughts on his lifelong quest for Dante materials.

Even after his death Zahm's support of the Dante collection continued. His estate, valued at about $10,000, mostly in stocks and bonds, was divided as follows: $1,200 was set aside for perpetual Masses to be said for his relatives and "eight or nine hundred dollars" was to be used to pay for outstanding book debts, return of his body to the U.S. and for burial. He went on to state: "It is also my will that the remaining portion of my estate be used to enlarge the Dante collection in the University of Notre Dame[,] Notre Dame Ind[.] by purchasing books, magazines and works of art on Dante not already existing in said collection as it has always been my desire to see my *Alma Mater* the possessor of the most valuable Dante Collection in existence."[19]

Dante at Notre Dame

It seems that initially Zahm kept the Dante books, at least the most valuable ones, in his office. In photographs of Father Zahm in his study at Notre Dame some of the early Dante editions can be clearly identified on his bookshelves. Zahm also put his personal bookplate in each volume, frequently covering up earlier *ex-libris* in the process, including several bibliographic and provenance notes in the earlier volumes that had been meticulously recorded by Acquaticci.

During his term as provincial Zahm appointed an architect named Von Herbulis to draw up plans for a library building. The plan called for a special room on the first floor for the Dante collection. The decor would be appropriately elaborate: Italian Renaissance furnishings and walls of richly veined wood capped with an elliptical vaulted ceiling and a frieze portraying scenes from the *Commedia*.[20] Unfortunately, fires on campus consumed the necessary building funds in repairs so the plans were abandoned. When Zahm left Notre Dame in 1906, despite bitterness about not having been renewed as Provincial, he did not take the Dante Collection with him. He had purchased the books for his *alma mater* and there they would remain. It is likely that after Zahm's departure the books were housed in the library which was the front half of the third floor of the Main Building; they may have been placed in a separate alcove as had been done earlier for the personal library of Professor J.A. Lyons and the 1,500 books donated by J.A. McMaster.[21]

The situation would change however when Paul Foik, C.S.C., came to Notre Dame in 1911 to serve as librarian. Six years later in 1917, using a new design by the architect Edward Tilton, Father Foik opened the doors of the new two-story Notre Dame Library building, appointed with marble throughout and a Greek-revival facade. The concept of a special Dante room was kept, but the revised plans placed it in the northwest corner of the second floor. A separate room was also included to house the artifacts and books Zahm had donated from his travels in South America. The completed Dante room was not so extravagant as first envisioned, but was tasteful nonetheless. An inventory taken shortly after the library opened listed the contents of the room as follows: 2 radiators, 1 light fixture, 1 table 4 ft. x 7 ft., 1 bronze statue, 4 chairs, 6 marble busts, 2 pedestals, 5 bronze busts, 2 large pictures,

17 cameos, 25 small pictures, 55 feet of shelving with folio cases, 2 easels, 1 curio case full of cameos, 1,800 volumes of Dante's works and 6 shades.[22] In 1922 Zahm's sister added a bust of her brother to the room.[23] Around this same time the value of the collection was appraised at $25,000.[24]

Zahm's endowment was received by Notre Dame's President, Father Burns, in June of 1922 [25] while his final purchases and the collection of autographed books, along with a few additional busts and medallions, arrived at Notre Dame from Holy Cross College in Washington, D.C., during July. The University immediately issued a news release stating the collection had received 2,000 additional volumes.[26] This massive acquisition and the new endowment stimulated Father Foik to focus on the collection. In his annual report for the academic year 1923–24 Foik estimated the Zahm bequest was about $4,000 and should yield about $300 in interest per year.[27] Apparently Father Foik was not told that the money had arrived a year earlier and that it was closer to $8,000.

While Foik was unsuccessfully attempting to obtain funds from the endowment for new acquisitions, he was also trying to organize the collection. There was no classification system other than size; the smaller books were on the upper shelves and the larger volumes on the lower shelves, with the overflow simply stacked on the floor and on window ledges. Nor was there any catalog of the materials. No one knew exactly which books were in the collection nor was there a method of accessing them other than by simply browsing.[28]

Foik's main concern, therefore, was to identify the books. He wrote to the Library of Congress requesting copies of their card catalog entries on Dante stating, "It is our purpose to turn out in due time a catalogue of the Zahm Collection of Dantiana."[29] Unfortunately the Library of Congress had very few of the volumes and the task turned out to be much greater than Foik first thought. He then wrote to Theodore Koch, a Dante scholar and the librarian at Northwestern University for information in English on Dante bibliography and the cataloging of Dante material.[30] Using a typed three-page list of books about Dante in English, Koch's catalog of the Fiske Dante Collection at Cornell and the few available Library of Congress cards, the head of cataloging reported that in April–June of 1923, "an attempt was made to catalog the English section of the Dante collection."[31] But the work was more than the cataloging section could handle, and the 1923–24 Annual Report stated that no progress had been made on cataloging Dante materials.[32]

In November 1924 Paul Byrne took over as Notre Dame Library director and once again attempted to gain access to the Zahm endowment. In his first annual report he wrote:

> If Father Zahm left the income from $4,000 to maintain his Dante Library this money should be made available for book purchases. Last year only two volumes were bought for the collection. One cost $3.25 and the other $90.00 and both were paid for from the general book fund of the Library. No additions have been made this year. The Zahm Dante Library holds a high place among Dante collections in America and it should not be allowed to lose this position.[33]

Over the next few years little was done with the collection until some of the Zahm endowment earnings were made available. The first recorded expenditure of the fund was during the 1926–27 academic year when a total of $9.80 was spent on Dante material. In the following years expenditures were $67.11, $15.48 and then nothing in 1929–30.[34] However, during that year the library hired Ellen Kistler, who later became head of cataloging, to begin creating catalog cards for the collection. The project was finally completed during the 1936–37 academic year.[35] During this period purchasing increased. In 1930–31 there was $233.61 spent on Dante, nothing was purchased in the following year but then from 1932–33 through 1935–36 expenditures were: $232.79, $228.14, $577.29 and $202.00. In 1936–37 purchasing dropped off to $24.82 with nothing spent in the following year and then $143 in 1938–39.[36] During this period the library purchased a copy of the facsimile of the 1472 *princeps* edition of the *Commedia* which Byrne called, "The most important addition in years to the Dante Collection..."[37] and three antiquarian titles were added: the Henry Boyd translation of the *Inferno* (Dublin, 1785), The *Commedia* edition 1787 (now lost) and Antonio Biscioni's *Prose di Dante e Boccaccio* (Florence, 1723).[38] With the start of war in Europe antiquary titles became difficult to find. Soon the war effort was affecting all library acquisitions as well as staffing and there is no further mention of early Dante imprints in the annual reports.

Another situation concerning the Dante collection that arose during this era was the problem of security. Specifically, Byrne was concerned about Father Thomas Brennan of the English Department, who held a class on Dante in the Dante room. Brennan apparently was careless with the materials and let students take volumes out of the collection. Some valuable materials were marked up and Byrne felt students had walked off with several others. Without mentioning names Byrne addressed this situation in the 1935–36 Annual Report. The resolution of the situation was that Brennan was expelled from the library, no further classes were taught in the Dante room, and an inventory of the collection was made.[39] During the inventory, which took place during 1938–39, all the books were stamped as belonging to the Dante Room and, without regard to provenance information, book pockets were pasted into the back cover of each volume.[40]

During the war and early post war years there is no direct mention of the state of the Dante collection in library annual reports or documents. However, from the Cataloging Department statistics we learn that three Dante volumes were cataloged in 1944–45 and during the academic years 1947–48 through 1951–52 there were 3, 11, 10, 37 and 11 titles cataloged.[41] No further statistics on Dante materials are mentioned in later reports. For the years 1954–55 through 1959–60 the Acquisitions Department listed the amounts spent on Dante items per academic year: $213.50, $111, $42.51, $29.85, $12.85 and $9.42.[42] After this time the reports are silent on acquisitions. Apparently during this period the collection was an independent entity without a curator or bibliographer. Departmental reports exist for other collections such as The Medieval Institute collection and the Department of Special Collections, but none mention or imply any responsibility for the Dante collection. Foik and Byrne had personally overseen the collection and discussed it in their annual reports but this was not the situation under the new Library Director Victor Schaefer (1952–1966). In fact it was probably because of a lack of supervision that in 1958–59 the eight *Commedia* incunabula editions were transferred from the Dante Collection to the Treasure Room oversize collection in room 208 of the library.[43]

When the library was transferred to the new Memorial Library building in 1963, Library Director Victor Schaefer disbanded the Dante collection. The statues, busts and other artwork were dispersed throughout the University and the books were moved to the general stacks. Apparently the majority of the Cinquecento editions were transferred to the Rare Book Room and can be identified because each book bears a call number label with the location designation, "Treasure Room." The Cinquecento editions that lack this designation were sent to the circulating stack collection. About a decade later the new University Provost, James Burtchaell, expressed his concern to the recently appointed Library Director David Sparks about the lack of regard for the Zahm Dante materials. During the next year, 1974–75, Sparks transferred all of the Zahm items that could be located in the stacks to the Department of Special Collections.[44] The following year a committee was formed to develop the use of the Dante collection. The members were: Thomas Werge of English, Dino Cervigni and Paul Bosco of Italian, Jeffrey Russell of the Medieval Institute and Anton Masin, special collections librarian.[45] The committee suggested the creation of a new Dante Room as the first step in reviving Dante studies at Notre Dame. Therefore, during the next academic year an open area behind the locked stacks in the Rare Book Collection was carpeted and a table and blackboard were added. A painting of Dante and Beatrice attributed to Luigi De Gregori was found and hung on the wall along with two prints of Dante and the area was called the "Dante Room."[46] The area still exists, although today it also houses the 12,000 negative microfilms from the Ambrosiana microfilm collection, and is primarily used for staff workspace or class presentations that require the use of items from any of the several special collections. Although the Zahm material is housed in locked cases nearby, patrons are required to consult the material in the Special Collections' reading room.

During the 1980s Dino Cervigni, a professor of Italian and a Dante scholar, who like Acquaticci came from the area of Macerata, took an interest in the collection. At this time, under the current Library Director Robert Miller, the Zahm endowment was reinstated, but yielded only a few hundred dollars a year. Laura Fuderer, the newly assigned bibliographer, worked with Professor Cervigni to order materials as funds allowed, especially recent editions and translations of the *Commedia*. In 1986, at Fuderer's suggestion, the Friends of the Library donated a copy of the lavish facsimile of the Berlin Dante manuscript containing illustrations by Botticelli, which was issued by Besler Verlag. Near the end of the decade Cervigni left Notre Dame and Fuderer resigned her bibliographical duties in the foreign languages to become the rare books librarian. Dr. Louis Jordan, head of Special Collections, curator of early printed books and Dante bibliographer, is currently working with Dr. Theodore Cachey, associate professor in the Department of Romance Languages and Italian Renaissance scholar, to organize and build the collection. During the 1992–93 academic year they acquired one of the few Cinquecento lacunae in the collection, the 1572 Sermartelli edition of the *Inferno* with the commentary of Vincenzo Buonanni. This edition was purchased with financial assistance from Medieval Institute book funds and represented the first early Dante edition purchased since the 1930s.

In 1993, Cachey and Jordan curated an exhibition of the Renaissance editions of the *Commedia*, "Renaissance Dante at Notre Dame: 1472–1629" which was displayed at Notre Dame 4 October–15 December 1993 and at the Newberry Library in Chicago 15 April–15 June 1994. They are also co-authoring a major catalog consisting of essays and full bibliographic descriptions of the Renaissance editions of the *Commedia*, which will be published during 1994–95. A conference, "Dante Now: Current Trends in Dante Studies," was also held in conjunction with these events, attracting many Dante scholars to Notre Dame.

APPENDIX

A Great Monument to Dante at Notre Dame University [47]

A propos of the sixth centenary of Dante's death, which is now being celebrated by the civilized world, we take pleasure in calling attention to the great library established in the Poet's honor at Notre Dame University.

Notre Dame has many and great treasures—artistic, scientific and literary—but among those which specially attract the [added: attention of the] visitor is its wonderful Dante Collection. This has long been recognized by competent judges as one of the most valuable and complete in the world.

In this collection [added: which owes its existence to the enthusiastic *Dantista*, Dr. J.A. Zahm,] is the better part of the famous Dante library of Giulio A[c]quaticci, the distinguished *Dantofilo* of Italy. Its owner spent many years in accumulating his library and proudly referred to it as one of the largest of its kind in Europe. It was certainly one of the rarest and most important, for it was particularly rich in incunabula. It embraced all the most precious editions of the *Divina Commedia* from that printed in Venice in 1477, by Vendelin da Spira, to those of our own time. Among them is the highly prized edition published in Florence in 1481 and enriched with the splendid engravings of [space left blank] from designs by Botticelli.

But the treasures of the Acquaticci library embrace but a small part of the Notre Dame Dante Library. For in it are all the chief translations of the Poet's works in more than thirty languages and dialects. Not the least interesting of these are versions of the *Divina Commedia* in Japanese. Commenting on the various Japanese translations of Dante's masterpiece, Dr. Zahm has expressed surprise and regret that there is so far no version of it in Irish. "I have," he said, "tried several times to get Gælic scholars to [several lines restating the previous two sentences are crossed out] undertake this work, but so far without success. At one time I hoped that Douglas Hyde would fill the *lacuna*, but a Gælic version of the *Divina Commedia* still remains a great desideratum in Dante literature. Is it too much to hope the world celebration of the sixth centenary of the great Florentine's death will stimulate some of our enthusiastic Gælic students to give us the long desired version of the *Divina Commedia* in Irish? This would be a worthy tribute to the Divine Poet from a son of the Emerald Isle."

Dr. [added: J.A.] Zahm, in whose honor the Notre Dame Dante Library has been named, is usually referred to as a man of science but, [added: those who know him best, inform us that] his first love was literature. An eloquent proof of this, aside from the numerous books that have come from his pen, is the wonderful Dante Collection at Notre Dame, to the securing of which the Doctor has devoted more than a third of a century of enthusiastic book hunting in all parts of the world.

The Zahm Dante Library does not, however, consist only of books. It is also notable for its splendid collection of works of art, [added: all of which illustrate the life and work of the supreme poet. Among these are] etching, steel and wood engravings, paintings in oil and water colors, busts and medallions in marble and bronze and terracotta. The central attraction of these works of art is undoubtedly a reduced replica of the colossol [sic] monument of Dante at Trent, pronounced by experts to be the most magnificent statue of heroic size in the Old World. Among the prints, hundreds in number, is the entire collection of a noted Dante lover in Florence.

Not counting the works of art, the books and brochures in this great Dante library, [added: as reported only] a month ago, exceeded three thousand in number. But, by an extraordinary windfall, this number has since been nearly doubled. For since then, Dr. Zahm, who is always seeking to enlarge the library whose upbuilding has always been for him a labor of love, has secured the complete library of one of the most enthusiastic Dantophilists in Italy. The exact number of items in this [added: superb] collection is two thousand one hundred and seventy-one. But what materially enhances its value is the fact that a large number of the books and pamphlets are autograph copies from their authors. It is safe to say that no Dante library in existence has ever received a single addition that is so large or so important as this, or one in which the Dante lover will find more genuine delight.

Among the numerous projects which, for some time [added: past, have engaged the] attention of the authorities at Notre Dame is the establishment of a Dante chair for the benefit of those who may desire to make a thorough study of the works of the Florentine poet. It is to be hoped that this project will be realized soon. Dr. Zahm has removed the chief difficulty by bringing together, as if by the wand of Prospero, the countless treasures of [added: his] magnificent library—a library, we make bold to say, which is the noblest monument to the *summo poeta* of which America can boast.

Dantofilo.

---

1. We would like to thank the Rev. James Connelly and Mrs. Jacqueline Dougherty of the Provincial Archives of the Congregation of the Holy Cross, Notre Dame, Indiana; Dr. Peter Lysy of the University of Notre Dame Archives and Ms. Laura Fuderer, rare books librarian, for their assistance in

gathering material for this article. Also, we thank Christian Dupont, who assisted with the research for this article, as well as with the writing of exhibition cards and mounting the cases for "Renaissance Dante at Notre Dame" who at the time of this writing was a Ph.D. candidate in theology. For a general biography of Father Zahm consult Ralph E. Weber, *Notre Dame's John Zahm: American Catholic Apologist and Educator* (Notre Dame: University Press, 1961).

2. John Cavanaugh, "Father Zahm," *The Catholic World* 114 (Feb. 1922): 12.

3. Jim Larrick, "The Dante Library," *The Notre Dame Scholastic* 87 (5 April 1946): 23.

4. Zahm to O'Connell, 5 February 1898, Papers of Bishop Denis O'-Connell, Diocese of Richmond Archives, Richmond, Virginia, UNDA.

5. O'Connell to Zahm, 27 January 1902, John A. Zahm papers, Box 1, folder 12, Provincial Archives of the Congregation of the Holy Cross. Hereafter cited as PA.

6. John A. Zahm papers, Box 1, folder 12, PA.

7. Zahm to O'Connell, 17 June 1902, Papers of Bishop Denis O'Connell, Diocese of Richmond Archives, Richmond, Virginia, UNDA.

8. John A. Zahm papers, Box 3, file 19, PA.

9. Zahm papers, Box 4, receipt 9 May 1901, UNDA.

10. Zahm papers, Box 4, 1 February 1903, UNDA.

11. See the letters quoted in Patrick J. Carroll, "Mind in Action," *The Ave Maria* NS 63 (15 June 1946): 756.

12. Zahm to O'Connell, 27 May 1902, Papers of Bishop Denis O'Connell, Diocese of Richmond Archives, Richmond, Virginia, UNDA.

13. Postcard from G. Acquaticci to Dominico Frascarelli, 22 June 1902, John A. Zahm papers, Box 1, folder 12, PA.

14. Zahm to O'Connell, 28 July 1902, Papers of Bishop Denis O'Connell, Diocese of Richmond Archives, Richmond, Virginia, UNDA.

15. Among Zahm's receipts is an American Express voucher from 1 December 1898 for the exchange of L50 for $9.71. Based on that rate L4,000 would come to $776.80. In 1991 dollars this was equal to $12,285 using the composite consumer price index in John. J. McCusker, "How Much is that in Real Money? A Historial Price Index for use as a Deflator of Money Values in the Economy of the United States," *Proceedings of the American Antiquarian Society*, 101 (Oct. 1991) table A-2 on pp. 329 and 332 and explanation on p. 312.

16. O'Connell to Zahm, 25 Nov. 1902, Zahm papers, Box 4, UNDA.

17. Zahm papers, Box 4, UNDA.

18. John A. Zahm papers, Box 2, folder 11, PA.

19. Last Will dated 6 Oct. 1917, Holy Cross College, Zahm papers, Box 1, folder 30, UNDA. Also in the same folder is a related letter from Sister Angelita of 18 Nov. 1921 and a copy of the Supreme Court of District of Columbia, Probate Court Appraisal of the Personal Estate of John A. Zahm, case number 28,687, administrative docket 65. For additional details concerning Zahm's Will see letters from Louis M. Kelly of 12 Nov. [1921], 26 Nov. [1921] and 14 Dec. 1921, Charles O'Donnell papers, PA.

20. Library Correspondence, UODL, Box 2, folder 1913–17, undated report, UNDA.

21. H.P.B., "The Lemonnier Library of the University of Notre Dame," *The Notre Dame Scholastic* 23 (14 June 1870): 629–632.

22. Library Correspondence, UODL, Box 2, folder library inventory ca. 1917–22, UNDA.

23. Letter to Sister M. Angeline, 20 January 1922, James A. Burns Correspondence, UPBU, Box 43, UNDA.

24. Library Correspondence, UODL, Box 2, folder L 1917–22, undated report, UNDA.

25. Father Burns to Louis M. Kelly, 10 June 1922, James A. Burns Correspondence, UPBU, Box 44, UNDA.

26. UDIS, Box 16 and Box 18, folder 9, 21 July 1922, UNDA.

27. AR, 1923–24, 2.

28. Byrne oral history, folder 1, p. 38, UNDA, and AR, 1936–37, unpaginated.

29. Foik to Dr. Putnam of the Library of Congress, 15 March 1923, Library Correspondence, UODL, Box 3, Zahm Dante Library folder, UNDA.

30. Foik-Koch letters, 5 January and 29 May 1923, Library Correspondence, UODL, Box 3, folder K 1922–24, UNDA.

31. AR, Cataloging Department, 1923–24, 3.

32. Library Correspondence, UODL, Box 3, Dante Library Select List, UNDA; Foik to O'Donnell 11 Dec. 1922, Charles O'Donnell Correspondence, PA; and AR, Cataloging Department, 1923–24, 2–3.

33. AR, 1924–25, "Recommendations for Improvement of Library Service," unpaginated.

34. AR, 1926–27, 10; 1927–28, 4; 1928–29, 12; 1929–30, 9.

35. Byrne oral history, folder 1, p. 38, UNDA; and AR, 1929–30, and 1936–37, both unpaginated.

36. AR, 1930–31, 11; 1931–32, 14; 1932–33, 21; 1933–34, 17; 1934–35, 5; 1935–36, unpaginated; 1936–37, unpaginated; 1937–38, 19; 1938–39, 10.

37. AR, 1936–37, unpaginated. As the actual amount spent on Dante during this year was only $24.82, it seems most probable that the funds to cover the cost of this volume had been encumbered in previous years and that

Byrne added it to this year's report because the book had actually arrived in the library during the 1936–37 academic year.

38. AR, 1938–39, 8.

39. Byrne oral history, folder 2, p. 4, UNDA; and AR, 1935–36, unpaginated.

40. AR, Cataloging Department, 1938–39, unpaginated.

41. AR, Cataloging Department, 1944–45, unpaginated; 1947–48, 5; 1948–49, 4; 1949–50, 2; and 1950–51, 2.

42. AR, Acquisitions Department, 1954–55, 12; 1955–56, 8; 1956–57, 6; 1957–58, 14; 1958–59 Supplementary report, 8 and 1959–60, appendix 2, 16.

43. AR, Medieval Institute, 1958–59, 10.

44. AR, 1974–75, 11.

45. AR, 1975–76, 17–18.

46. AR, 1976–77, 13 and AR, Department of Special Collections, 1976–77, 1 and 13. According to Anton Masin's budget figures in the 1977–78 Annual Report for Special Collections, p. 15, the cost of the carpeting was $462.62. This sum exceeded the total amount spent from the Zahm fund for Dante books over the previous twenty years!

47. John A. Zahm papers, Box 2, folder 11, a five-page handwritten essay, PA.

The Latin American Library
of Father Zahm

RAFAEL E. TARRAGO

Introduction

In the March 1917 issue of the *Pan American Bulletin* it was reported that Dr. J.A. Zahm had presented his South American library to the University of Notre Dame.[1] Three months later, *Library Journal* quoted the note in the March issue of the *Pan American Bulletin*, adding a description of major titles in the Latin American library of Father Zahm. The *Journal* called this collection "one of the most select private collections in the United States, containing many rare volumes, representing a search of the most remote bookstalls of Europe, North and South America."[2] This select collection included classical works such as *Colección de Documentos Inéditos de Indias*, *Colección de Libros Raros y Curiosos*, *Memorias de los Vireyes* [sic] *del Perú*, and publications of the "missionary explorers" of the sixteenth to the eighteenth centuries.

The intention of the University was to preserve the library of Father Zahm intact in a special room of the new library building, where special courses in South American history and commerce were to be offered. The note in the *Pan American Bulletin* announced that those special courses would be under the direction of Father John O'Hara, C.S.C., whose South American studies had begun when his father served as United States consul at Montevideo, Uruguay, and who had travelled extensively through Argentina, Brazil, and Uruguay.[3] The South American history courses were to be a prerequisite for a degree in foreign commerce, and three years of Spanish were also to be required of students enrolled in this program.

The main purpose of this essay is to narrate the story of the development of Zahm's library, from its beginnings until its donation to the University of Notre Dame. Then I shall explain what became of the grand plans for a special Latin American library and why the Latin American history courses heralded by the *Pan American Bulletin* and *Library Journal* in 1917 never blossomed into a Latin American studies program. Finally, I shall provide a sampling of the library that Zahm collected, and gave to the University of Notre Dame with great hopes for its development as the core of an area studies program.

The Story of the Latin American Library of Father Zahm

In the correspondence of Father John A. Zahm, C.S.C., in the Notre Dame Archives there are no records of purchases of Latin American books or books about Latin America. The fact that in those archives one can find a great deal of correspondence related to his Dante collection makes one suspect that Zahm did not acquire his Latin American books through dealers in Europe or Latin America. However, he himself claims in one of his books that early in his life he developed an interest in the history of the Spanish conquest of America, and the work of the Spanish missionaries of the sixteenth century, and that this interest was greatly enhanced by his visit to Mexico in 1881.[4]

After he left the University of Notre Dame in 1906, Zahm went to Holy Cross College, in Washington, D.C., and travelled widely in South America. His first trip to South America took him to the Spanish Caribbean, Venezuela, Colombia, Panama, Ecuador, Peru, Bolivia, and finally, down the Amazon River. By his own account, he retraced when possible the tracks of the Spanish conquerors. After his return to the United States he wrote two travel books based on his observations which show a vast knowledge of Latin American history and Spanish and Spanish American literature. At this time he also contributed unsigned book reviews and a series of articles on El Dorado under the pen-name, J.A. Manso, for the *Pan American Bulletin*. Zahm returned to South America in 1913, this time with the ex-president of the United States, Colonel Theodore Roosevelt, in what is known as the Roosevelt Scientific Expedition to South America.[5]

Father Zahm and Teddy Roosevelt in the Brazilian wilderness.

We know little about how Zahm went about collecting his books on Latin America, and there is nothing about this in his papers. In his book of travels in Venezuela and Colombia, *Up the Orinoco and Down the Magdalena*, he makes favorable comments on the second-hand bookstores of Santa Fe de Bogota, Colombia, where he claims to have acquired some of the most prized volumes in his Latin American books collection.[6] A press release to Catholic newspapers of 22 February 1917, announcing the donation of his Latin American books to the library of the University of Notre Dame, mentions his acquisition of an original edition of the Jesuit Manuel Rodiguez's *El Marañón y Amazonas* in an old shop in Chachapoyas, in the heart of the Andes, and of his finding a copy of Padre Carvajal's account of the discovery and first exploration of the Amazon in a second-hand bookstore in Lima.[7]

In a letter to Father Cavanaugh, President of Notre Dame, dated in early 1916, John O'Hara (later Father O'Hara) says that Zahm had promised to give to Notre Dame his Latin American books. In the same letter he says that Zahm had suggested that the University of Notre Dame should acquire the services of Dr. Vicente G. Quesada to teach Latin American history. Dr. Quesada was never hired by Notre Dame, and in the fall of 1917 O'Hara was made professor of South American history at Notre Dame.[8] While completing his final year of theological studies, O'Hara studied under the historian, Dr. Peter Guilday, at the Catholic University in Washington, D.C., and prepared articles and commentaries on Latin American history for the newly established *Catholic Historical Review*. In Washington, D.C., he worked with Zahm, helping him do an inventory of the collection of books on Latin America that Zahm eventually donated to Notre Dame.[9]

In his book, *Along the Andes and Down the Amazon*, Zahm says that the United States was no longer a debtor nation, and that nowhere was this country to find a better outlet for excess capital than in South America. He proposed that well organized banks and steamers must be followed up by cultivating intimacy and friendship with Latin Americans.[10] O'Hara believed in the value of a grand exchange of people and commerce between the nations of the Western Hemisphere. In the summer of 1917 he registered at the University of Pennsylvania for courses in Latin American relations, Caribbean interests of the United States, and practical finance, and when he organized his foreign commerce program at Notre Dame it was in essence a Latin American commerce program, intended to be a promoter of inter-American commercial exchange.[11]

The program leading to the degree of bachelor of philosophy in foreign commerce introduced into the College of Arts and Letters at Notre Dame under the direction of O'Hara and the inspiration of Zahm began in the fall of 1917. Courses in this program included a year each of foreign commerce, of Latin American history, and of ocean traffic and trade, and three years of a foreign language.[12] This foreign commerce program combined the growing student interest in business and foreign commerce and Latin American studies. Basically it embodied the educational elements that Zahm had indicated to be required for United States businessmen conducting business with Latin Americans in the last chapter of his *Along the Andes and Down the Amazon*. It was in order to support this program that he gave his Latin American collection to the University of Notre Dame, standing behind O'Hara, and promising his guidance.[13] The University published a pamphlet describing the course of studies for the Foreign Commerce Program, entitled *How Notre Dame Prepares the Trade Ambassador*.[14]

On 1 December 1917 the *Notre Dame Scholastic* published a note announcing that the Department of South American History had received from the Rev. Dr. Zahm, C.S.C., its founder, a collection of volumes, photographs, and slides dealing with South America.[15] In his thesis *Forces Affecting the Development of Libraries at the University of Notre Dame, 1843–1968*, Brother John Federowicz, C.S.C., mentions the housing of the Zahm South American collection in the new library of the University of Notre Dame.[16] In his annual library report for the year 1920–21 Father Paul J. Foik reports that the "Library of South Americana" had been classified, but had yet to be accessioned and cataloged.[17] Four years later, however, Foik's annual report indicates that the South American Collection had been relegated to the Brownson Room, on the third floor of the library, and that while most of it had been classified in the past, few of the books in it had been accessioned, and none of them had been cataloged.[18] Two years later, Library Director Paul R. Byrne says in his annual report for the year ending 30 June 1926 that because of insufficient staff only a small beginning had been made in the cataloging of the "Zahm travel collection" and the "South Americana," and that he hoped that within a year "both" of these valuable collections would be completely cataloged.[19] From these sources it can be deduced that by 1926 the Zahm Latin American Collection, which was going to be preserved intact in a special room of the 1917 library, had been relocated and dispersed.

O'Hara was strengthening his position as an authority in the field of foreign trade and Latin American studies. In the August 1919 issue of the *Hispanic American Historical Review* he joined with five other Latin American specialists in a symposium on the teaching of history of Hispanic America in the educational institutions of the United States. In the fall of 1919 he taught courses on exporting and the history of Latin America at Notre Dame. His dream for Notre Dame was a school of foreign commerce emphasizing business with South America that would be heavily supported by the business people engaged in this rich trade, and that would enable Catholic Notre Dame to exchange not only students, but cultural traditions with the universities of Latin America. But the financial means were not there. In the school year 1920–21, with the creation of the College of Commerce, the Department of Commerce in the College of Arts and Letters was discontinued. Spanish remained one of the favorite languages of the commerce students, but mastery never seemed to be their aim; the history of South America soon lost out in the rush for more practical courses.[20]

Zahm wrote four books related to Latin America: *Up the Orinoco and Down the Magdalena, Along the Andes and Down the Amazon, Through South America's Southland,* and *The Quest of El Dorado.* The first three are travel books, but they contain an immense amount of carefully selected historical material. Through these books he became the first English-speaking American Catholic author to write a non-partisan appraisal of South America's history and culture.[21]

Zahm's books do not provide a list of his Latin American collection. One way of reconstructing his Latin American library is to search in the catalog of the Hesburgh Library for the books listed in the bibliographies of his four works on Latin America, and then locate those bearing his personal book plate. In this manner I have identified 34 titles in Zahm's Latin American library, many of them important sources for the study of the history of Spanish America. The following list is the product of that exercise, and the titles included give some idea of Zahm's interests and the quality of the collection he contributed to the Notre Dame Library.

A Catalog of the Library

Acosta, Joaquín. *Compendio histórico del descubrimiento y colonización de la Nueva Granada en el siglo desimosexto.* Bogota: Librería Colombiana, 1901. Second edition of this history based on chronicles of the Spanish conquest of what today is Colombia.

Acosta, José, S.J. *The Natural and Moral History of the Indies.* London: Hakluyt Society, 1880. 2 vols. (Works Issued by the Hakluyt Society, 60 and 61). Reprint of the 1604 printing of an English translation of Acosta's *Natural and Moral History* (1590), the first "scientific" work on the Americas.

Acuña, Christóval de. *Nuevo descubrimiento del Gran Río de las Amazonas.* Madrid: Imprenta de J. C. García, 1891. Second edition of a chronicle of the exploration and settlement of the Amazon region, first printed in 1641. It includes a biographical note on its author.

Agassiz, Louis. *A Journey in Brazil.* Boston: Ticknor and Fields, 1868. Account of the travels and scientific observations of Professor Agassiz in Brazil in 1865.

Amich, Fray José. *Compendio histórico de las trabajos, fatigas, sudores y muertes que los ministros evangélicos de la Seráfica Religión han padecido.* Paris: Librería de Rosa y Bouvet, 1854. A history of the Franciscan missions in Peru. It includes an account of the Franciscan missions in Bolivia by Fray Ceferino Mussani, *Noticias historicas sobre las misiones de la Republica de Bolivia.*

Casas, Fray Bartolomé de las. *Historia de las Indias.* Madrid: Imprenta de Miguet Ginesta, 1875. 5 vols. First edition of this influential work by the man who did most during the sixteenth century for the rights of native Americans. It is worthy of note that this *Historia de las Indias,* although non-printed, circulated in manuscript copies and influenced most printed chronicles and histories of the Spanish conquest of America written in the sixteenth and the seventeenth centuries.

Castellanos, Juan. *Historia del Nuevo Reino de Granada.* Madrid: Imprenta de A. Pérez Dubrull, 1886. 2 vols. (Colección de Escritores Castellanos). First edition of this chronicle in verse of the Spanish conquest of what today is the Republic of Colombia by one of the conquerors.

Chantre y Herrera, José, S.J. *Historia de las misiones de la Compañía de Jesús en el Marañón Español, 1637–1767.* Madrid: Imprenta de A. Avrial, 1901. First edition of a manuscript chronicle of the Jesuit missions in the province of Maynas in what was called the Kingdom of Quito (today, Ecuador), written by a Spanish Jesuit in the 1790s.

Colón, Fernando. *Historia del Almirante Don Cristóbal Colón.* Madrid: Imprenta de T. Minueza, 1892. 2 vols. in one. (Colección de libros raros y curiosos que tratan de América, 5 and 6). Biography of Christopher Columbus by his son. Important because it is the only contemporary source that asserts that Columbus visited Iceland. Curiously, this work written in Spanish was first printed in Italian in Venice, in 1571.

Cruz, Fray Laureano de la. *Nuevo descubrimiento del Río de Marañón llamado de las Amazonas.* Madrid: Biblioteca de la Irradiación, 1900. First edition of a chronicle of the Franciscan explorations and missions in the Amazonia written by a Franciscan priest in 1651.

Fernández de Navarrete, Martín, ed. *Colección del los viajes y descubrimientos que hicieron por mar los españoles.* Madrid: Imprenta Nacional, 1858. 5 vols. Important compilation of documents and accounts of Spanish explorations of the sixteenth century. The editor has written connecting texts.

Fernandez de Oviedo y Valdés, Gonzalo. *Historia general y natural de las Indias.* Madrid: Imprenta de la Real Academia de la Historia, 1855. 4 vols. First printing of an influential history of the Spanish conquest of America by a courtier and royal officer in Santo Domingo. It was one of the earliest histories of the Spanish conquest.

Fernández Piedrahita, Lucas. *Historia general de las conquistas del Nuevo Reino de Granada.* Bogota: Imprenta de Medardo Rivas, 1881. Chronicle of the Spanish conquest of what today is the Republic of Colombia, first printed in Madrid in 1688. This edition has an interesting introduction by the editor.

Fuentes, M.A., ed. *Memorias de los vireyes* [sic] *que han gobernado el Perú.* Lima: Librería Central de Felipe Bailly, 1859. 6 vols. Compilation of the account of their administration written by the viceroys of Peru, held at the National Library in Lima as of 1859.

Goering, Anton. *Vom Tropischen Tieflande zum Ewigen Schnee.* Leipzig: Adalbert Fischer's Verlag, 1892. Travelogue on Venezuela, profusely illustrated.

Hernández, Pablo, S.J. *El extrañamiento de los jesuítas del Río de la Plata y de las Misiones del Paraguay por decreto de las misiones del Paraguay por decreto de Carlos III.* Madrid: Librería General de Victoriano Suárez, 1908. (Colección de libros y documentos referentes a la historia de América, 7). Analytical study of the expulsion of the Jesuits from southern South America in 1767.

Herndon, William Lewis, and Lardner Bibbon. *Exploration of the Valley of the Amazon Made under Direction of the Navy Department.* Washington: Robert Armstrong, Public Printer, 1853–54. 2 vols. Account of the exploration of the Amazon and its tributaries by two U.S. Navy lieutenants. It was printed as a U.S. Senate report.

Herrera, Antonio de. *Historia general de los hechos de los castellanos en las islas y Tierra Firme del Mar Oceano.* Madrid: Oficina Real, 1730. 8 vols. in 4. Second edition of a history of the Spanish conquest of America, first printed in the seventeenth century.

Humboldt, Baron Alexander von. *Personal Narrative of Travels to the Equinoctial Region of America during the Years 1799–1804.* London: George Bell and Sons, 1907. Translation into English from the French of the author by Thomasina Ross. These travel and scientific accounts contain many insightful observations about Spanish America on the eve of its wars of independence from the Spanish Crown.

La Condamine, M. de. *Relation abrégée d'un voyage fait dans l'interieur de l'Amérique Méridionale.* Paris: Veuve Pissot, 1745. Account of the 1735 Franco-Spanish expedition to South America to measure a meridian at the Equator. Bound together with *Lettre à Madame sur l'émeute populaire excitée en la Ville de Cuenca au Perou*, and *Pieces justificatives pour servir de preuve a la pluspart des faits allégués dans la lettre précédente*, dated 1746 and 1745. This volume does not have Zahm's personal book plate, but it is mentioned in the press release of 22 February 1917 to Catholic newspapers announcing Zahm's gift of his South American library to the University of Notre Dame.

La Condamine, M. de. *Relation abrégée d'un voyage fait dans l'intérieur de l'Amérique Méridionale.* Maestricht: Jean Edme Dufour and Philippe Roux, 1778. This edition of the account by La Condamine of the Franco-Spanish expedition to the Equator does not include the information on the incidents at Cuenca that make the 1745 Paris edition so valuable for the study of that expedition.

MacGillivray, W. *The Travels and Researches of Alexander von Humboldt*. New York: Harper, 1846. A condensation of the travel narratives of Baron von Humboldt in Spanish America and Asiatic Russia.

Martyr, Peter. *De Orbe Novo*. Paris: Ernest Leroux, 1907. (Recueil de voyages et de documents pour servir a l'histoire de la géographie, 21). French translation of one of the first accounts of Columbus' voyages.

Martyr, Peter. *Fuentes históricas sobre Colón y América*. Madrid: Imprenta de la S.E. de San Francisco de Sales, 1892. 4 vols. Spanish translation of the writings of Peter Martyr on Columbus by Dr. Joaquín Torres Asensio. The introduction by the translator documents the mood toward Columbus in Spain and Spanish America at the time of the fourth centenary of his first voyage to the Americas.

Nuñez Cabeza de Vaca, Alvar. *Relación de los naufragios y comentarios*. Madrid: Librería General de Victoriano Suárez, 1906. 2 vols. (Coleccion de libros y documentos referentes a la historia de America, 5 and 6). The author of these accounts of his explorations in southern North America (*Naufragios*) and of his administration as governor of Paraguay (Comentarios), one of the most interesting personalities during the Spanish conquest of America, had them printed in Spain in 1555.

Pacheco, Joaquín, and Francisco de Cardenas, eds. *Colección de documentos inéditos relativos al descubrimiento, conquista y organización de las antiguas posesiones españolas en América y Oceanía*. Madrid, 1864–84. 42 vols. Monumental collection of documents, letters, and reports at the Archivo de Indias. This collection facilitates research on early Spanish America.

Rodríguez, Manuel, S. J. *El Marañón y Amazonas. Historia de los descubrimientos, entradas y reducciones de naciones*. Madrid: Imprenta de Antonio González, 1684. A chronicle of the explorations and missions along the Amazon by the Jesuits. Bound with *Compendio historial e índice chronológico peruano y del Nuevo Reino de Granada*, by the same author.

Simón, Fray Pedro. *Noticias historiales de las conquistas de Tierra Firme en las Indias Occidentales*. Bogota: Casa Editorial de Medardo Rivas, 1882–92. 5 vols. First edition of a chronicle of the

Spanish conquest of what today is Colombia. The manuscript was held at the National Library, in Bogota.

Ulloa, Antonio de. *Noticias americanas: entretenimientos físico históricos sobre la América Meridional, y la Septentrional Oriental.* Madrid: Imprenta Real, 1792. Description and commentaries of the regions of North and South America visited by the author, member of the Franco-Spanish expedition that measured a meridian at the Equator in 1735 in South America, and later, first Spanish governor of Louisiana. This volume does not have Zahm's book plate, but it is mentioned in a press release to Catholic newspapers announcing his gift of his South American library to Notre Dame.

Ulloa, Antonio de, and Jorge Juan. *A Voyage to South America.* Dublin: William Williams, 1758. 2 vols. in one. Translation from the Spanish into English of the account of travels in South America by the two Spaniards in the Franco-Spanish expedition to measure a meridian at the Equator in 1735. This important source for the political and economic state of South America at the beginning of the eighteenth century does not have Zahm's book plate, but it is mentioned among the books that he gave to the University of Notre Dame in 1917 in a press release of 22 February of that year.

Vedia, Enrique de, ed. *Historiadores primitivos de Indias.* Madrid: M. Rivadeneyra, 1877. 2 vols. (Biblioteca de autores españoles, 22 and 26). Compilation of chronicles and accounts of the Spanish conquest of America, including Herman Cortes's *Cartas de relación*, Francisco Lopez de Gomara's *Historia general de las Indias*, and those of Bernal Diaz del Castillo, Cieza de Leon, and Zarate. This title is mentioned in the University press release of 22 February 1917 to Catholic newspapers on the Zahm gift.

Vega Inca, Garcilaso de la. *Comentarios reales.* Madrid: Oficina Real, 1723. Second edition of this chronicle of Peru by the son of a Spanish conqueror and an Inca princess. This is the first part of a work that told the story of the Inca Empire and of its conquest by the Spaniards. In these *Comentarios reales* the author chronicles the building of an empire in South America by his maternal ancestors. It includes an unpaginated table of contents and an index.

Vega Inca, Garcilaso de la. *Historia general del Perú.* Madrid: Oficina Real, 1722. Second edition of this chronicle. In this *Historia general*, second part of a corpus concerning the formation of the Inca Empire

and its conquest by the Spaniards, the author chronicles the Spanish conquest. It includes an unpaginated table of contents and an index.
Whymper, Edward. *Travels amongst the Great Andes of the Equator.*
New York: Charles Scribner's Sons, 1892. Travelogue on Ecuador, profusely illustrated.

---

1. "Pan American Notes," *Pan American Bulletin* 44 (March 1917): 375.
2. "South American Library Presented to University of Notre Dame," *The Library Journal* 42 (June 1917): 455.
3. "Pan American Notes," *Pan American Bulletin* 44 (March 1917): 378.
4. John R. Zahm, C.S.C., *Through South America's Southland* (New York: D. Appleton and Company, 1916), vii.
5. Ralph E. Weber, *Notre Dame's John Zahm* (Notre Dame: University of Notre Dame Press, 1961), 190.
6. Zahm, *Up the Orinoco and Down the Magdalena* (New York: D. Appleton and Company, 1910), 302.
7. "Press Release to Catholic Newspapers," Zahm Papers, Box 3, UNDA.
8. Thomas T. McAvoy, C.S.C., *Father O'Hara of Notre Dame* (Notre Dame: University of Notre Dame Press, 1967), 46.
9. Ibid., 55–57.
10. Zahm, *Along the Andes and Down the Amazon* (New York: D. Appleton and Company, 1912), 522–25.
11. McAvoy, 58–59.
12. Philip S. Moore, C.S.C., *Academic Development, University of Notre Dame: Past, Present and Future* (Notre Dame, IN, 1960), 100.
13. McAvoy, 54.
14. *How Notre Dame Prepares the Trade Ambassador* (Notre Dame, IN: n.p., n.d.)
15. "Local News," *The Notre Dame Scholastic* 51 (1 December 1917): 167.
16. Brother John Federowicz, C.S.C., "Forces Affecting the Development of Libraries at the University of Notre Dame, 1843–1968" (Master's thesis, Kent State University, 1968), 87.
17. AR, 1920–21, 11.
18. AR, 1923–24, 16.
19. AR, 1925–26, 6.
20. McAvoy, 88–89.
21. Weber, 190.

Dollars, Donors, and Determination: Collection Building in the Notre Dame Libraries

MAUREEN GLEASON

Three events, 30 years apart, mark the history of collection building in the University Libraries of Notre Dame during the twentieth century: the Library Survey conducted by Frank Walter in 1920; the Wilson-Lundy Survey of 1950; and the Collection Analysis Project carried out in 1980. By reviewing these surveys and tracking their results during the intervening years, a picture emerges of how Notre Dame's collections developed in response to a changing University. We may look at the first period, 1920 to 1950, as the time when the foundation of the collections—major sources, standard works, periodical runs—was gradually built due largely to the determination of the librarian. The second period saw the initiation of more specialized collecting geared to serve the needs of a rapidly expanding University, with broader participation in, but no real organization of collecting. The period after 1980 is the time when the growth of endowment expanded the possibilities for collecting, and collection development assumed a more professional cast, but also when expectations grew apace.

The Walter Survey, 1920

In view of the lack of endowment and losses by fire and otherwise, the library is surprisingly good. It is unusually free from really worthless materials. It is probably fairly adequate for the immediate

> needs of most of the courses. Its faults are those of omission rather
> than commission...an excellent aggregation of individual titles rather
> than a collection showing deliberate correlation.[1]

So wrote Frank Walter about the Notre Dame Library in 1920. Walter, a widely respected librarian who served as director of the library at the University of Minnesota from 1921 to 1943, was engaged to survey the library and make recommendations for its improvement. He praised its fine special collections on Dante, Ireland, South America and botany, and was especially impressed by its rich collection of Catholic periodicals, recommending that the latter be indexed to better fulfill their potential as scholarly resources. Weaknesses were noted, though, in the social sciences, and even in philosophy (history was stronger), and particularly in modern works and foreign language materials. He remarked on the need for more good literary editions, especially in European literature, and suggested greater duplication of books for class use. He strongly recommended greater faculty involvement in book selection, saying that the librarian could not do it all, which suggests that the latter individual was indeed largely responsible for collection building at the time. Walter also offered the University's location as an argument for stronger collections at Notre Dame, for the library was without easy access to other large collections. Walter's estimate suggests a well-selected, though limited collection geared to the obvious educational needs of a growing college that was not yet a real university. Despite pockets of potential excellence, it was in no sense a research collection.

Walter's description of the collection was largely qualitative. Another perspective can be gained by examining its size and rate of growth in comparison with other academic libraries. During the first part of the twentieth century, many American colleges were in the process of becoming universities, a choice which would determine the nature and size of the collections they would build. At the start of the century, the collecting energies of Jimmie Edwards, Notre Dame's first librarian, had given Notre Dame a respectable place among U.S. academic libraries, only a few of which had anything approaching research collections. In 1900, with 55,000 volumes, Notre Dame was among the 20 largest American academic libraries listed by Danton.[2] In that same year, it was tied for 14th in size among 70 libraries whose statistics were charted by Edelman and Tatum, placing it in the top 20 percent.

By 1920, however, it was only in the top 36 percent;[3] the mean annual growth between 1900 and 1920 of 17 libraries recorded by Danton was 15,707, and with an annual average growth of only 2,550, Notre Dame was clearly falling behind by the time Walter conducted his survey.[4]

Statistics during this period, of course, may be viewed with some skepticism, and, in any case, the size of Notre Dame's collection as reported at various times suggests erratic growth. When Paul J. Foik, C.S.C., was appointed librarian in 1912 after Edwards' death, the number of volumes increased as Foik gathered the books that had been "stored away in various corners of the main building," disposing of duplicates, and cataloging the rest. Records also indicate that Foik's selections prior to Walter's visit were often *ad hoc* purchases to meet immediate need, each of which required approval of the University president. The nature of collection building may be glimpsed in Foik's request for permission to buy books on corporate finance, of which the library had nothing, in order to supply Professor Plante's class; or to buy an "almost out of print" book, *Mathematical Theory of Eclipses* for $2.50. Foik's own judgment was that the "library was exceedingly weak in philosophy and the technical sciences" where "works of permanent reference" were needed.[5]

Building the Foundation, 1920–1950

Since Father Foik was transferred to St. Edward's College, Austin, Texas in 1924, the collections during most of the period between the Walter and the Wilson-Lundy Survey in 1950 were under the care of his eventual successor, Paul Byrne. This period saw the expansion of graduate education and faculty research in universities. Edelman and Tatum state that "the close relationship between the quality of graduate education and research and the collections and services of the university library...is the dominant theme in the development of American university library collections."[6] Unfortunately, Notre Dame did not grow as rapidly as did many other academic libraries in this 30-year period. Whereas the library was in the top 36 percent of the Edelman-Tatum list of libraries in 1920, by 1950 it was in only the top 55 percent. Philip Moore, C.S.C., in his *Academic Development: University of Notre Dame: Past, Present, and Future* laments the library's slowness of growth, stating that, in contrast to the average of 16 years for university library collections to double found by Fremont Rider, Notre Dame's took 25 years, from 1924 to 1949. Moore continues: "Looking back today upon the library resources and other conditions essential to genuine graduate work, especially on the doctoral level, we must conclude that in the 1920s Notre Dame was over-ambitious or over-extended in most of the fields in which advanced programs of study were offered."[7] Lacking resources to finance library and other support for graduate study, the University drastically reduced doctoral programs to systematic botany and organic chemistry in 1932, and it was not until after World War II that serious efforts began to match library resources with the increasing numbers of graduate programs. The growth rate of virtually all libraries slowed during the Depression years of the early 1930s but began to rise again shortly afterward. Notre Dame's did not; collections grew by 18.6 percent between 1931 and 1936; by 11.1 percent from 1936 to 1941. Although growth during the 1940s increased to 43.8 percent, its relative size among comparable academic libraries declined between 1920 and 1950.[8]

The state of a library's collections, their size and nature, is naturally dependent on funding, not only its amount, but also its source and how it is allocated. During the first half of the twentieth century, Notre Dame, like many academic libraries, was almost entirely dependent on student fees, and the inadequacies of those fees is a constant complaint of the librarians. In 1919, Father Foik complained to the President of the University that the University's support for its library could not meet the North Central Association requirements; in 1920–21, the student fee for library support was $3.00. It was the same in 1925–26, and librarian Paul Byrne echoed Foik's earlier warning that it did not meet the minimum standard of the accrediting agencies of $5.00 per student. By 1929–30, the fee had increased to $6.00 and the persistent recommendation of the librarians to include summer school students had been heeded. Six dollars was still the fee ten years later, and complaints of its total inadequacy had become a regular feature of the annual report. A brighter note is at last sounded in 1946–47, when the library was able to buy more books than ever before. The increase in funding was due, to some extent, to money that was not spent during the war years, but also to $20,000 from the Alumni Fund (a significant amount in a year when library materials and binding expenditures amounted to a little over $44,000), and to fees resulting from increased enrollment.[9]

The library's financial straits through the years of course reflect in some measure those of the University. Wilson and Lundy track the percent of the University's educational and general expenditures used to support the library. The American Library Association's minimum standard for this widely accepted measure of universities' support for their libraries was 4 percent; during the period 1934/35 to 1949/50, Notre Dame fell below this in only one year, and in 1949/50 the University devoted 6 percent of its educational and general expenditures to library support. However, Wilson and Lundy also point out that the standard applied to all academic institutions and made no allowance for support of graduate study and research. They offer the examples of Duke and University of North Carolina which regularly spent over 7 percent of their educational and general expenditures in order to build research library collections.[10]

The allocation of available funds (to various departments and for various purposes) provides a clue to the kind of collection that was being built. The first allocation, in 1920–21, was simple: one-half of the budget remained with the librarian, divided equally between periodicals and reference books; the other half was divided among the colleges, with Arts and Letters receiving 25 percent, Science, 22.5 percent, and Commerce, Engineering, and Law, each 17.5 percent. Such a division is interesting in light of the distribution of enrollment in 1920: 26.7 percent of the students were in engineering; 31.3 percent in commerce; 17.6 percent, law; 14.3 percent, arts and letters; 10.1 percent, science.[11] The library distribution reflects the assumption that the practice-oriented programs had lesser need for library materials despite their larger enrollments, and perhaps as well reflects assumptions about the nature of an academic library collection. In general, during the next 30 years, the portion of the budget assigned to the colleges grew somewhat at the expense of that for general library collection support, with the amount spent on periodicals shrinking somewhat, a striking contrast to what was to happen during the second 30-year period. Among the colleges, Arts and Letters' share swelled to 63.2 percent of the budget by 1937–38. By that time, however, the single-college allocation was replaced by departmental allocations, and the growth in Arts and Letters' share may be due to its greater number of departments, as well as its increased enrollment.

Donated funds, usually for specific subjects, as well as gift books, were critical factors in shaping collections during this period. During the 1920s, donated funds approached 60 percent of the total spent in some years. Individual gifts, for instance those of Father Nieuwland for chemistry and Father Miltner for philosophy, provided as great a share of the acquisitions budget then as a present-day gift of $40,000 would of the libraries' current acquisitions budget.

Special appropriations from the University frequently supplemented departmental allocations and reveal something of the University's view of collecting priorities in any given year. Some of these appropriations were for a particular purchase. Others targeted subject areas: in 1924–25, amounts for communications, mathematics, boy guidance, and architecture; a few years later, for education and sociology; in 1936–37, $2,815 for biology and $1,817 for philosophy; in 1938–39, for biology, political science, engineering and mathematics. The previous year, special appropriations for chemistry, philosophy, and political science amounted to 48.5 percent of total expenditures. Although the amounts do not seem significant today, given the meager budgets of those years, they had a major impact on the distribution of funds in any given year. The shifting mix of subjects favored, however, suggests a response to pressing needs or faculty demands, rather than fixed intentions regarding the nature of the collections being built.

Exchanges of materials published on campus for periodicals published elsewhere were a significant source of support for the periodical collection during these years and were made possible by the founding of the *American Midland Naturalist* at Notre Dame in 1909. Currently, only about 3 to 4 percent of the libraries' serial subscriptions are received on exchange; contrast this with 1920, when 84 percent of periodicals were the result of exchanges. Paralleling the gradually diminishing significance of exchanges in libraries generally are the trends at Notre Dame: by 1932, the portion had dropped to 42 percent of the total, by 1943, 29.3 percent. Nevertheless, exchanges were a mainstay of the collection in the 1920s and 1930s, and the existence of long runs of some serials in the present collection are attributable to this acquisition method.

One source of funding, of great significance now, was scarcely heard of at Notre Dame during the period from 1920 to 1950. Although a few of the outstanding academic libraries were well-endowed early in the century (the Yale Library spent endowment income of $25,000 in 1906),[12] before 1960 Notre Dame had only four endowments, and those were comparatively small. In the 1920s, the Dante endowment, established with a gift from John A. Zahm, C.S.C., to support his Dante collection, was the only named endowment, although Foik's effort to raise money for an Irish collection resulted in an expendable fund of about $1,500. It is not until the 1940s that we find mention of a "small, but growing endowment."[13] Of those endowments for which there are clear records, the Corbett for Medieval Studies (1933) and the Yawman for Business (1946) were the only others established during this period.

What sort of collection was being built with the monies available, who was building it, and were there conscious efforts to evaluate its quality and direct its course? Despite recommendations in library literature extolling the virtues of collection development policies, such policies were rare during this era. The intentions governing Notre Dame's collecting must be deduced from occasional statements, and from the evidence of collecting activity. Foik expressed what served as a collection policy in saying that he wanted to acquire: 1) "sources and fundamental documents in English and foreign languages, along with contemporary works useful in discovering truth;" and 2) "choice of the best new books in all fields to act as a stimulus." He expanded this by describing the principles that determined the allocation of funds, namely: the number of departments in each college; the need of those departments; the importance of classes in each department; and the provision of a reserve fund for the librarian.[14] Evidence from the annual reports suggests that similar intentions influenced collecting under Byrne, Foik's successor. The librarians believed that they shared with the faculty responsibility for the education of students and the promotion of scholarship, and therefore great selectivity and judgment in building a collection to promote those aims were imperative. Such an attitude is fairly typical of college librarians during these years.

In addition, certain persisting collecting principles emerge from a review of what was actually acquired between 1920 and 1950. The acquisition of major sources and standard works in all fields established the basis for a strong collection. For example, the purchases of the following are noted with pride: *Dictionary of National Biography*, *Grove's Dictionary of Music and Musicians*, both in 1927; and later, *Monumenta Germaniae Historica, Royal Society Transactions* from 1665 forward, *Rolls Series, Catalogue of the Bibliothèque Nationale, Annales de la Propagation de la Foi*, 1822–1930 (specifically identified as a strengthening of those Catholic sources for which a particular responsibility was felt), *Hensius Allgemeines Bücherlexikon*, 1700–1892, *Colonial Archives of Pennsylvania, British Museum Catalog*, and many more. There were also constant efforts to fill in back runs of periodicals. Like many libraries early in the twentieth century, Notre Dame did not take serials seriously as a scholarly resource, and often did not bind and retain even those that were acquired. As a result, the struggle to fill in broken runs is a recurring theme during the first half of the century. In 1940–41 after three years of unsuccessful pleas to the University administration for a special grant of $5,000 to fill such lacunae, money was taken from the book fund, to the intense dissatisfaction of the departments which saw their allocations cut. By the 1930s, of course, regular recourse to interlibrary loan was made to supply what was not owned, but it was regarded as something of an embarrassment. The 1940–41 Annual Report notes that refusals of loans from other libraries had reached a new high, and said "Notre Dame cannot go on indefinitely expecting other schools to supply us with material which should be on our own shelves."[15]

Of course, acquisitions were not confined to original sources, and new secondary works were also bought. Some of these were academic in nature; when up to $2,000 was donated in 1933–34 to purchase books from the Yale University Press catalog, all but $400 worth were already in the collection, indicating regular acquisition of the output of major university presses. But the lists of the most circulated books that appeared regularly in the annual reports and in the student newspaper, the *Scholastic*, indicate that currently popular authors' works were also being bought. In 1937, *Gone with the Wind* was most in demand, and works of such authors as Cather, Hemingway, Tolstoi, and Undset appeared regularly, as did those of such vanished favorites as Donn Byrne and Edgar Wallace. By the 1930s, the *New York Times Book Review* was being used as a selection tool.

Among the deficiencies cited by Walter were those in foreign language materials. Although it is hard to determine the extent to which efforts were made to remedy this in the years following his survey, books published abroad were certainly purchased regularly. In 1923–24, for instance, the librarian reports that "advantage is being taken through our French importer...to build up the French language and literature section as the franc is at present much depreciated."[16] The distress reported by the librarian when World War II disrupted overseas purchasing is evidence of its significance for collecting. Notre Dame joined other libraries in a cooperative effort to meet this challenge. In 1942, a committee of librarians arranged with the British and U.S. governments to bring in journals from Germany, France, Italy and German-occupied countries up to the amount of $250,000 for total receipts. Notre Dame requested 44 of these titles, of which it was granted 40, although it is not clear how many actually appeared on the library's shelves. The library's annual reports during the war also complain of the difficulty of obtaining foreign books. After the war, the library had some success in obtaining books from Italy, France and Belgium. Notre Dame alumni serving in the armed forces were contacted to obtain volumes from Germany and Austria, but their efforts were largely futile. The French and Russians had snapped them up, they reported.[17] Not all agreed with these efforts, however, and some years later, one of the librarians complained that the purchase of foreign literature does not stimulate students to read—a sign, perhaps, of the persistent tension between building an undergraduate collection and supplying the research needs of graduate students and faculty.[18] In reality, failures in the latter aim are reported as well. The 1928–29 Annual Report writes of the growing demand for specialized graduate material, and in 1934–35, the librarian reports that the library is not meeting this demand, especially in the case of sets in biology and physics.

Efforts were made to build to collection strength in those areas where Notre Dame had a special responsibility. Foik had used the Irish National Foundation, which he established, as a vehicle for gathering a collection of Irish materials, and there are frequent references to keeping up the strengths of the Catholic Americana collections. Sadly, Byrne also complains that the Dante endowment (apparently controlled by the University administration) is not being used, to the detriment of the library's outstanding Dante collection.[19]

In common with other academic libraries during this period, Notre Dame officially regarded book selection as a faculty responsibility. However, getting the faculty to participate in selection was a greater problem than their domination of selection, judging from the number of times the issue arises in reports and surveys. One way that individual faculty members inevitably influenced the nature of the collections was by the donation of their own libraries. In 1933–34, Professor Martin McCue, dean of the College of Engineering, left the library 1,000 volumes in mathematics and engineering, and in the same year the library received 1,200 volumes featuring works of drama, poetry, Dante, Washington, Lincoln and Polish history and literature from Charles Phillips, teacher of literature, director of plays, champion of the cause of the Polish people. Being the beneficiary of such specialist collecting made a great difference to a relatively small collection that had been meagerly funded. And other gifts continued to enrich the collection. Daniel Hudson, C.S.C., contributed hundreds of volumes acquired not only by virtue of his editorship of *Ave Maria* but also through his contacts with literary figures. Father John A. O'Brien, a noted preacher who eventually came to live at Notre Dame, gave thousands of volumes, many associated with his educational work, but also others dealing with politics, World War II, philosophy, as well as a group of titles on the late Revolutionary period in Mexico. The collections benefitted from more unexpected donors such as Joseph Kotchka, retired steelworker from Pittsburgh, who annually provided books on a variety of topics including aviation, Russian and German politics and the languages of Hungary and Poland.

Periodic efforts, both fortuitous and planned, were made to evaluate the quality of certain parts of the collection during the period between surveys. In 1934–35 such an assessment criticized the absence of the works of the foremost economic theorists of the pre-modern period. On the other hand, great satisfaction was taken in the results of checking Finotti's *Bibliographia Catholica Americana, 1784–1820* for which a new edition was being prepared. Notre Dame owned 103 titles, including five not identified on the list for the 2d edition which covered 1729–1830. In philosophy, Notre Dame's holdings in 1938 were compared with those of 25 other Catholic colleges, and the library was determined to be second in overall size of collection, and third in quality, based on a select bibliography. These assessments were, for the most part, sporadic and unrelated to specific collection improvement actions. In 1939, however, the library needs of the College of Engineering were thoroughly surveyed, apparently preparatory to a significant enhancement of the engineering collection. It was concluded that the book collection was "pitifully small and out of date," but that solid holdings in society transactions and proceedings contributed to a more substantial serial collection. The assessment was based on bibliographies compiled by faculty members, as well as a bibliography of books for an engineering school library issued by the Society for the Promotion of Engineering Education. As a result of this evaluation, several hundred books and theses in various engineering and mathematics fields, 1,000 standard technical books for course use, and many reference handbooks were ordered.

Wilson-Lundy Survey

Father Moore describes the situation at the University in the late 1940s:

With the ending of World War II, the development and expansion took up where they had left off in 1938, with notably increased tempo. Better qualified Faculty members have been continuously recruited, library resources built up, laboratory facilities expanded, sponsored research tremendously augmented, symposia, lectures, and publications multiplied and the quantity and quality of the student body increased. Doctoral programs have more than doubled from 7 to 15...[20]

Recognizing these changes, the foreword to the Wilson-Lundy survey states:

The Library of the University likewise felt the impact of these forces and underwent certain changes occasioned by them. In order that the Library might be further developed to meet the demands made upon it, the Administration of the University requested the American Library Association in the spring of 1950 to make a survey of the Library.[21]

This survey was conducted by Dr. Louis Wilson, dean emeritus of the Graduate Library School of the University of Chicago and by Frank

A. Lundy, director of libraries at the University of Nebraska, who, after preliminary planning, spent November 1–14, 1950 on campus. The purpose of the Survey, as stated in its final report was: 1) to determine the present effectiveness of the library in playing its proper role in support of stated objectives of the University; and 2) to make practical recommendations for both short and long term changes and development for the guidance of library officers and University administrators in making the library a more productive and efficient agent in the learning, teaching and research functions.[22]

Naturally, the collections loomed large in the aspects of the library that were to be examined. Wilson and Lundy began this examination with three observations: 1) Notre Dame did not establish a library until 1873, 30 years after the school opened; 2) the 1879 fire destroyed that library; and 3) vigorous development of graduate study had taken place since 1940 (thus intensifying the demands on the collections). In light of this, they compared Notre Dame library statistics with a mix of 24 other academic libraries; public, private, and Catholic. Notre Dame was 23d in total volumes, 17th in volumes added annually, 17th in materials and binding expenditures, and first in per student expenditure for books. Its rate of growth was almost normal for academic libraries (18,014 volumes were added in 1949–50), but it had started from a very small base, and an unusually large number of volumes (mostly duplicates) had been discarded during reclassification from Dewey to Library of Congress during the late 20s and early 30s (63,215 between 1927 and 1950).[23] In commissioning the Wilson-Lundy study, Notre Dame appeared to have ambitions for its library that were no longer exclusively those of an undergraduate institution. This new goal would require more than ordinary resources.

Wilson and Lundy employed an array of methods to assess the collections, and assessment results as reported by them provide some insight into those collections at mid-century. They relied on standard bibliographies in traditional fields, and on studies of academic library holdings in those fields in order to gauge the extent to which Notre Dame measured up to comparable libraries. In general, the smaller and more selective the list used, the better the library's showing: 100 percent of the 46 periodicals in *Books for Catholic Colleges* were currently subscribed to; 73 percent of 19 works in economic and social history in *Guide to Historical Literature* and 77 percent of 26 in cultural history

128

in the same work were owned; the library had 90 percent of the listings for Brownson, Cather, Twain, James, Emerson and Hawthorne in the "Bibliographies, Individual Authors," section of *Literary History of the United States*. Of the more specialized research works, Notre Dame's holdings usually ranged from 30 to 40 percent, and this proportion did not compare well with major university libraries. This was true even of fields particularly relevant to Notre Dame programs, such as those in *Progress in Medieval and Renaissance Studies* and the "History of Christianity" segment of *Guide to Historical Literature*. Somewhat surprising, however, is the fact that Notre Dame held 67 percent of the 2,357 works in Hawkins' *Scientific, Medical and Technical Books Published in the U.S. 1930–44; Supplement, 1945–48*, which may suggest a more systematic attention to the collections in fields which were served by branch libraries. In a comparison of Notre Dame's holdings of the most cited scientific periodicals, however, the library ranked 45th of 55 major university libraries.

Wilson and Lundy also asked faculty members to identify their greatest collection needs,[24] and it is worth noting the frequency with which periodicals and foreign materials appear on these lists, reflecting changing academic emphases to which collecting practice had not yet adequately responded.

Wilson and Lundy proposed a goal for library collecting: "...a challenge, not to fill out certain sets or to provide special rare materials which can be exhibited to visitors with pride, but to have at hand the materials that are fundamentally essential to the University's daily teaching and research." They recommended that:

1. Books for general reading be provided in greater number and made accessible in library reading rooms and dorms.

2. Reference collections and bibliographic apparatus be considerably increased.

3. The collection of federal, state and foreign documents be built up and administered to make them accessible.

4. All units of the University making use of audio-visual materials examine the program of acquisitions and administration to provide them more effectively.

5. Exchanges be constantly reviewed to derive maximum benefit from the University's excellent list of publications.

6. The director, library committee, departmental librarians, department heads, and department library committees concern themselves with problems of acquisition and of fruitful cooperation "in order that the particular information desired by a scholar may be secured at the particular time he needs it."

7. A Friends of the Library group be organized and Officers of the University and the Notre Dame Foundation assist in bringing the needs of the library to the attention of interested friends.

8. The University raise the annual appropriation for books, periodicals and binding to $100,000, and to secure basic materials now lacking it appropriate a special fund of $25,000 annually for five years to be used each year as follows: for basic books, $10,000; for back files, $10,000; for new subscriptions, $1,500; for microfilms, etc., $2,000; and for federal, state and foreign documents, $1,500.[25]

Meeting New Demands, 1950–1980

The library director who succeeded Paul Byrne in 1952, Victor A. Schaefer, was faced with the task of collection building in light of the Wilson-Lundy report. Indeed the chapter titles used by Wilson and Lundy dictated the divisions used by the department heads in their annual reports of progress made as late as the 1960s, and the improvements they reported under "Resources for Instruction, Research, and Publication" seem modest, but steady. Schaefer delayed attention to the collection until the faculty could be surveyed once again, and of course, acquisitions were limited by the money available. The University's financial response to the Wilson-Lundy recommendations, while not immediate and total, can be detected in increased funding and greatly accelerated collection growth over the next 30 years. In contrast to the 43.8 percent increase in size between 1940 and 1950, the collections increased by 109 percent between 1950 and 1960, and by 98.7 percent during the following decade. It is true, of course, that other libraries were growing as well. Although between 1967 and 1987 Notre Dame's holdings grew by 119 percent as compared to the median increase among Association for Research Libraries' members of 102 percent, relative ranking improved only marginally since Notre Dame's base was smaller.[26] In 1950 Notre Dame was 69th in size among the

126 libraries listed by Edelman and Tatum; in 1975, it was 63d among 122.[27]

This growth was made possible, of course, by a significant increase in funding, which had, in fact, begun by the time of the Wilson-Lundy study. Reflecting the expansiveness of higher education, particularly in the 1960s, the library's acquisitions expenditure grew by 268.3 percent during that decade, compared to 49.5 percent during the 1950s, then dropped back to 131.2 percent during the 1970s. In fact, by the end of the '60s, overexpenditures had become a serious problem for the library and the University, fueled by the growing costs of serials which were absorbing an ever-greater portion of the acquisitions budget. At the same time, more of that budget was being allocated to departments, and by 1954-55, some shift from arts and letters to science is noticeable, related of course to the rising cost of serials.

Each of the decades between the Wilson-Lundy report in 1950 and the Collection Analysis Project in 1980 is marked by distinctive trends that left their mark on the collections. In response to the Wilson-Lundy recommendations, the Main Library was divided into humanities, social sciences, and business and economics reading rooms in the early 1950s, and each was staffed by librarians. This focused collecting activity, and there were efforts to evaluate the collections in the light of student needs, and to strengthen weaknesses. The business and economics collections were regarded as particularly weak. Sources such as *Choice* and the *Lamont Library Catalog* were used as selection tools, and an effort was made to gradually acquire all the periodicals in the *Readers Guide* and the *International Index*. In the 1950s, purchasing in support of international relations programs began in earnest. In 1953–54, for example, several hundred titles on economics and history in Russian, Polish and Ukrainian were purchased, and about that time special appropriations for "Society studies" and international relations began and continued into the 1960s. Filling in of periodicals and sets identified as necessary by faculty continued. Major collections of sources, such as the titles in the Evans' *American Bibliography* (1639–1820) began to appear in microform during this period, and the library used this means to expand its research capability.

By 1960–61, the Acquisitions Department is complaining of the "unbroken climb in the cost of books, periodical subscriptions and binding," and also of the increase in the rate of production of printed materials. By 1964, the Chemistry/Physics Library is lamenting the rising cost of subscriptions, and we hear that support for science and engineering collections is imperiled [28] despite the successful effort to establish a research level collection in mathematics at the time of the opening of the new Computing Center and Mathematics Building in 1962. Economy measures ensued; duplication of little used and expensive reference materials was curtailed; backruns of only the highest priority journals were acquired; and for the first time, we hear of a serials review when the Architecture Library began examination of its serials list. Never before had the list of serials been systematically reduced rather than expanded.

Themes that have become familiar are sounded for the first time in the 1960s; for instance, the University's propensity to expand programs without providing money for library support. It was during this time that the Department of Psychology was founded, and the master of business administration degree offered for the first time, and apparently the library was strained by new demands without corresponding resources.

In 1968–69, the early depletion of the acquisitions budget resulted in a crisis meeting of the University vice presidents for business and for academic affairs, the assistant vice president for academic affairs, the comptroller, assistant comptroller, the director and assistant director of the library, and the head of the Acquisitions Department. The following measures were taken: the expenditure of funds from academic department accounts were made subject to the approval of the library director; placement of new subscriptions was to be "rigidly selective"; cancellations were to be considered; and the creation of a contingency fund under the control of the director was also to be considered.[29]

All was not grim during the 1960s, however, for that was when regular grants from external sources began to support collections. As a result of the National Defense Education Act, funds for English, government and international studies, history, mathematics, philosophy, sociology and Soviet studies were received annually. The National Science Foundation provided funds, especially for the mathematics and philosophy collections, and the Ford Foundation supported collections in human development and Western Europe.

The acquisition of microforms which had begun to expand during the previous decade grew even more rapidly during the 1960s, as witness the change from 478 reels of microfilms acquired in 1964–65 to 3,872 in 1968–69. At the end of this period, in addition to acquiring microform collections which supported research, the library began to retain some of the more heavily used periodicals only in microform—a practical, though not a widely popular decision.

It was also at this time that the Notre Dame Library Association, one of the innovations recommended by Wilson and Lundy, at last came to be. At the suggestion of Father Theodore Hesburgh in 1959, it was adopted as a special project of the Women's Advisory Council "to enlist the interest and support of all the friends of Notre Dame, to encourage them to become acquainted with the problems of the library and to assist in interpreting the program and the service of the library to others...with the object of enlarging and enriching the resources of the library."[30] Initially, it was composed principally of "the women of the Notre Dame family"—the Women's Advisory Council (generally wives of men serving on boards and councils of the University); the mothers of present students; and the wives of alumni, faculty members, and friends. Actually, however, many men were members. At first the Association adopted as an aim the upgrading and replacing of heavily used segments of the collection; for instance, providing critical and easily readable editions of standard American and English literary works. Almost immediately, however, it decided to focus on the purchase of rare books. In 1961, the Notre Dame Library Association had an income of $72,833 from membership fees and gifts; it invested $50,000 and used $20,000 to purchase books.[31] The Association published an annual from 1961 to 1963 which included at least one article on some special feature of the collections, a list of donors, a financial report, and descriptions of major library collections such as the Trohan, the Ford, the John Bennett Shaw and others, apparently to encourage prospective donors. Unfortunately, shortly after this, the Association curtailed its national activities and became a more modest local organization, perhaps as a result of a change in the University's fundraising strategies.

The early years of the 1970s saw a continuing crisis in the financing of collections and more attention being paid to the method of accounting for acquisitions expenditures. Inflation had become a major factor, and steps to control its impact were studied. The results of a study of the book budget were presented to the University administration, and a freeze was imposed on all book funds in February 1972.

Stimulated by the struggle over library funding that failed to keep up with expanding University programs, a new director of libraries, David Sparks, appointed in 1971, experimented with new methods of allocation. Sparks had devised a mathematical model for book fund allocation soon after his arrival, and in the ensuing years data for that model were collected and applied in a test mode to "show the proportionate impact of the various teaching departments and colleges...on the budget of the University Libraries."[32] In 1975 Professor Raymond Brach of the College of Engineering developed a computerized version of this model, which, with some modifications became the basis for a redistribution of the book funds over a three-year period. The acquisitions budget had also been restructured to provide an overall monetary allocation to each academic department covering books, continuations and serials, and the transfer of funds among these components was allowed. The chief purpose of the redistribution, which was actively urged by the University provost, was to, (as Sparks put it) correct "the grave imbalance" in the growth of expenditures for science and engineering. In 1975–76, book funds for Memorial Library, which supported the Colleges of Arts and Letters and Business, grew by 4.71 percent, while those for the science and engineering libraries grew by 34.07 percent. In the year following the changes, funds for Memorial Library were up by 16.47 percent and those for the science and engineering libraries only by 4.17 percent. Sparks comments: "This was a direct effect of reallocation of book funds and demonstrates that the process has been effective."[33]

Serials costs were the main culprit, rising to over 50 percent of the acquisitions budget in 1974–75, where they had been 42 percent only two years earlier; they consumed 78.6 percent of the science and engineering libraries' budget by this time. The need to control serials costs had been a recommendation of the study completed by the Committee on University Priorities (COUP) in 1973, and in 1973–74, the first of several library-wide serial reviews took place, resulting in the cancellation of 589 titles costing $6,396.

Serials were not the only problem during these years, however. Between 1966 and 1972, the book funds rose on an average of 3.37 percent annually, while book prices rose by 9.41 percent. In 1973, the libraries were forced to cancel their first approval plan, (a university press plan with the Richard Abel Company begun in 1967) because the general fund to which it was charged could no longer cover its costs.

Among the positive developments occurring during the 1970s was a new organization of the collection development operation. At the start of the 1970s most books were ordered on the initiative of individual teaching and research faculty members who sent orders to the Acquisitions Department where they were searched in order of arrival until the designated book allocation ran out. The annual reports of the 1960s give evidence of problems interfering with effective book selection. Library administrators complain the librarians are not sufficiently interested in selection activities, that they are absorbed by procedural matters. The librarians complain of a lack of time and unresponsiveness to their efforts on the part of academic departments. In fact, the 1965–66 Annual Report describes a procedure calculated to discourage the humanities librarians' participation in selection: they are to read reviews, etc., then submit suggestions to the head of humanities, who then gives them to the assistant director, who sends them to the head of the appropriate academic department! That this lack of participation was not universal, however, seems clear from another report that year where the chemistry/physics librarian is said to do practically all of the selection. In 1974, to promote more systematic, better planned selection, a Technical Services Task Force recommended the creation of the Order Department which was to serve as a "window on the campus" for collection building activities. A Committee on Collection Development was also formed by Sparks, its membership composed of librarians each of whom had liaison responsibilities to an academic department.[34] Although the changes were not drastic, their clear aim was to provide a structure through which the libraries could assume greater responsibility for collection development.

The 1970s were noteworthy for the acquisition of several large collections, in which the then provost, James T. Burtchaell, C.S.C., played a large role. Through the good offices of Astrik L. Gabriel, director of the Medieval Institute, in 1971–72 the Jarry collection of 13,000 French monographs, journals and pamphlets, particularly strong in medieval materials was purchased for $10,500 from Canon Eugene Jarry, professor of medieval studies at the Institut Catholique, Paris. The 1973–74 purchase of the Stevens collection from the

Philadelphia Divinity School strengthened the Protestant theology and liturgy collection. There was also the 1975 purchase, made possible by the gift of an anonymous donor, of the stock of the ADCO Book Exchange (Goldfadden), some 125,000 items which enormously expanded the sports collection. The libraries also acquired at this time the collection of the Center for Applied Research in the Apostolate (CARA), mostly African, Church-related materials. It was during the 1970s that the agreement was reached whereby the collection of Milton Anastos, noted Byzantine scholar, would come to Notre Dame at his death. The Anastos collection of over 40,000 volumes is still with Professor Anastos in Los Angeles, but new additions are now represented in Notre Dame's catalog. Microfilms of the works in Milan's Ambrosiana Library were acquired by the Medieval Institute during this period, and are now part of the libraries' collection.

Although the increase in the University's appropriation for the libraries grew only modestly during the 1970s, these acquisitions as well as special funding strengthened identifiable collections. Provost's grants of up to $70,000 contributed to acquisition of source materials in American history, and the improvement of the art and music collections which were too weak to adequately support the University's expanding academic programs in those fields. The challenge grant received from the National Endowment for the Humanities in 1978 contributed greatly to collection building in the humanities. It amounted to $400,000 to be matched by $1,200,000 in permanent endowment funds, and thus its effect continues to be felt today. It permitted retrospective purchasing of monographs, replacement of books long missing, the acquisition of major catalogs and bibliographies, and was applied to the collection priorities identified by the various humanities departments.

Surveys toward the end of this period revealed that undergraduates were still concerned about the currency of the collection and the availability on the shelves of wanted items. Faculty doubted the adequacy of support for research, and the responses of faculty in the Colleges of Arts and Letters and Business seemed more negative than their colleagues' in the other colleges. Teaching and research faculty involvement in selection continued to vary greatly among departments and individuals.

Financial support for the libraries had never achieved the dramatic boost that Wilson and Lundy suggested was necessary to support the research aspiration of the University, the libraries' share of the University's educational and general expenditure rising from 4.38 percent in 1975–76 to 4.5 percent in 1979–80. Although the fundraising Campaign for Notre Dame had a goal of $10 million for the libraries, only $7 million had been raised. Endowments had increased, however, from approximately six in 1970 to twenty-seven at the end of the decade.

Librarians were certainly more involved in collection development. Twenty liaison officers were given part-time assignments to work with academic departments in collection building and a bibliographer (for fine arts) was assigned full-time to the Collection Development Department (formerly the Order Department). However, a survey showed that, apart from the branch librarians, these liaisons did not feel collection development to be an integral part of their library position.[35]

By this time, awareness of the critical nature of preservation was growing, but the libraries had taken only very halting steps toward a preservation program. A survey of 6,752 items for condition of binding and paper resulted in the projection of nearly 100,000 volumes which would eventually require rebinding or replacement and close to 120,000 with severely yellowed and brittle pages. Despite the obvious need, the appointment of a part-time preservation officer in January of 1980 was not successful in achieving the desired results.

A number of evaluations revealed weaknesses in the provision of standard academic materials. A check of *Books for College Libraries* (1973) done in 1977 revealed that Notre Dame did not own 17.4 percent; when *Choice*'s Outstanding Academic Books for the years 1970–1977 was checked, 26.6 percent were not held, including 42.4 percent of the science titles. In other words, in the provision of current academic titles, the collections seemed to be getting worse.

Collection Analysis Project

By this time, the libraries had a new director, Robert C. Miller, who came in 1978; the funding situation looked more promising, especially with the growing numbers of endowments; and collection development as a vital library function had come into its own. These circumstances led to the libraries' inauguration of the Collection

Analysis Project (CAP) in 1980, 30 years after the Wilson-Lundy survey. CAP was a year-long self-study of collection related matters and was assisted by the Office of Management Studies (OMS) of the Association of Research Libraries which provided a conceptual model for analyzing the collection, a manual describing methods of analysis, and training by two OMS representatives.

The study began by comparing Notre Dame with other university libraries. Notre Dame was 20 percent to 48 percent below the median of its fellow ARL libraries in all categories: total volumes, volumes added, microforms, current serials, expenditures, binding, etc. Comparing Notre Dame's holdings to participants in the National Shelflist Count (a count of titles based on a shelflist measure) showed them to be proportionately stronger quantitatively in philosophy, theology, mathematics, and the sciences; weaker in foreign languages and music. This initial survey identified questions that required investigation: was the financial base sufficient to support research collections? were allocations appropriate? was selection methodology effective? how to cope with growing demand? The CAP committee noted the judgment of the 1974 North Central Association accreditation team: "For a doctoral university the library has substantial deficiencies in its holdings (and in its financial support)."[36]

In addition to describing the state of the collection, CAP analyzed environmental developments and trends; examined goals and objectives; and appointed individual task forces on budget allocation, operating practices in collection development, collection assessment, preservation of library materials, and resource sharing. Forty-nine recommendations finally emerged which may be grouped into those dealing with financing, with staffing, with collection evaluation, with preservation, and with cooperation. The financing recommendations emphasized control of the budget so that continuing commitments did not consume an inordinate share (for serials a generous limit of no more than 65 percent was suggested); the gathering of data for sound allocation decisions (although no use of a formula); and the most flexible use of endowment income possible. Various ways of strengthening the liaison/bibliographer structure were recommended, as was the appointment of at least one additional bibliographer. The importance of regular assessments was stressed, and the conduct of an availability study recommended. Strengthening the preservation program was regarded as important, as was the filling of the position of preservation officer. The ideal of cooperation was endorsed, as was the sharing of information between interlibrary loan and collection development.[37]

Coping With Change 1980–1993

The years following the completion of CAP saw constant change in the libraries' environment, which reduced the likelihood that CAP recommendations would be implemented precisely as written. CAP did, however, highlight many issues critical for contemporary collection development and provided a sense of direction which moved collecting forward. Seven bibliographers, in American Catholic studies (1980), theology/philosophy (1982), language and literature (1982), business (1984), Latin American, government and international studies (1986), medieval and classical studies (1987) and music (1993) have joined the fine arts bibliographer who was appointed in 1979. Although each of these positions is structured somewhat differently, and three are shared with other library departments, their existence signals a more systematic approach to collection building. Collection development as an organizational entity has also been strengthened, and now exists as a formal department with its own head within the Collections/Technical Services Division. Support staff has been added to collection development: a library technical assistant in 1980–81; a divisional assistant with substantial collection development assignments in 1986; and a half-time assistant to the medieval and classical studies bibliographer in 1991. From the time the first collection development student assistant was hired in 1981–82, the student hour allotment has grown from less than 700 per year to 1,850 in 1992–93. Established in 1979–80, the Standing Committee on Serials in 1985 became the Collection Development Committee, a body whose advisory role in budget and policy matters has grown.

At the time of CAP, the libraries' first general approval plan was brand new, established in direct response to the recognition that Notre Dame's acquisition of current academic books was seriously deficient. In the intervening years, this form of acquisition has proven effective. The Harrassowitz plan for German books was initiated in 1983, and in the years following, much smaller plans for Russian, Latin American, Irish, French, Spanish and small press books.

That endowments and their use would be crucial in collection building efforts was recognized by CAP, who recommended reserving endowment for extraordinary collection building efforts. The University's expressed intention in the early 1980s to match library materials inflation with increases in appropriations led briefly to optimism that this could be done. But inflation soon overwhelmed the additional amounts provided by the University, and it soon became clear that the ordinary budget needs of the various subjects would require regular budgeting of endowment funds. The six named endowments of 1960 increased to twenty-seven by 1980, to seventy-six by 1990 and to eighty-nine by 1993. In 1979–80, $98,600 in endowment income was expended, 8.9 percent of total acquisition expenditures; income in 1993–94 will be more than $778,000, and is expected to comprise approximately 25 percent of acquisition expenditures. All of these funds have made a difference in the libraries' ability to address needs beyond the minimal, and the very largest have helped to shape research collections. The libraries' Latin American, philosophy and theology, English and American literature, fine arts, and science collections have all benefitted from these large endowments.

The CAP analysis reveals an awareness of the continuing strain rising costs will place on the libraries' acquisitions budget. Although there was a non-obligatory serials review in 1980, the emphasis during the early 1980s was on expanding a serials list that, never healthy, had been decimated by the cancellations of the previous decade. In 1986–87, however, for the first time, new subscriptions had to be paid for by money transferred from a department's book allocation, and 1987–88 saw a library-wide cancellation project based on departmental quotas. More such cancellation projects followed in 1989–90 and 1991–92, the latter targeting the very expensive titles, mostly in science, that account for such a large percentage of the cost increase. Actually, since 1980 nearly 3,000 new subscriptions have been placed, versus 875 cancellations. It is also true, however, that the ratio of new subscriptions to cancellations was 4.2 to 1 between 1980 and 1989, but 1.9 to 1 since then.

No account of collection building would be complete without note of changes taking place in formats acquired. Videos were not collected by the Notre Dame Libraries before 1985; now there are several hundred. The first electronic product, *INFOTRAC*, a bibliographic database, was acquired in 1985; the libraries now subscribe to nearly 25, in a variety of formats.

The cooperation praised by the CAP report is highly spoken of, but remains a minor factor in collecting. The most noteworthy endeavor that has taken place was Notre Dame's participation, with Indiana and Purdue Universities, in pilot tests of the North American Collections Inventory Project sponsored by the Association of Research Libraries and funded by the Lilly Endowment in 1983. Conspectuses were completed describing Notre Dame's collection in several subjects, and the results are maintained online in the Research Libraries' Information Network. This work has had very little influence on the libraries' collecting practices, however.

Ultimately the CAP recommendations on adopting a preservation program were taken seriously, and the progress on this front is obvious. Since 1990, there has been a preservation officer, and a preservation unit staffed by three people has been set up. In 1991, Notre Dame was awarded a three-year NEH grant to enable the libraries to microfilm, and thus preserve, their outstanding Medieval Institute collection, a recognition of the value of this collection to the scholarly community.

Throughout this narrative, quantitative comparisons of Notre Dame's collections to those of other universities have been made, and these should be carried forward to the present. The libraries' share of the University's educational and general expenditures has not grown—it was 4.3 percent in 1991–92—but that figure must be viewed in light of the fact that it placed Notre Dame 18th among 106 ARL libraries. In contrast to the poor showing at the time of the CAP report, a comparison of Notre Dame statistics with the ARL median is much improved, except for number of microforms, and money spent on binding. From figures 20 percent to 48 percent below the median in 1979, the libraries are now substantially above the median in volumes added, and only 4 percent to 7 percent below in other measures. Notre Dame's overall ARL index (an index calculated from measures of library holdings and expenditures) in 1980 placed it 95th; it was 55th in 1991–92. Although that figure may be inflated somewhat by the large numbers of records for titles being simultaneously added to the catalog by tape loading, and influenced by the inclusion of Law Library statistics, nevertheless the general upward tendency is one indicator of collection health.

The story of the University Libraries of Notre Dame's collections is not yet finished and its outcome is hard to predict. Will the tiny assortment of books that has grown to more than two million volumes today continue its ever accelerating growth, or will technological developments lead to a new kind of library in the next century? Will the role of the selector who once examined each potential addition for its merit and affordability and who now is one of many managing often sizeable funds and making macrodecisions, diminish in importance? Will interlibrary loan, a resort to which was once an embarrassment but which now is a vital component of library service, change its nature as individual collections recede in importance? Will new sources of funding supplement current arrangements, just as regular appropriations have replaced student fees and endowment has become more important than occasional gifts? Is it possible that the libraries of the twenty-first century will be as different from the libraries of 1993 as the latter are from the library of Foik's day?

---

1. Frank Keller Walter, "Report of a Survey of the University of Notre Dame Library" (Notre Dame, Ind., 1920), 8.

2. J. Periam Danton, *Book Selection and Collections: a Comparison of German and American University Libraries* (New York: Columbia University Press, 1963), 87.

3. Hendrik Edelman and G. Marvin Tatum, Jr., "The Development of Collections in American University Libraries," *College and Research Libraries* 37 (1976): 50–55.

4. Danton, 88.

5. AR, 1911–12, 9.

6. Edelman and Tatum, 34.

7. Philip S. Moore, *Academic Development: University of Notre Dame: Past, Present and Future* (University of Notre Dame, 1960), 137.

8. Growth figures taken from "Collection Analysis Project: Final Report" (University of Notre Dame Libraries, 1981), 3–23.

9. Information on finances, events and activities taking place in the library during given years are taken from the library's annual report for those years, unless otherwise indicated.

10. Wilson/Lundy, 161–62.

11. *University of Notre Dame Bulletin* XXXV, no.3 (1939–40): 49.

12. Merrily E. Taylor, "The Yale University Library 1701–1978," in *Encyclopedia of Library and Information Science* (New York: Marcel Dekker, 1982) 33: 273.

13. AR, 1945–46, 3.

14. AR, 1920–21, 4–5.

15. AR, 1940–41, 2.

16. AR, 1923–24, 4.

17. AR, 1945–46, 4.

18. AR, Biology Library, 1937–38, 5.

19. AR, 1924–25, 6.

20. Moore, 139.

21. Wilson/Lundy, vii.

22. Ibid.

23. Ibid., 36.

24. See ibid., 38–58 for a list of deficiencies perceived by academic departments.

25. Ibid., 60–61.

26. Richard Hume Werking, "Collection Growth and Expenditures in Academic Libraries: a Preliminary Inquiry," *College and Research Libraries* 52 (January 1991): 11.

27. Edelman and Tatum, "Development of Collections," 50–55.

28. AR, Assistant Director for Science and Engineering Libraries, 1964–65, 3.

29. AR, Acquisitions Department, 1968–69, 2–3.

30. "The Notre Dame Library Association," (Notre Dame, Ind.: n.p., n.d.), Notre Dame Library Association notebook, ULND.

31. Ibid.

32. AR, 1975–76, 22.

33. AR, 1976–77, 18.

34. AR, 1973–74, 8–9.

35. Information on collection development operations from the 1970s to the present is taken from the internal files of the Collection Development Department.

36. "North Central Association Accreditation Report," *Notre Dame Report* 4 (1974): 142.

37. University Libraries of Notre Dame, "Collection Analysis Project: Final Report" (Notre Dame, Ind., 1981), 1–22.

Library Directors
University of Notre Dame

Robert C. Miller, 1978–

David E. Sparks, 1971–1978.

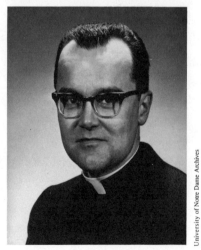

Rev. James W. Simonson, C.S.C.,
1967–1971.

Victor A. Schaefer, 1952–1966.

Paul R. Byrne, 1924–1952.

Rev. Lawrence V. Broughall, C.S.C., 1924.

Rev. Paul J. Foik, C.S.C., 1912–1924.

James F. Edwards, 1873/74–1911.

Rev. John A. Zahm, C.S.C., 1874–1876 (College Library).

Rev. Joseph C. Carrier, C.S.C., 1866/67–1873/74 (College Library).

Notre Dame's Contribution to the Order of Knowledge in America

SOPHIA K. JORDAN

"If classification *per se* is not knowledge, it is certainly the most important method of dealing with knowledge."[1]

Introduction

During the last part of the nineteenth and well into the twentieth century, library literature experienced a deluge of articles, dissertations, and books on the theory and practice of classification. Many of the classification schemes advanced during this period were put into practice; few, however, survive today. While various theories and practices of classification were around long before the height of this activity, this period was to mark the transition from diversity to standardization both in theory and in practice.

In the history of American classification schemes, the place of Catholic theoreticians and practitioners has been neglected. The fact that the history books are relatively silent with regard to the contributions Catholics made to the formation of intellectual life within the academy has been accounted for by the political and sociological conditions that prevailed at the turn of the century. These conditions restricted the recognition, and in some cases the formation, of a Catholic intelligentsia. Amidst this sociological and political background, the

American academy experienced dramatic changes and libraries were caught in the midst of those changes.

The changes had more than an accidental effect on the nature of the academic library. The most significant change was the university's shift away from a common curriculum to a subject-discipline approach to learning. This shift implied not only the introduction and expansion of research and graduate/post-graduate education, but also a shift in the order of learning. Since the connection between habits of learning and the order of knowledge is reflected in books, the philosophical shift in the universities did not leave their libraries untouched. It was this change in the academy which was directly responsible, even if invisibly, for the birth of standardized classification—schemes reflecting the inherent character of the developing patterns implied in specialized knowledge.

The need to respond to changes in the academy in the late 1880s motivated the two standardized classification schemes, the Dewey Decimal (DC) and Library of Congress (LC) classifications. As American Catholic academic institutions contemplated what it meant to be Catholic in that intellectual milieu, Catholic libraries and librarians framed the same question in terms of theories of classification. By the late 1930s this issue catapulted Catholic librarians into the intellectual arena of their profession. At the center of the debate for Catholic institutions were the inherent difficulties and inconsistencies of the theology and philosophy classes in both DC and LC classifications. In both schemes, religion was treated as a subjective experience; a philosophical remnant reflecting the disposition of the American founding fathers. Religion was a choice and that choice did not depend on any epistemology or hierarchy of knowledge. Beyond the obvious limitations caused by the inherently Protestant nature of the Library of Congress and of Amherst (where DC originated), Catholic library use of either of these schemes revealed the fundamental difficulties involved when attempting to fit a literature which expressed a dogmatic or hierarchical order onto a classification conceived with a subjective orientation.[2]

Unfortunately, the rapid and thorough adoption of the two systems left little time for American Catholic institutions to engage in the debate before they, too, accepted a general classification. The two most common general classification schemes were thus debated only in the larger academic arena and were irrevocably set in their arrangements for religious materials 50 years prior to Catholics becoming actively engaged in the profession. Although their initial response was limited, somewhat diffuse, and not at all organized to represent the needs of Catholic academic libraries, Catholic librarians had much to say and began to respond to both classification schemes.

The founding of the Catholic Library Association (CLA) in 1921 and the *Catholic Library World* (*CLW*) in 1929 was critical in raising the collective voice of Catholic libraries.[3] From their initial criticisms of the two general classifications, the question of a uniquely Catholic classification scheme would emerge. The debate for a modified DC began at the Notre Dame Library with Father Foik in 1916. Foik carried that debate not only into the library school here, but also to the national level and urged active involvement by librarians in proposing alternative Catholic classification schemes. The issue reached its zenith from the late 1930s through the early 1950s as the Notre Dame Library provided the background for supporting and developing the alternative classification scheme of Jeannette Murphy Lynn. By the late 1950s and early 1960s, changes in libraries and in the Catholic Church began to dismantle the very elements which had necessitated a unique Catholic classification. Notre Dame Library then stood on the other side of the debate as the director of the library, Victor A. Schaefer, argued against any further need for an alternative classification scheme.

The contributions of American Catholic librarians to the evolution of standardized classification schemes in America have been long forgotten among cataloging practitioners. Nor is it a history reflected in the standard readings. It is a history, however, well worth recounting for it is evidence that Catholic libraries and librarians were actively engaged in the debates concerning the intellectual life of the academy; and that the library and librarians at the University of Notre Dame played a prominent role in each of the historical events that shaped that history.

Catholic Intellectual Tradition and the Order of Knowledge

Why is classification of any concern to the Catholic intellectual tradition and to a library specifically? How did Catholic libraries in America deal with the classification of knowledge prior to the Dewey

Decimal and Library of Congress schemes? What degree of success did the alternative classifications have in Catholic libraries?

One would expect, *a priori*, that with their long tradition as keepers of books Catholic institutions and libraries would have designed a standardized classification scheme. The centrality of the Vatican, strong scholastic influences, and long-established doctrinal teaching lend themselves naturally to such a view. One can imagine, if not a centralized classification, then at least one that reflected the various religious orders and/or affiliations, i.e., a classification scheme for Jesuit libraries, one for Benedictine monasteries, another for the Dominicans and Franciscans, and so on. Although an attractive and reasonable claim, history fails to substantiate the thesis.

One might further expect that as Catholic institutions transported libraries to the New World they also transported a classification scheme from the Old World. While old bookplates and institutional markings remained on the books in transit, there is no evidence that their original order and/or arrangement was preserved in their new location. One finds instead, in the early years of American Catholic libraries, a diversity of library practices.[4]

The Order of Knowledge at Notre Dame

By the time Catholic institutions and libraries were experiencing growth, a network of classification schemes was being established and beginning to be shared. There were two individuals whose concern with the classification of knowledge and whose work in their own libraries provided some of the earliest evidence of this at Notre Dame. The provenance of several books in the University Libraries of Notre Dame was traced to collections belonging to Father Simon Bruté (1779–1839) and Father Joseph Maria Finotti (1817–1879).

Father Simon Bruté was a leading book collector. Trained as a philosopher, he had studied various philosophical treatises dealing with the order of knowledge. He had described and cataloged his own collection of 8,000 books according to a certain view about class divisions. A printed catalog of his collection and its divisions came out in 1901. Bruté was affiliated with several institutions and their libraries, institutions connected to the early years of Notre Dame. These were Saint Mary's Theological Seminary of Saint Sulpice in Baltimore,

Maryland (founded 1791), Mt. Saint Mary's College in Emmitsburg, Maryland (founded 1808), and the Vincennes Theological Seminary in Vincennes, Indiana (founded 1838 by Bruté a year before his death).[5] Based on book provenance and evidence from correspondence, it does not require a great leap of faith to assume that just as books exchanged hands among the various institutions which he served, so too did his classification scheme.

Father Finotti described his library's collection and its arrangement in his *Manual to the Library of Georgetown College, 1847*. The first catalog based on Finotti's description was published in 1868 by Father James Curely. From his description we know that the books were arranged in alcoves according to the curriculum. A system noting the alcove, the case, and the fixed shelf position was designed. This was a simple system repeated in almost every library. It would be the familiar curricular arrangement which would become the precursor to subject classification. This same pattern is evident in the early arrangement of books at Notre Dame.[6]

When Notre Dame was founded in 1842, books were a rare commodity, and there was little need for a separate library. Up to 1873, students depended upon textbooks that had been collected by faculty in their respective teaching areas, student clubs or literary societies. The College Library headed by Father Nicholas J. Stoffel did not come into existence until 1851 and then it only contained basic reference works and course materials directly supporting the curriculum. Recognizing the importance of a circulating library for the use of the students, in 1873 Father Lemonnier appropriated the libraries from each of the literary societies and several of the different departments of the University where collections had accumulated. He did not incorporate the College Library. Lemonnier thus formed a library housed in the Main Building, the Circulating Library, and appointed James F. Edwards as librarian, probably in 1873. During this early period there is no evidence suggesting any theoretical concern for ordering or classifying any of the libraries' collections. One can only speculate that either it was not perceived as an issue or that a system was already in place and working adequately.

Concomitant with his desire to see a circulating library, Lemonnier began initiating a series of changes at Notre Dame that would echo the larger trend in academic institutions and force the issue of classification.

Between 1874 and 1875, the distinction between the high school and college curricula was strengthened when the present classifications of freshman, sophomore, junior, and senior were adopted. In the following year subject divisions and graduate/post graduate courses were introduced.[7] By 1897, the University was divided into four units—arts and letters, science, engineering, and law—and by 1905 they were renamed respectively the College of Arts and Letters, the College of Science, the College of Engineering and the College of Law.

The concern for a classification scheme that coordinated and reflected the character of learning emerged at Notre Dame soon after the curricular model was replaced with the subject-disciplinary model. Prior to these academic changes, the curriculum provided the chief organizing principle for the various library collections. The earliest accession book covering the period from 1872–1908 confirms this.[8] Annotations on the front verso of the flyleaf list for each year the individuals responsible for accessioning. The recto of the first page reveals the divisions of the curriculum and the dates indicating changes and/or the addition of subject areas. Each subject division has a reference to a page number where the accessioning for the discipline was entered. Recorded there also are the dates representing when the various private libraries of the faculty were absorbed into the new Lemonnier Library. As one inspects the accession entries, ample evidence exists that there was no theoretical principle operating. Titles and authors are entered as received and an accession number assigned. The volumes were located in the appropriate alcove for a specific subject and shelved in accession order. Remarks by student assistants in the library attest to the difficulties associated with keeping the books in accession order.

The Fire of 1879 forced Edwards to centralize the collections. In October 1881, the two libraries, the Lemonnier Circulating Library and the College Library, merged into the Lemonnier Library.[9] There is a printed catalog of the Lemonnier Circulating Library just after the Fire. It lists 770 titles arranged by author, except for anthologies which were arranged by title. Still at this point, the organization did not reveal any concern with the inherent difficulties of a theoretical classification.[10] But the Fire of April 13, 1879, provided Notre Dame with a window of opportunity for the emergence of a classification system. Just as these events were taking place locally, Melvil Dewey published his decimal classification system anonymously in 1876 under the title "A Classification and Subject Index."[11]

Clearly, from examination of the 1909 accession book, the library was struggling with translating the organization of the collections based on a curricular model to a classification scheme based on fixed subject divisions. The difficulties were more than those associated with a practice. They were those associated with struggling for a theory of classification. The early attempt to introduce a new scheme of subject divisions in conjunction with changes in the College Divisions was a mixed experience. The 1907 accession book distinguishes 17 class divisions. Each class was subdivided by language (Latin, German, English, other) and then either alphabetically by author or by accession number. This system attempted to express in a comprehensive fashion a system of notation, a hierarchy of knowledge and a classified shelf position. It was difficult to maintain once the collection began to grow and the accession books reveal a mix-and-match strategy using the previous system and that of incorporating Dewey. Shortly thereafter, Edwards sought a "professional" librarian to convert the collections. In 1907 Florence M. Espy was hired as cataloger and Paul Byrne as her student assistant.[12] From 1907–1918, Melvil Dewey's Condensed Accession Book was used, providing explicit instructions to the librarian for incorporating the "old fixed system, alcove, range and shelf" into the new system with class headings. Dewey divided a library collection into nine independent classes or special libraries. These, in turn, were again divided into nine special divisions with nine further distinct sections. Thus, there could be a total of 81 sections each for theology and philosophy into which the entirety of its intellectual content was to fit. Dewey did not use them all. In his first edition, one division and twenty-three sections remained free in philosophy; in theology, all nine divisions and nine sections were attributed. Dewey had also proposed a subject index for use with the new classification. The purpose of the index was to "fix" a concept by locating the most appropriate term. The subject term or heading referred to the class for which it acted as a sign. The subject index has evolved into our present-day subject heading list.[13]

In 1907, new titles were classed both by the old system and the Dewey notation with the traditional division of the accession book retained, but expressed by Dewey notation. In a 1909–1910 report

Edwards noted that the library of 5,000 volumes had been fully cataloged and Miss Espy had clearly expressed her preference for the Dewey notation over the past practice:

> Do you intend to have the books in the French language or in Spanish or German in sections apart from the final arrangement or do you wish there to be—history in history, literature in literature, religion in religion, along with the books in English as they now are—Most librarians prefer the present method...Today, I begin in History. The correct order in which to take the books is:
> Religious biography
> Secular biography
> Maps—genealogies...
> I can take the books as they stand on the shelves, if it suits you better...I can go back to the obsolete system but I hate to do it. We catalogers cut the food, but we expect the man at the desk to chew it a little.[14]

Beyond organizing the collection, Edwards had little concern for cataloging. It was not until Father Paul J. Foik's arrival that Espy's witticisms were translated into a theoretical concern for classification and Notre Dame became actively engaged in the larger debate with other Catholics. Father Paul J. Foik, C.S.C., was librarian from 1912–1924. The contributions he made to the history of classification could not be gleaned from his description of his early years: "To pick up a science piece meal and then to apply it without any preliminary experience was the case when I became the librarian at Holy Cross College."[15] Paul Byrne, already at Notre Dame, and Foik were to become fast friends. This teacher and student became compatriots in the theoretical investigation of classification. In a letter to Paul Byrne who was studying at Albany, New York at the time, Foik writes:

> I am especially grateful to you for copies of library material and other data which you sent. This year I am going to devote a certain amount of time to study to see if I cannot map out at least a partial course of Library Science. I am building up my library material on the subject. If you can be of any service to me in furnishing names and authors of the texts used in the New York library school I will be only too happy. I can see great possibilities in this kind of work here at the University...I am conveniently situated here in the Middle West and

if needs be can call lecturers in when particular topics useful to the library student are to be handled.[16]

Byrne and Foik continued such correspondence and exchanges of lecture and course material. No accidental association existed between the need for a theory of classification and the need for professional librarians in Catholic institutions. Foik admitted that at the heart of the librarians' intellectual formation was the question of the theories of knowledge and he had this to say regarding the profession:

The trained librarian is a man of ideas. He has plans, he sees more clearly, the possibilities of development, he has laudable ambition that he desires to seize. The untrained man has none of these because he has generally neither the energy nor love for his work.[17]

Sometime between 1916 and 1918, Foik was to go through at least two versions of a modified schedule for Dewey's religion class [200–260.19].[18] Each of these was developed subsequently to the classification in use in the 1907 accession books. How widely Foik's modification may have circulated remains a matter for speculation, but some version of these early notes were still being circulated after Lynn's classification had been developed.

The first paper was on Catholic Revisions of the Religion Section of Dewey, by Miss Anne M. Cieri, College of New Rochelle, New York. Miss Cieri briefly described and compared the revisions of the Brussels Institute, Father Foik, Father Martin, Mrs. Lynn, Father Kane, Miss Pettee, and Father Blanc.[19]

This quote from 1940 reveals, first, that Catholics had proposed and circulated alternative schemes; and, second, that Foik's modification was one among several alternatives being proposed for general incorporation into Catholic libraries. Each of Foik's versions circulated among other libraries for comment while most certainly making its way into the classification and cataloging of the Notre Dame Library and the library school classes.

The first mention of a library school occurs in the 1916/17 *Bulletin*.[20] A certificate was acquired for two years of work and a Bachelor of Library Science (BLS) at the end of four years. The courses were divided among bibliography, cataloging, and administration. The Dewey Decimal system with comparative studies of other systems was listed under the course description for cataloging. The library school offered its first courses in classification in 1916. The school lasted intermittently between 1916 and 1923 experiencing a brief hiatus from 1923 to 1924. It resumed in 1933, until it was finally closed in 1953. By 1917/18, library school course descriptions for classification noted a larger number of alternative schemes for comparison with Dewey:

> Lectures, class practice work, and required readings. Dewey decimal system. Comparative studies are also made of other systems, especially the Cutter expansive system. The Cutter-Sanborn system of author tables is used in connection with the Dewey System. Adaptations of the Dewey System by the Institution Internationale de Bibliographie of Brussels.[21]

It should be noted that even though the LC classification schedule for philosophy, B-BJ, was published in 1910, there was no mention of its being reviewed for Catholic libraries. Not until 1927, when the Library of Congress published the schedule for theology, (BL-BX), would the entire classification scheme gain wider acceptance and implementation in Catholic academic libraries. The library school at Notre Dame continued to raise issue with the various theories of classification. By early 1920, Foik's concerns for classification and cataloging had moved from problems at Notre Dame into a more public arena—the National Catholic Educational Association and the State of Indiana. The Public Library Commission of Indiana replied to Foik's concern on the appropriateness of using Dewey in a letter dated September 30, 1920. We read:

> We much appreciate your statement concerning the Dewey classification for use in a theological library. Not having seen it put to such use, I was a little bit uncertain as to what to recommend.[22]

A growing concern to place Catholic librarians at the center of the intellectual issues of academe and librarianship motivated Foik to propose the formation of what would become the Catholic Library Association at the 1919 meeting of the National Catholic Education Association:[23]

With the approval of the Secretary General and the President of the Department of Colleges and Secondary Schools of the Catholic Educational Association, I have the pleasure to present here a preliminary report showing the necessity for the establishment of some organization within the association dealing with library problems as they affect education.

The mere possession of a reasonable number of good books in our educational institutions will not insure satisfactory results. There is need of scientific training and certification of librarians...Since the school library bears a certain definite relation to education, it is clear that the trained librarian can help in the solution of educational problems...[24]

Foik was named the first president of the CLA and retained that title from 1919 until 1928. His aspirations toward improving Catholic librarianship centered on the intellectual formation of the librarian and his/her ability to practice and to theorize about the profession, and nothing needed more speculative work than that of the classification issues related to theology and philosophy.

Troubled by the difficulties of cataloging, in 1922 Foik hired Anna A. Kosek as head of Cataloging and Paul Byrne, who returned as reference librarian. Hiring a cataloger and a reference librarian was not coincidental. Rather, it was intentional and necessary. The relationship between the work in cataloging and in reference mirrored for Foik the very relationship of how the library worked in the academy. From 1920 until his departure in 1924, Foik continued to speak eloquently and passionately about the relationship of the academic librarian to intellectual formation in the academy:

If the development of a library is to keep pace with the growth of the University in general, then opportunity must be given the librarian to meet the demands of both faculty and students. This can only be successfully accomplished by the employment of experienced and competent assistants. A reference librarian and a cataloguer have become indispensable; and steps are being taken to fill both these positions in the coming year.[25]

Moreover:

> It is becoming that a leading university such as Notre Dame should
> attempt to marshall the forces of Catholic education in a work that
> has been too long neglected. In this effort, there have been two means
> employed: (1) the establishment of the Catholic Library School
> during the summer session, (2) the foundation of the Library Section
> of the Catholic Educational Association...Thus the Library School
> will give scientific training in librarianship, the Library Section of
> the Catholic Educational Association will apply that knowledge in
> the discussion and solution of specific problems...[26]

The debate about librarians' intellectual engagement in the academy
took on particular force in the case of the theoretical issues of a
classification system. Unfortunately, Foik left for Texas on the eve of
that engagement, but not without leaving a legacy and vision for Notre
Dame to implement:

> There is no more pressing need in Catholic education today than the
> work of organizing and developing our school libraries...The attitude
> of all standardizing agencies as to the importance of the library is
> unmistakable evidence of the trend of thought on this subject.
> Catholics should not be followers but leaders in this movement
> because the library is after all the heritage of the ages of faith.[27]

The task of instruction at the Library School fell upon Paul Byrne;
in the 1924 catalog he is listed as its sole instructor. In the intervening
years, Byrne had completed his education and garnered extensive
experience as a librarian. He had completed a BLS from New York
State Library School in Albany, had worked at Ohio State University,
the New York State Library and in 1924 returned to his intellectual
home.

At just about this time, concern for Catholic classification was
widening, and in a 1926 article by Lester Kuenzel we find the first
expression of the related need for Catholic subject headings:

> We know of no library organization that has worked out a system of
> subject nomenclature which can be applied to the LC and DC systems
> of classification and which is capable of consistent logical expansion.

157

The Library of Congress has the best thus far devised; the Belgium plan seems to me far inferior to it...

We must consider tradition and terminology of primary importance. They are quite distinct but so interwoven that they determine, in a great measure, our nomenclature in the sacred sciences. Tradition has given us the material and terminology has given us the form. Our terminology is the vehicle whereby the thought and feeling of one age passes down to another age.[28]

The topic had been broached, but only to disappear from discourse as silently as it had appeared. Whether Kuenzel's work introduced the topic of subject headings prematurely or whether it simply had the wrong readership is open to debate. What is important is the centrality of subject headings for a classification scheme, and that meant Catholic subject headings for a Catholic classification scheme. It was raised again when Edna Becker wrote from her experiences at Fordham University in 1933 agreeing with the questions raised by Kuenzel, but once again it faded. Its resolution will be described later.

The Library of Congress and Catholic Classification

In 1927, the Library of Congress had just published its schedule for religion, BL-BX. Unlike Dewey, the divisions within the classes were more numerous and by virtue of its notation, better able to express more complex relationships, allowing it to adapt and to expand. Byrne was librarian at Notre Dame at the time. His years of studies with Foik, his experience as a cataloger, and his theoretical familiarity with the inherent difficulties of Dewey's class for theology left him little choice than to experiment with the new schedule. Byrne was so anxious to replace the deficiencies of the Dewey Decimal system with an expandable notation that in 1928, only one year after the LC schedule appeared, he hired a new head of cataloging to convert the entire collection. Notre Dame was the first Catholic library, not previously using the LC scheme, to convert on the basis of the value of a single schedule. No other Catholic academic library converted so early. Catholic University of America did not convert until 1937. With the advent of the schedule for theology, there was a new wave of Catholic criticism and engagement.

In 1928, other attempts at developing closer relationships between the Library of Congress and the Catholic library world were forming. William Warner Bishop of the Library of Congress sent four American librarians to help the Vatican Library reclassify its collection. The product of that association was the Vatican *Norme* of 1931.[29] The *Norme*, which attempted to superimpose a Catholic terminology onto a Protestant organization, resulted in a hybrid classification that has since been abandoned. There was some hope early on that it would emerge as an authority on theology and have some weight in effecting changes in LC's theology schedule. Unfortunately, American Catholic libraries did not respond enthusiastically and the *Norme* did not fulfill the hopes of a full collaboration in the United States. The association between the two great libraries, however, did spur American Catholic librarians to increased activity in identifying an appropriate alternative classification for their intellectual tradition.

The librarian whom Paul Byrne had hired in 1928 to head cataloging during the conversion to LC was Jeannette Murphy (Lynn), a freshly graduated librarian out of the University of Wisconsin.[30] Lynn was born on September 27, 1905 in Boulder, Montana. She received her BA in sociology from Tabor College in 1926 and, in 1928, a certificate of Library Science from the University of Wisconsin. Her first professional appointment was at the University of Notre Dame. From 1928–1932, she worked on converting the Notre Dame collection from Dewey to LC. She then took a one-year appointment (1932–1933) at Saint Mary's College, Notre Dame, Indiana before she entered the Graduate Library School at the University of Chicago. Lynn completed her master's at Chicago in 1935 and from then until 1937 was head cataloger at the Cossitt Library in Memphis, Tennessee before moving to become librarian of Siena College in Memphis (1937–1939). From 1952–1954, she was secretary and editor of the CLA and from 1954–1959, chief cataloging and classification librarian at the Crerar Library.

Lynn was already versed in both the DC and the LC schemes, although she had not yet had occasion to use the newly issued theology schedule prior to her arrival at Notre Dame. In concept, the task before her was simple: convert Notre Dame Library's collection from DC to the more expandable LC. The translation from most other subject classes was relatively straightforward, but the intellectual and mechanical difficulties in translating the theology and philosophy schedules were something else entirely. The conversion of the Notre Dame Library was not completed under Lynn.[31] Her experience here, however, motivated her to find a solution for Catholic libraries in general. Her graduate library studies at the University of Chicago centered on resolving the intellectual and mechanical difficulties she had encountered at Notre Dame. In the two years that she pursued her degree, she continued to visit and study the Notre Dame Library. Her efforts resulted in a master's thesis based on her work and experience at Notre Dame. It would change the face of the debate and the history of American classification.

From the Catholic perspective, the predominant weaknesses in the two general classifications were the Protestant character of their divisions and the subsequent vocabulary for the accompanying subject headings. The net result of the inadequate capability of the classification scheme to express the unique Catholic tradition was a failure which manifested itself in the most practical and basic manner—the system failed to provide access because it misplaced books intellectually and thus physically. References to the machinations required to make the theology schedule work are replete in the Cataloging Department's portion of the annual reports from 1922 through 1932. A theoretical naivete cannot divorce itself from practical consequences in the organization of knowledge.

Catholic libraries' and librarians' responses to the DC and LC schemes were a mixture of acceptance and criticism. As well as confusing the intricacies of many doctrinal issues, the terms and the organization of the classes excluded entire areas of Catholic intellectual and institutional history. The general weaknesses of both systems were most aptly expressed by Lynn:

> The Dewey outline for religion has not been revised or expanded, in general, since its first publication. It provides in the last (13th) edition a total of 908 divisions for the entire literature of religion. One hundred and forty-two of these are devoted to the Young Men's Christian Association, sixty-seven to the Catholic Church in all its aspects. In one American library alone it has been estimated that there are approximately fifty thousand books on Canon Law, for which Dewey provides a single combination of numbers without subdivision, 348.[32]

160

While preferring LC over DC, Lynn recognized the need for modifications to its theology schedule, before it could be used by Catholic libraries:

> The only considerable attempt at a classification of religion is the schedule of the Library of Congress. Both Catholic and Protestant Libraries have found the schedules confused and unsuited to their needs. Non-Catholics have felt that too much space has been devoted to the Catholic topics, to the neglect of Protestant literature, while Catholic libraries find that the approach and terminology of the tables do not conform to the long established usage of Catholic theologians, and that the progression of the outline fails to coincide with the consensus of Catholic scholarship.[33]

The weaknesses in each system were clear from the beginning. If the trend was toward a standardized general classification, a determination was necessary as to what accommodations had to or could be made to them so that American Catholic libraries were not left behind in comparison to their Protestant counterparts. This was the growing concern of Catholic librarians in and outside of Notre Dame. By 1933, the still very young *CLW* clearly showed a preference for the Library of Congress scheme.

The forces favoring the LC's classification had been in motion for almost a decade, but Lynn's "Alternative Classification" was the first systematic Catholic modification to the whole schedule intended for wide circulation. With the appearance of Lynn's work, in 1938 Victor A. Schaefer converted Catholic University of America's (CUA) Library to LC. Moreover, to facilitate and encourage widespread adoption he initiated a cooperative venture with the Library of Congress to provide original cataloging for Catholic books not currently nor likely to be cataloged by the Library of Congress. This combination of events—Lynn's "Alternative Classification," the Library of Congress's responsiveness to Catholic intellectual issues, and CUA's initiative to provide retrospective cataloging and catalog cards for dissemination to Catholic libraries—put a stamp of approval and official acceptance of the LC scheme for Catholic libraries.[34] Unfortunately, the initial enthusiasm and support for the modified LC and its attempt to resolve inherent theoretical issues would wane over the years and Schaefer, once a staunch supporter, would by the time he came to Notre Dame as director in 1952, stand on the other side of the Catholic classification issue.

Catholic Subject Headings

The alliance being built between *CLW* and the Library of Congress reached its pinnacle in 1936, when Theodore Mueller, the librarian of Congress, began a series of responses in *CLW* to criticisms and suggestions for revisions in LC's subject headings. The question of Catholic subject headings was brewing and several articles appeared urging work in this area. These were the conditions in 1937 when Lynn published her master's thesis, "Alternative Classification for Use with the Library of Congress Classification" and in 1938, when Oliver L. Kapsner was asked by the CLA to undertake the preparation of a list of Catholic subject headings. One last theoretical concern needed to be re-vivified in order to complete the whole of classification theory. The remaining piece in this history of standardized classification schemes in Catholic libraries was the issue of subject headings, and it, too, had Notre Dame connections. Kapsner, a young seminarian from Saint John's College, Collegeville, Minnesota, registered for the 1925 Library School summer classes; his teacher was Paul Byrne. Byrne never had a more attentive student. While Kapsner stayed only one summer at Notre Dame, what he learned from Byrne and the library environment motivated him to continue library studies. In 1929, four years prior to Lynn's arrival there, Kapsner took summer classes at the University of Chicago Library School. During the course of his studies at Chicago, he made numerous trips to use and to study the Notre Dame Library. Although he never received a library degree, his degree in philosophy and his ongoing interest and practice as a librarian made Kapsner a central figure in this history of Catholic classification schemes in the 1930s.

In the same circular which had gone out to Catholic institutions in October of 1938, initiating the cooperative with the Library of Congress, Schaefer added: "it may be necessary at times to depart from LC practice especially in subject headings..."[35] The topic which had first been broached by Kuenzel was handed over for a solution to Kapsner in 1938 by the Catholic Library Association.

The Library of Congress classification scheme was finally propelled into dominance among Catholic libraries by the arrival, in 1942, of Oliver Kapsner's *Subject Headings*,[36] the last element needed to refine both DC and LC classifications. Earlier attempts had been made at articulating the problem, but none had devised a systematic and hierarchically ordered class of subject headings characteristic of the Catholic tradition. Kapsner's herculean task produced a controlled vocabulary which was not only better suited to the history of Catholic theology and teaching, but retained its hierarchical structure. The first edition proposed some 2,300 new subject headings and by the time of the fifth edition there were 7,000. When the fifth edition was reissued in 1981, however, the subject headings were reduced again to 3,000.

Later Years

Between 1950 and 1980, Catholic libraries were typically cataloging at two levels—one general for all non-Catholic books and one specialized for those books in theology and philosophy. This was no less true at Notre Dame. Lynn's work went through a second and final edition in 1954. Kapsner's went through five editions by 1973, and its final revision in 1981. Both have since been out of print and have come under severe criticism for being outdated. In the forward to the second edition of Lynn's work, Kapsner draws our attention to the effect Lynn had on the history of Catholic classifications in America:

> The publication of the first edition of *An Alternative Classification for Catholic Books* denoted a turning point in Catholic library progress. Previously, libraries with large collections of Catholic literature had to fit the books into inadequate class schedules. This unfortunate situation was remedied by the appearance, in 1937, of the Lynn masterpiece.[37]

In 1942, while head of the Preparations Department at the Catholic University of America, Schaefer had this to say about Kapsner's *Catholic Subject Headings*:

> There are examples where changes in the LC list are necessary; changes in terminology rather than in the fundamental ideas contained in the heading...Or differences in terminology due to different beliefs

or non-beliefs...The problem confronting catalogers of Catholic books is a complete understanding of the content and the underlying ideas of the Library of Congress list...A basic weakness of *Catholic Subject Headings* is due to its seemingly great reliance on topics treated in dictionaries rather than in books...The *Catholic Subject Headings* has been compared heading for heading with the public catalog at the Library of Congress and the examples could be multiplied. The statistical analysis made seems to show that Catholic subject headings fail to make a notable addition to, or improvement to the LC list.[38]

When Paul Byrne ended his directorship of the library in 1952, he was replaced by none other than Schaefer. The same man who had spoken so favorably about the alternative classification scheme, encouragingly about the need for a modified subject heading departing from LC, and inventively for cooperative efforts, would in 1942, stand on the other side of the debate. Schaefer remained at Notre Dame until 1966. In a 1954 review article, he revisited the issue of Catholic classification and subject headings. Soon afterward Notre Dame abandoned the use of Kapsner's subject headings. Schaefer's striking opposition was only a sign, however, in a series of events soon to take place within librarianship and the Catholic Church which closed the chapter on the great classification debate.

Schaefer's review article was not favorably received among Catholic librarians. His understanding of the relationship between words and ideas was brilliantly challenged, however, by a graduate student at a Catholic institution. Hagler's rebuttal to Schaefer appeared in *Catholic Library World*:

This classification [Lynn's classification], which takes the half and half division of the LC tables consistently away from the side of subject grouping and toward the desideratum of denominational classification, violates but little, if at all, the principle of subject arrangement. We see more and more in our own day that while the religious treatises, written from the points of view of the denominations, may concern themselves with the same term or verbal reference, they are quite likely to deal with two entirely different subjects! A knowledge of semantics is certainly not lost to a classifier in these fields; and a classification which allows him to arrange material by viewpoint can be a welcome relief from a system which bundles unlikes together for the sake of loosely applied terms.

A quarter of a century ago, it seemed that the grasp of the Dewey Decimal and Library of Congress (LC) classification on public and research libraries, respectively, had become so strong that any newly proposed scheme was fore-ordained to a bleak existence as the mere mental gymnastics of some theorists. Standardization of a sort—the fondest hope of many a librarian—seemed possible among North American libraries, because the great discussions about classification came at a time when the profession in this country was still quite young, and could swing with some degree of unanimity to the few best systems proposed.

The ultimate function of any book classification, however, is the logical, systematic arrangement of materials in accordance with the needs of the users. This axiom of the library profession was probably never in danger of being forgotten but it was glossed over by the great appeal of standardization, the results of which have been beneficial to general libraries. Practical demands of specialized inquiry in our ever-growing research libraries, however, while not loosening the grasp of the "standard" systems in any way, have added a new dimension to the whole question of classification.

Paradoxically enough it is in the "general" or academic library in Catholic institutions of learning that almost invariably one finds itself doing a grave disservice to its academically minded users when its classification imposes on them a number and arrangement of divisions foreign to the patterns of thought that they are developing. This is precisely what the commonly used general classifications do, notably Dewey and Library of Congress.[39]

It was a brilliant rebuttal, but in the face of other events, it did little more than slow down the closing chapter on the issue. The final outcome of a uniquely Catholic classification scheme was mixed. Much of the momentum dissipated when LC finally adopted and accommodated the criticisms by Catholics. The extent to which criticism from Catholics waned can be explained by the several successive forces which worked to dismantle the debate. These included the changing intellectual character of Catholic learning since Vatican II; disinterest in theories of classification in favor of *praxis*; democratization of education within Catholic universities with a leaning toward "objective" disciplines, which unwittingly had the effect of collapsing theories about the hierarchy of knowledge; and, finally, the general demise of original cataloging. The Second Vatican Council, 1962–1965, had muted many theoretical and literary distinctions between Catholicism and Protestantism which had motivated the need for a specifically Catholic theological classification.[40] The Lynn-Peterson classification was based on a pre-Vatican II theology. The final outcome of the debate is thus more a story of successive dismantlings in intellectual life rather than a finished conversation.

Lynn and Kapsner continued to make contributions to the discourse among librarians for improvement in classification and cataloging practices, not merely to reflect Catholic needs in the academy, but to raise the theoretical issues within librarianship that are all too often forgotten in times of "technological" shifts. Their words are powerful and remind us that theoretical issues are never silent, even when masked behind the assumption of standards and practices. No one system can provide Catholic libraries with the needed richness in terms and classes for cataloging its books. Clearly, this is true for any general system of classification which attempts to classify in a special area. The modifications and constructions of systems by Catholic librarians to obtain a more accurate representation of their tradition was fundamentally eclectic in the early years. In an article for *Catholic Library World*, Lynn says of that eclecticism:

> Eclecticism is a dangerous attitude in philosophy, and it is not an easy road for the librarian, but with the increasing expenditures and the functional standards now being applied in all school activities, eclecticism in the choice of techniques is the library's clearest hope.[41]

It was an eclecticism she witnessed and experienced at the Notre Dame Library and which would make a significant and lasting contribution to American Catholic libraries. From theoretician to practitioner, the Notre Dame Library not only contributed to the shape of the history of American Catholic classification, but it also played out that very history to its end.

---

1. Bohdan S. Wynar, *Introduction to Cataloging and Classification.* (Littleton: Libraries Unlimited, 1971), 195.

2. The Library of Congress was responsible for devising the classification scheme which bears its name. While the schedules were constructed by independent scholars in their respective subject areas, it was the Library of Congress' collection which dictated the consequent divisions. Similarly, the Dewey Decimal scheme was devised by Melvil Dewey while he was at the Amherst College Library.

3. There is some discrepancy on the founding date for the Catholic Library Association. It rests on which date (1921 or 1931) represents the first official meeting. Foik had first proposed the organization in 1919 at the National Catholic Education Association. At that time only 86 institutions had joined the consortium which would become the CLA. Because so few Catholic institutions initially participated, and even though those who did were active, it is the later date which is often cited as the official beginning. See Paul J. Foik, C.S.C., "The College Library in Relation to College Work," *Catholic Educational Association Proceedings* 16 (1919): 183.

4. The number of articles and books tracing early Catholic American libraries and their collections are not numerous. I have indicated only a few sources that may be of interest to the reader: E.B. Adams, "Two Colonial New Mexico Libraries," *New Mexico Historical Review* 19 (1944): 135–167; Fr. H. Alerding, *A History of the Catholic Church in the Diocese of Vincennes* (Indianapolis: Carlon & Hollenbeck, 1883); William Stetson Merrill, "Catholic Libraries and Librarians in the United States," *Catholic Builders of the Nation*, vol. 4, (Boston: Continental Press, 1923); Dorothy May Norris, *A History of Cataloguing and Cataloguing Methods 1100–1850, with an Introductory Survey of Ancient Times* (London: Grafton, 1939); and the Rev. George E. O'Donnell, *St. Charles Seminary Overbrook 1832–1943* (Philadelphia: Jefferies & Manz, 1943).

5. Notre Dame's early history is connected with these institutions and their libraries, as well as others, in a variety of ways. The University of Notre Dame Archives is replete with correspondence on topics ranging from issues regarding the curriculum, faculty, the nature of an education, and the need for books. Beyond connections regarding how to manage and direct an educational institution, there is correspondence about book acquisitions and exchanges. The more obvious connection is, of course, that Bruté had worked as a part-time librarian at each of these institutions and had in each case been responsible for organizing and classifying the collections. Thus questions about the organization of education and knowledge was freely exchanged among the fledgling Catholic institutions. See E.D. Seeber, "The Bruté Library in Vincennes," *Indiana Quarterly for Bookmen* 4 (1948): 81–86.

6. Edwards had a copy of Finotti's catalog. We know this because after the Fire of 1879, he attempted to purchase the Finotti collection on the basis of the printed catalog. While he was unsuccessful in acquiring the entire

library, several volumes were purchased or donated and grace the present Notre Dame collection. See *Notre Dame Scholastic* 13 (August 23, 1879): 12.

7. The University Archives contains a variety of documents each identifying different dates for initiating the changes in the curriculum. The earliest date which mentions these changes is 1867 and is found in the corresponding annual report. The papers of Fr. J.C. Carrier [CCR1 Box 2], however, suggest an earlier date, while the work of Bernard J. Lenoue, "The Historical Development of the Curriculum of the University of Notre Dame," (Master's thesis, University of Notre Dame, 1933) suggests the 1870s as a clear demarcation. Pinpointing the exact date within a decade may be a moot point. More important is recognizing that the shift to a subject-discipline structure was an issue as early as the 1860s and that it was implemented by 1875.

8. Accession Records, ca. 1872–1908: The accession book does not indicate in which library these titles were housed. This would not have been necessary since each of the various libraries prior to 1881 served a particular curricular division. I was able to confirm this by tracing accession entries under various curricular divisions to the bookplates of the separate libraries. Oversize Box 4, Lemonnier #1–19,069, UODL,UNDA.

9. *Notre Dame Scholastic* 15 (October 21, 1881): 111; Ibid., 18 (October 5, 1879): 74. This, too, is confirmed by the changed entries in the Accession Record.

10. Fr. Stoffel was responsible for the management of the College Library. Nowhere in the various archival materials in our possession does he discuss matters pertaining to the work of the library. The only clue we have to the relative position of the College Library is his remark suggesting that the College Library was of little interest among the students, faculty, and administration: Fr. Nicholas J. Stoffel, CSFL, UNDA.

11. [Melvil Dewey], *An Historical Pamphlet: The Original Prospectus of the Dewey System, Amherst 1876, reprinted from Dr. Ernest Cushing Richardson's Copy* (New York: The Brick Row Book Shop, 1941). Dewey had actually devised his system in 1873. The publication was delayed for three years while he was engaged in converting the Amherst Library.

12. The names of Espy and Byrne appear as the last entries in the Accession Record for 1908, Accession Records, ca 1872–1908, UODL, Oversize Box 4, UNDA, and in both the *Annual Report* and *Annual Catalogue of the Officers, Faculty & Students of the University of Notre Dame* for that year.

13. The intimate relationship between subject index (heading) and classification is not new. Dewey's genius was to devise a classification scheme which could articulate and systematize the relationship. Careful examination will reveal that the subject-classification is a recasting of the familiar subject-discipline relationship.

14. James F. Edwards, "Book and Periodical List," CEDW, 27–28 Box D, UNDA.

15. Foik to Rev. J.A. Heiser, C.S.C., Holy Cross College, February 2, 1917, CFOI, B 1915–1916, Miscellaneous F (1917–1922), UNDA.

16. Foik to Byrne, Albany, New York, September 30, 1915, Ibid.

17. Paul J. Foik, "Memorandum Regarding Librarian," June 20, 1916, p.4, CFOI, UNDA.

18. "Classification of Religion," UODL, Miscellaneous Reports, Box 11, Folder 26, UNDA.

19. *Catholic Library World* 12 (1940/41): 28.

20. *Bulletin of the University of Notre Dame*, No. 7 (1916/17): 130.

21. Ibid., no. 8 (1917/18): 204–205.

22. Paul J. Foik, UODL, Folder: Misc. L, 1917–1922, UNDA.

23. Ibid.

24. Ibid., 3.

25. AR, 1920–1921, 12.

26. Paul J. Foik, "Report on the Library Summer School and Other Activities," p. 2, UODL, Foik, 1923–24, Box 1, Folder 3, UNDA.

27. Ibid., 2–3.

28. Lester Kuenzel, "Uniform Subject Nomenclature for Use in Catholic Libraries," *Library Journal* 51 (1926): 1084–85.

29. Biblioteca Apostolica Vaticana, *Norme per il catalogo degli stampati* (Vatican: Typis polyglottis, 1931). For articles dealing with the effect the *Norme* had on Catholic libraries and cataloguing see: J.C.M. Hanson, "Cataloging Rules of the Vatican Library," *Library Quarterly* 1 (1931): 340–346; also his "Review of the Vatican *Norme*, 2nd ed.," *Library Quarterly* 9 (1930): 360–361; Edward Roche, "The Vatican *Norme* as an Aid to the American Cataloguer," *Catholic Library World* 18 (1946/47): 107–110; and Coleman J. Farrell, O.S.B., "Vatican Library Shows the Way," *Catholic Library World* 9 (1937): 20–22.

30. Although she was hired under her maiden name, Murphy, I will refer to her by her married name, Lynn.

31. The January 22, 1931 issue of the *Notre Dame Scholastic* notes that between 1929 and 1931 the collection was reclassed from Dewey and Cutter notation to the Library of Congress. The chief cataloger at the time was Jeannette Murphy. The General Library Circulation register for 1929–1931 lists all accessions, first with their Dewey number, then with their LC designation. This clearly suggests that newly acquired books were classed in both schemes until a retrospective conversion could be made of the entire collection.

32. Jeannette Murphy Lynn, *An Alternative Classification for Catholic Books: A Scheme for Catholic Theology, Canon Law, and Church History; To*

be Used with the Dewey Decimal, Classification Decimale, or Library of Congress Classification (Milwaukee: The Bruce Publishing Co. and Chicago: American Library Association, 1937), 4.

33. Ibid., 5.

34. Victor A. Schaefer, "The Catholic Cooperative Cataloging Service," *Catholic Library World* 11 (1940): 139–43.

35. Ibid., 142.

36. Oliver L. Kapsner, O.S.B., *Catholic Subject Headings* (Collegeville: St. John's Abbey Press, 1942). See also his "Catholic Subject Headings: A Friendly Reply," *Catholic Library World* 12 (1942): 174–178, 185–188.

37. Lynn and Charles Gilbert Peterson, *An Alternative Classification for Catholic Books*, 2nd ed. (Washington, D.C.: Catholic University of America Press, 1954), 4.

38. Victor A. Schaefer, "Catholic Subject Headings: A Review Article," *Catholic Library World* 14 (1942–43): 77–81, 84.

39. Ronald A. Hagler, "Some Applications of a Theory of Classification," *Catholic Library World* 28 (1956–57): 71–73, 104.

40. A survey of Catholic libraries was conducted by John F. Macey and John C. Benyo. The data it gathered revealed how many Catholic libraries which had used Lynn's "Alternative Classification" and/or Kapsner's "Subject-Headings" prior to Vatican II had subsequently abandoned it. John F. Macey and John C. Benyo, "*Quo Vadis* Specialization? The Current Status of Catholic Schemas in Light of Vatican II and OCLC." *Cataloguing and Classification* 8 (1987): 105–120.

41. Lynn, "The Future of Cataloging and Classification," *Catholic Library World* 13 (1941–42): 139.

Rare Books and Special Collections at the University of Notre Dame

LAURA FUDERER

The Early Years

The first evidence of the existence of early printed books at Notre Dame appeared in a program published for the Silver Jubilee in 1869.[1] A section on "The College Library and Museum" noted that among the estimated 10,000 books on campus were "old and rare works" including an *Iliad* published in Basle in 1520 and a Tertullian and a St. Cyprian "of about the same date." Of 24 imprecisely identified books, the University Libraries today own 16 that may be the same versions. These may be either the originals which survived the fire of 1879 or replacements, typically gifts in response to the reconstruction efforts of Librarian Jimmie Edwards. For example, the 1869 list included *Dublin Review*; one of the earliest responses to Edwards' plea for donations was a complete set of *Dublin Review* given by Father Hudson, editor of *Ave Maria*. One book known to have survived the fire is a single volume of the 21-volume *Histoire de l'église* by Bérault-Bercastel (Maestrichte: P.L. Lekens, 1791). Scrawled in pencil on the front flyleaf are the words, "A Relic from the fire of Notre Dame. Burning of College etc. 1879." A letter dated 1937 explains that the book was returned to the University by a California alumnus whose cousin, Daniel Maloney, "was a student at the University at the time of the big fire of 1879, and the book was rescued by him from the library room of the Main Building during the fire."[2]

For a young college founded deep in what had so recently been Indian territory, Notre Dame's library collections were unusually European in character. This was due in part to the connection with the French Mother House of the Congregation of Holy Cross in LeMans, but also to the international as well as national breadth of Edwards' soliciting and collecting. Since the earliest printed books are necessarily European, Notre Dame may have had more early European imprints among its rare books than the typical midwestern college of the nineteenth century.

The French connection appears in the Rare Book Collection today in books that bear the ownership stamp of the Congrégation de Sainte-Croix, such as *Institutions Liturgiques* by Prosper Guéranger, Abbot of Solesmes. Printed in LeMans and Paris from 1843 to 1847, this two-volume set is inscribed by the author, "Offert par l'auteur à la Bibliothèque de N.D. de Sainte-Crois au Mans." From the library at LeMans this book was presumably carried or sent by Holy Cross priests or brothers to the college they had so recently established in Indiana. Whether these books were acquired before or after the fire is debatable. After all, 500 books did survive, not to mention the estimated 3,000 volumes which, according to the Silver Jubilee program, were located "in a great many special libraries in and about the college."[3]

When the new Main Building was opened in 1882, the Lemonnier Library, including the 500 books that survived the fire, occupied the front projection of the third floor. Presumably rare books and manuscripts were also located there, either on the open shelves, locked away in private offices or cabinets, or perhaps displayed in the glass cases visible in a photograph reproduced in the 1895 Golden Jubilee program. The program describes the various categories of the 50,000 volumes, adding that there were "among them many old books, including a translation of the bible [sic] into German...having been printed seven months before the birth of Martin Luther."[4] This may refer to volume two of a Bible printed by Anton Koberger in Nuremberg in 1483, now one of Notre Dame's collection of 81 incunabula. It may be the first official reference to an incunabulum at the University. The 1895 program mentions this Bible again in connection with Notre Dame's exhibit at the 1893 Columbian Exposition (i.e., World's Fair in Chicago). It was part of "a small but rich selection from the precious historical treasury of Bishops' Memorial Hall [including] many rare

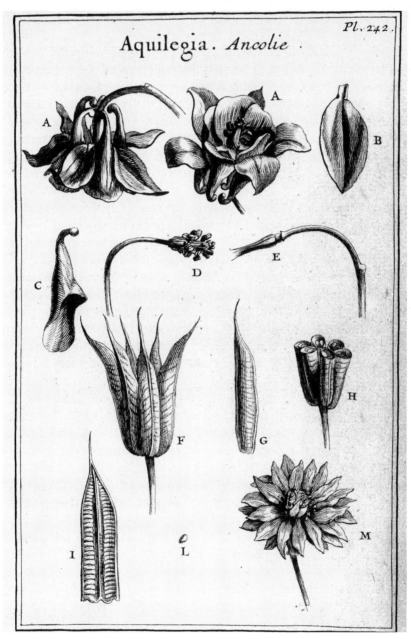

*Plate 242 from vol. 3 of Élémens de Botanique, ou, Méthode pour Connoître
les Plantes by Joseph Pitton de Tournefort (Paris: De l'Imprimerie Royal,
1694). Located in the Department of Special Collections, University Libraries
of Notre Dame.*

old Bibles published in the German language long before the birth of Luther."[5] Also among these may have been a two-volume Bible published by Sensenschmidt and Frisner around 1476–1478.

In his campaign to rebuild the library collections and Bishops' Memorial Hall Edwards canvassed the country for donations. One of the first to respond in addition to Father Hudson (mentioned above) was William Onahan of Chicago.[6] Among the books he donated was *An Exposition of the Lord's Prayer* by Archbishop Robert Leighton (London: James Nisbet, 1836), which was added to the reconstructed Bishops' Memorial Hall and today appears in the Rare Book Collection; the flyleaf bears the stamp, "Wm. J. Onahan, Chicago."

Another individual answering Edwards' plea was a Lieutenant Colonel A.J. Dallas, U.S. Army, who contributed several books translated into Native American languages by early missionary priests such as Eugene Vetromile and Albert Lacombe.[7] These volumes are among some 40 such prayer books, catechisms, and Bibles in Cree, Ojibwa, Lakota, and other languages now in the Rare Book Collection. Ten copies of translations by Frederic Baraga, later Bishop of Sault St. Marie (and believed by some to be a saint), include volumes given to Edwards by Bishop John Vertin of Marquette.[8] The front cover of *A Short Compendium of the Catechism for the Indians* by Nicholas Louis Sifferath, "Missionary of the Ottawa and Otchipwe Indians," contains the pencilled note, "Gift of Father Sifferath, July 1897, Adrian, Mich." Possibly connected with this gift are the nine linear inches of manuscript translations of religious texts into French, German, Latin, and Native American languages by Sifferath; these form part of the present Modern Manuscripts Collection. The books are complemented by *History of the Catholic Missions among the Indian Tribes of the United States, 1529–1854* by John Gilmary Shea, a friend of Edwards and another donor to the University. Shea's papers, including a manuscript draft of this book, are now in the University Archives.

Another friend of Edwards was Archbishop Robert Seton, who donated several fine rare books that display his religious armorial bookplate. Seton's grandmother, Elizabeth, was the first American-born saint. On the flyleaf of the 1795 edition of *Du Contrat Social* by Rousseau Seton wrote, "My grandmother (afterwards known as Mother Seton) used this volume at a period of her early married life when she was so unfortunate as to become somewhat enamored of the French infidel literature..." He also donated his grandmother's Bible, a Douai version published in Philadelphia in 1805.

Also thanks to Edwards the Rare Book Collection now contains many volumes from the library of Orestes Brownson and his son, Henry, from whom they were acquired. Besides Brownson's own works are many books by European authors whom Brownson introduced or interpreted to the American reading public in his periodical, *Brownson's Quarterly Review.*

The Rev. Paul J. Foik, C.S.C., succeeded Edwards as librarian, and an unusual collection was purchased during his tenure by President John Cavanaugh, C.S.C. In 1913 archaeologist Edgar J. Banks sold 100 cuneiform tablets written ca. 2300 B.C. to Cavanaugh for $250. Banks wrote that they were worth much more than that, but "I have received so many kindnesses from you, and have enjoyed coming to Notre Dame so much that I do not wish to profit on these."[9] In 1916 Banks offered Cavanaugh a Babylonian cylinder written for King Nebuchadnezzar ca. 600 B.C. for $500; Cavanaugh agreed to put it on display in the new library in hopes of "securing the necessary funds" to pay for it.[10] The cylinder and 80 of the tablets now constitute the Department of Special Collections' collection of ancient documents.

Special Collections in the New Library of 1917

When the new library building was constructed in 1917, one room housed Father John Zahm's Dante Collection, which included a remarkable number of fifteenth and sixteenth-century editions of *Divine Comedy.* Zahm also gave the University his Latin Americana and travel collection. Although some of the handpress editions now belong to the Rare Book Collection, at that time they may have been part of the circulating collection. Both the Dante and the Latin American collections appear for many years among reports of collections gradually being cataloged. In his survey of the library in 1920 Frank Walter noted "the fine special collections the University possesses on Dante, Ireland, South America, Botany, Woman, etc."[11]

Apart from references to various donations of special collections, rare books as such were not mentioned until the annual report of Librarian Paul Byrne in 1937/38. In the first official recognition of a place called "Treasure Room," Byrne observed:

> For years we have gradually been gathering into one secure place, the rare books in the library collection. Little of this material had ever been cataloged or listed in any way. Rather large gifts of this kind came from the libraries of the late Father Charles O'Donnell, Professor Charles Phillips, and Eugene McBride. During the past two years, as time allowed, this material has been fully listed and cataloged...[but for 100 titles]. In the collection appears, [sic] not only rare books and association copies, but also finely printed works, valuable not because of the matter, but because of their format. There are now 991 volumes in this Treasure Room.[12]

In this brief paragraph Byrne answered two of the commonest questions asked about rare books and special collections: what are they? and where did they come from? Notre Dame was and still is typical of academic and other research libraries in that donations constitute a major source of its rare book acquisitions. As for definition, by referring to association value and fine printing Byrne recognized that a variety of criteria may determine a book's rarity and those criteria may vary from one institution to another. What Notre Dame considers a valuable association may not be significant to another place.

Ten years later the Treasure Room was being called "Rare Book Room," as indicated by a floorplan of the library in 1948 that shows the room on the second floor.[13] Also located on that floor were the Dante Room, the Medieval Institute, and the Art Gallery. The 1947/48 Annual Report of the new head of cataloging, Pauline Ramsey, included "Rare Book Room" in cataloging statistics for the first time. Also listed was a "Memo" collection, which may have been the beginnings of the Notre Dame Collection, along with 44 theses which appeared as a separate category. Eventually the Notre Dame Collection included books and periodicals published on campus, monographs authored by the faculty, and all the theses and dissertations submitted for degrees at the University.

Another milestone for rare books at Notre Dame was the year 1956/57, when for the first time an individual was given special responsibility for them. The librarian of the Medieval Institute Library, Dr. Francis D. Lazenby, added "curator of the Treasure Room" to his list of titles and a separate section for the room in his annual report on the Medieval Institute Library. Rare books appear to be located in Room

207, Oversize Room 208, and the "Grill." No mention is made of the Dante Room.

Under Lazenby's curatorship rare books received the sort of professional attention that the richness of the collections at Notre Dame warranted. The 1956/57 Annual Report was the first to mention exhibits using rare books and special collections; one exhibit was on the Shaw Collection of Lafcadio Hearn and the other drew from the Greene Botany Collection and the Treasure Room for "The History of the Herbal." This report was the first to mention a medieval manuscript ("Facetus of John the Cistercian," fifteenth century); use of the collections (109 requests, more from students than faculty, and mostly for term papers and thesis purposes); and the existence of a Notre Dame Collection, one of the largest collections in the Department today. Located in Room 205, the Notre Dame Collection included manuscripts such as Sorin's papers and the early records of the University as well as books and theses. (Manuscripts and records relating to Notre Dame have all been transferred to the University Archives since that time.) The following year, a fourth title was added to Lazenby's name as he became "Custodian of the Notre Dame Collection."

Also in the following year (1957/58) Lazenby began to make Notre Dame's treasures accessible beyond the campus by contributing records to published sources. These included *Census of Medieval and Renaissance Manuscripts in the United States*, Goff's *Incunabula in American Libraries*, a list of modern American authors published by the Modern Language Association (probably *American Literary Manuscripts*), and others in succeeding years. In addition Lazenby may have been the first librarian from Notre Dame to participate in sessions devoted specifically to rare book management at the annual conference of the American Library Association.

Although a large portion of the rare book and special collections have come from donations over the years, selective purchasing has been a part of new acquisitions as well. In the early years under Edwards and Foik, the distinction between purchases and donations is not always clear. Byrne's reports reveal shrewd advantage taken of the used book market. In 1932/33 he wrote:

A careful watch has been kept this year on second and remainder lists. Thru[sic] these sources we have been able to pick up a few very valuable history sources...At auction in New Jersey we secured a copy of Catherine Stewart's 'New Homes in the West.' This rare work deals in part with the Pottawatamies [sic] around Notre Dame and St. Joseph Michigan[sic: no comma]. There is no copy in the Library of Congress and the only copy in the Middle West is in the Chicago Historical Society Library. Other valuable titles for research in history were Father D'Acuna's Voyage and Discoveries in South America, Las Casas' Popery, truly displayed in its bloody colors; Archbishop Salpoint's Soldiers of the Cross and Moreau's Les Pretres Francais Émigres aux État[sic] Unis.[14]

These titles, all now in the Rare Book Collection, added to the University's holdings in Latin Americana and Catholic missions among the Indians of North America. Byrne also mentioned purchasing titles by the Grabhorn Press which, together with Pennsylvania University Press, "have been publishing in moderately priced editions certain very rare Americana...of great use to the research students in American history." Notre Dame owns 44 Grabhorn titles today.

During World War II foreign purchases, an important source of rare books, were virtually cut off. In his report for 1943/44 Byrne observed that the destruction of millions of books in England and the theft of thousands of books in France, Belgium, Holland, and other "Nazi dominated countries" make American libraries all the more "a treasure house of European culture."[15] Continuing that theme in 1944/45, he commented, "As a result of the destruction of many rare books and periodicals libraries are now restricting the loan of their more valuable material."[16]

With no lists of major acquisitions or gifts appearing in the annual reports for the years immediately after the War one sees little added to rare books or special collections apart from a notable gift from Raymond E.F. Larsson [see below]. With the arrival of Victor Schaefer in 1952/53 and for the next 20 years the library experienced an explosion of purchasing in what one Acquisitions report called "an era of abundance." The following are examples of acquisitions by either donation or purchase: in 1952/53, Diderot's 35-volume *Encyclopédie*, *La Chine Illustré* (1670), and *The Four Gospels* engraved by Eric Gill; in 1953/54, *Liber providentia*...by Pico della Mirandola (1508) and two incunabula; in 1954/55, three more incunabula, a thirteenth-century manuscript by Peter of Riga, *Index Librorum prohibitorum* (1596), and so on for six pages in that year alone. Long lists of donors and of major acquisitions that included medieval manuscripts, incunabula and other early printed books, specialized bibliographic reference sources, eighteenth-century imprints, expensive facsimile sets, etc., continued through the 1960s. In 1958/59 Schaefer reported that the library owned 32 incunabula (after Lazenby transferred the eight Dante editions to Room 208). Much of the purchasing resulted from the establishment of the Medieval Institute and from the Institute librarian's assumption of responsibility for the Treasure Room. The purchasing was not restricted to medieval universities (a strength of the medieval collections), however, but ranged over the classics, English and American literature, sciences such as mathematics and chemistry, and other fields.

Donations

The Library at Notre Dame has relied heavily on donations throughout its history, and this was especially true in its early decades before the existence of an annual book budget. Several early donors are mentioned above, including Zahm who was one of the first to donate an entire collection to the University.

Another early donor was Edward Lee Greene whom Notre Dame accommodated in retirement in exchange for his library of 4,000 volumes and herbarium of 65,000 specimens. The arrangement was made at the instigation of Father Julius Nieuwland, Notre Dame professor of botany and chemistry, former student of Greene's, and inventor of synthetic rubber. Nieuwland contributed his enormous collection on botany and together, "The resources of Greene and Nieuwland were said to have made Notre Dame one of the best universities in the country at which to study botany."[17] These collections apparently were moved into the new biology building when it was built in the 1930s and then transferred to the Department of Special Collections after the Memorial Library was built in 1963. The Edward L. Greene Collection on Botany constitutes one of the Department's major collections, while hundreds of Nieuwland's early printed books on botany appear in the Rare Book Collection.

In 1928/29 Charles Wightman of Evanston, Illinois, donated 456 oversize art books. The fine gift was anticipated by Byrne who wrote in the 1926/27 report:

> We are promised a collection of elephant folios from C.A. Wight-
> man...[which with those of Father Zahm] will make a valuable
> working library for the Art Department and the Art Gallery.[18]

The special strength in Ireland noted by Walter in his 1920 report
on the library was enhanced in 1931 when Francis O'Neill, retired
General Superintendent of Police in Chicago, wrote to President
Charles L. O'Donnell, "Having passed the 83rd milestone on the way
to eternity, I am disposed to carry out a long-considered intention."[19]
He offered his library of 1,500 volumes on Irish studies to O'Donnell
in September, and in October the collection was on campus in Byrne's
care. The gift had been anticipated by Foik as early as 1923/24, when
he referred to it in the annual report for that year. In the 1931/32 report
Byrne wrote:

> The largest and most valuable gift came from Captain Francis O'Neill
> of Chicago. This library consisted of 1500 volumes on Irish literature
> and Irish Music. Many of the works are out of print and extremely
> difficult to secure and the collections[sic], while small, is said to be
> one of the finest in this locality. About one half of the collection has
> already been cataloged and placed on our shelves for use.[20]

In circulation for many years the collection was recently reunited and
named for its special strength, "Captain Francis O'Neill Collection of
Irish Music." The 1952 survey of the library notes that this collection
supplemented "The Hiberniana Collection, originally known as the
Catholic Reference Library of America, [which was] exhibited in 1892
[sic] at the World's Fair in Chicago and later was deposited at Notre
Dame."[21]

Over the years the library at Notre Dame developed an extensive
collection of modern first editions of English and American authors,
once again largely due to donors. In 1935/36 an estate gift of 2,500
such volumes was bestowed by alumnus Eugene McBride ('16), whose
gift bookplate was designed by the then head of the Architecture
Department, Professor Kervick. Another alumnus, John Paul Cullen
('22), began a series of donations of first and signed editions in the
1940s that continued through the 1960s. His initial gift included 29
letters between himself and Sherwood Anderson in addition to 286
books.

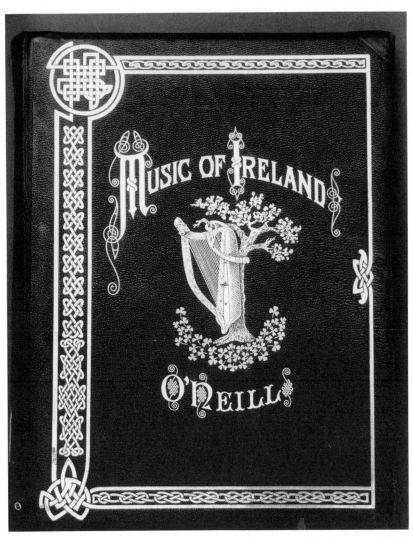

The cover of O'Neill's **Music of Ireland: Eighteen Hundred and Fifty
Melodies: Airs, Jigs, Reels, Hornpipes, Long Dances, Marches, etc., Many
of which are now Published for the First Time,** *collected from all available
sources, and edited by Capt. Francis O'Neill; arranged by James O'Neill
(Chicago: Lyon & Healy, 1903). Located in the Department of Special
Collections, University of Notre Dame.*

In 1952/53 alumnus John Bennett Shaw ('37) began a long association with his alma mater. After graduating from Notre Dame Shaw
became a successful rare and used book dealer. His earliest gifts were
modern first editions and out-of-print books. By 1959/60 he was
regularly sending first editions on a loan basis, including a collection
of 300 books by and about Lafcadio Hearn. In 1965 he sold his extensive
collections of G.K. Chesterton and Eric Gill to the University for less
than market value. The "John Bennett Shaw Collection of G.K.
Chesterton" contains over 2,000 books and periodicals by or about
"G.K.C.," including almost every work listed in the definitive bibliography by John Sullivan (whose library forms the bulk of the collection). Coincidentally, the dust jacket of the Sullivan bibliography was
designed by Chesterton's friend and one-time neighbor, Eric Gill. The
"Eric Gill Collection" at Notre Dame consists of almost 2,000 items
relating to the English sculptor, typographer, engraver, and writer who
lived from 1882 to 1940. The collection includes books, pamphlets,
broadsides, posters, prints, greeting cards, sketches, woodblocks,
photographs, and most of the publications of the Golden Cockerel Press
and the St. Dominic's Press. Shaw purchased most of this material from
Gill's brother, Evan. Shaw went on to become the world's foremost
authority on Sherlock "Holmesiana."

Also in the 1950s Robert H. Gore, Sr., began giving Notre Dame
early American coins and rare books on orchids, benefactions that have
continued along with substantial funding by his son, Robert Gore, Jr.
Gore, Sr., became interested in orchids when he served as Governor
of Puerto Rico under Franklin Delano Roosevelt. The extensive collection of orchid books includes Frederich Sanders' *Reichenbachia*, an
elephant-size portfolio of 192 chromolithograph plates printed from
1888 to 1894. The "Robert H. Gore, Jr., Collection of American
Numismatics" now contains some 4,400 items ranging from colonial
issues to paper currency.

Special Collections after 1962

When the new 14-story library opened, the Department of Rare
Books and Special Collections occupied rooms on two floors of the
west wing of the building. The outer room contained wall cases for
exhibits, while the long reading room was designed in the style of a

gentleman's club with plush red carpeting, wood panelled walls, glass-enclosed bookshelves, and deep black leather chairs. The third room contained the bookstacks, and a basement offered further space for storage.

Apparently the department had no curator for several years, although as assistant director of libraries for the Humanities Division, Lazenby had responsibility for the Rare Book Room and signalled his continuing interest in the field by attending at least one more rare book pre-conference. His 1964/65 report enumerated the Ford, Shaw, Dillon, and Descartes collections as well as 4,500 volumes (presumably the Rare Book Collection), which were in the third room. The Notre Dame Collection (approximately 4,000 volumes) was moved into the basement.

In 1968 Victor Schaefer returned from a sabbatical after retiring as library director and assumed the position of director of Special Collections and curator of Rare Books. Much of his annual report for 1968/69 dwelt on the "International Sports and Games Research Collection," which was moved into the Department of Special Collections when space became available in the basement.

Over the next decades other special collections and miscellaneous materials from elsewhere in the libraries gravitated into the department. In his first report as library director in 1971/72 David Sparks wrote the following about special collections:

> ...the organization of materials on both the first floor and the underground level was completed and set into a usable array...the culmination of several year's[sic] work of sorting, sifting, moving, and transferring a mass of material into the underground level of the Department...[22]

For some reason the Zahm Dante Collection had been placed on the fourth floor when the new building opened. Not until 1974 were the early and other rare editions retrieved and placed in the department as a special collection. Likewise the Greene Collection on Botany was transferred from the Biology Department to become another special collection. Rare books were being sought and transferred from circulating collections such as that of the Department of Architecture.

In 1973/74 for the first time the name "Department of Rare Books and Special Collections" was used in an annual report and a librarian,

Anton Masin, was hired exclusively to head that department. In 1975/76 Sparks recorded that in order to emphasize the public service aspects the department was reporting to the Public Services Division. This same year Masin reported 2,000 visitors, 800 uses, and 4 classes, and the establishment of a committee of scholars to develop the use of the Dante Collection through an organized program of Dante studies. The following year a new "Dante Room" was established, but unlike the elegant room in the old library it was merely classroom space with two conference tables occupying one end of the rare book stacks.

During Masin's tenure through the 1970s Rare Books and Special Collections experienced burgeoning growth in acquisitions and use. In the 1977/78 Annual Report Sparks observed:

> But a few years ago the Rare Book Room was the least used, most somnolent part of the University Libraries; it seems now to have become, under Mr. Masin's enthusiastic administration, one of the most active.[23]

In 1978/79 Masin reported 6,000 visitors and 4,675 items used. He was mounting exhibits and producing exhibit catalogs. For the first time there was a budget for preservation of rare and special materials. The disposition of uncataloged backlogs stored in the department was a perennial concern.

The burgeoning use experienced a sudden decline in 1978/79, however, for a few reasons that Masin identified in the annual report. Interestingly, one reason averred was the national gas shortage. The campus of Notre Dame was and still is a popular tourist site; the towering mosaic of Jesus Christ on the Hesburgh Library facade is said to be the most photographed object in northern Indiana. Throughout the year, but especially on football weekends, the Department of Special Collections has thousands of visitors pass through the Exhibit and Reading Rooms. The gas shortage in the late 1970s adversely affected tourism and as a consequence visitor statistics in Special Collections went down. Another reason for the decline in use was a new restriction limiting access to the "Dante Room" to classes and groups using department materials. A third reason was the transfer of most of the sports monographs to the libraries' circulating collection.

Another accomplishment of this period was the installation of security equipment by Honeywell. Unfortunately, the new security system failed to deter the burglary of gold coins that were on display in 1980/81. The loss was covered by insurance.

In 1983/84 former Director David Sparks replaced Masin as head of the department. The uncataloged backlogs continued to be a priority, and collection development policies were written for the largest collections. A new collection called Catholic Americana was established with the acquisition of thousands of parish histories and Catholic pamphlets, due to the efforts of Bibliographer Charlotte Ames. After some years of retrospective purchasing, gaps in the Notre Dame Collection were filled and offprints systematically solicited from faculty. In 1984/85 an additional room in the basement was acquired and the International Sports Research Collection was moved into the new quarters. In 1985/86 a grant from the National Endowment for the Humanities financed the conversion of the records for the Greene Collection on Botany to computerized form available in the national database known as OCLC, as well as the preservation of its pre-1800 volumes.

Acquisitions Since 1962

In 1966 a large purchase from the Rev. Elias Denissoff included some 500 titles relating to philosopher René Descartes. The many seventeenth-century editions were cataloged for the Rare Book Collection.

Over the years Notre Dame's collections in religion, especially liturgy and theology, have grown by the absorption of collections being disposed of by seminaries and other church-related institutions. One such was a collection of some 150 theology and classics books printed from the sixteenth to the eighteenth centuries. Donated to Notre Dame in 1972/73 by Dr. Patrick T. Conley of Cranston, Rhode Island, the volumes were acquired from a sale of the library of the Dominican House of Studies in Washington, D.C. Also in 1972 Dr. Astrik L. Gabriel, director of the Medieval Institute, secured one of the largest individual purchases made by the Notre Dame Library to that time, the library of Canon Eugéne Jarry. The Canon was a retired professor of medieval studies at the Institut Catholique in Paris; the oldest of the 15,000 volumes were added to the Rare Book Collection.

The collection of incunabula, which now numbers 81, also depended largely on donations. For a period of 11 years one incunabulum a year

185

was donated by Gabriel. The first was *Opuscula* by Vincent of Beauvais, printed by Johann Amerbach in 1481. In 1993 Gabriel donated his extraordinary collection of 262 sixteenth-century imprints, at least one publication for every year of that century.

Besides rare books, donations of unusual (i.e., "special") materials in recent decades greatly expanded the number of collections in the department. A collection of 2,000 issues of American newspapers from the eighteenth to the mid-twentieth centuries was donated to the libraries in 1972/73 by Arnold C. Hackenbruch, an alumnus of the Department of Architecture. In 1976/77 the collection of cuneiform tablets (mentioned above) together with the Babylonian cylinder were transferred back to the libraries from the Art Gallery. In 1977/78 Captain Harold F. Haynes donated his collection of some 750 titles published by the Folio Society, Heritage Press, Imprint Society, Limited Editions Club, and Nonesuch Press. In 1984/85 a St. Louis medical librarian, Suzy Conway, decided to make her collection of over 400 works by Edward Gorey available to the students here because her brother, Robert ('66), graduated from Notre Dame. In addition to books, Conway had acquired greeting cards, beanbags, T-shirts, a beach towel, and a jigsaw puzzle, among other unusual formats. Supplemental funding provided by the Conways has enabled the department to continue adding to the collection original pen-and-ink drawings, miniature books, and other items by Edward Gorey. In 1988/89 Theodore S. Weber ('45) provided the funds to purchase a collection of 12,000 paperbacks and other materials relating to Penguin Books. It encompassed all but 41 of the books published from 1935 to 1965, several thousand published into the 1980s, and catalogs, promotional items, and miscellanea such as a bust of Hemingway.

The 1990s saw a series of donations that recalled the tradition of "Hibernian" collection development promoted in the early years of the century by Foik. In 1990 an anonymous donor financed the acquisition of a collection of 74 rare books relating to the Irish Rebellion of 1798. The following year Thomas C. McGrath of New Jersey donated his collection of early printed maps and sea charts of Ireland. The majority of the 84 beautifully framed prints were produced by the great map-makers of the seventeenth century and a smaller number were done in the sixteenth and eighteenth centuries. The same year Notre Dame was fortunate to be chosen as a recipient for the new facsimile of *The Book of Kells* by The Wild Geese, an Irish cultural organization. Also in 1991 Dr. Charles Wolf donated his collection of Irish postage stamps, which was complete to date and has been enhanced by him yearly since then.

A recent estimate showed that the Department of Rare Books and Special Collections contains over 67,000 books and approximately 18,000 non-book items. Being on the ground floor near the entrance to the Hesburgh Library, it has remained a popular place; in 1991/92 nearly 3,000 visitors used some 2,400 items. The collections undoubtedly will continue to grow as long as alumni and others think fondly of the University of Notre Dame.

---

1. Joseph A. Lyons, comp., *Silver Jubilee of the University of Notre Dame, June 23rd, 1869*, 2d ed. (Chicago: E.B. Myers, 1869), 71–2.

2. John Lacey to Paul [Byrne?], July 1, 1937, in pocket of box containing Bérault-Bercastel, Rare Book Collection, University Libraries of Notre Dame.

3. Lyons, 71.

4. *A Brief History of the University of Notre Dame du Lac, Indiana, from 1842 to 1892 Prepared for the Golden Jubilee to be Celebrated June 11, 12 and 13, 1895* (Chicago: Werner Co., [1895]), 201.

5. Ibid., 250.

6. Sister Damien Tambola, "James F. Edwards: Pioneer Archivist of Catholic Church History of America" (Master's thesis, University of Notre Dame, 1958), 58.

7. Ibid., 65–6.

8. Ibid., 84.

9. Edgar J. Banks to John Cavanaugh, April 6, 1913, Office Files, Department of Special Collections, ULND.

10. John Cavanaugh to Edgar J. Banks, May 11, 1916, Office Files, Department of Special Collections, ULND.

11. Walter, 9.

12. AR, 1937–38, 5.

13. *Use Your Library: A Guide to the Resources and Services of the University of Notre Dame* (Notre Dame, Ind.: University of Notre Dame Library, 1948), 4.

14. AR, 1932–33, 19.

15. AR, 1943–44, 9.

16. AR, 1944–45, 4.

17. John Federowicz, "Forces Affecting the Development of Libraries at the University of Notre Dame, 1843–1968" (Master's thesis, Kent State University, 1968), 90.

18. AR, 1926–27, 7.

19. Francis O'Neill to Charles O'Donnell, Sept. 18, 1931, Presidents' Papers, UNDA.

20. AR, 1931–32, 10.

21. Louis R. Wilson and Frank A. Lundy, *Report of a Survey of the Library of the University of Notre Dame for the University of Notre Dame November 1950–March 1952* (Chicago: American Library Association, 1952), 31.

22. AR, 1971–72, 13.

23. AR, 1977–78, 18.

Style and Symbol:
Library Buildings at Notre Dame

MARSHA STEVENSON

The building that an institution chooses to house its library can offer important clues to the school's self-perception and to the image it wishes to portray to the outside world. As tangible monuments to scholarly dedication, libraries typically are among the most ambitious and prominent structures on a campus. They can bear eloquent architectural witness to a school's academic aspirations, and frequently are designed to impress students and faculty with the importance of learning within the institution's priorities. Libraries have both benefitted and suffered from this special place accorded them, since a grandiose exterior is not necessarily consistent with the goal of a functional interior.

Two main library buildings have been constructed on the Notre Dame campus. The first, built in 1917, is the present home of the School of Architecture. The second, opened in 1963 and dedicated a year later, is now called the Theodore M. Hesburgh Library but originally was known as Memorial Library. Each has a unique story to tell in terms of architectural history, the campus' intellectual ambience and values, and the influential personalities of the period.

At Notre Dame, as at other academic institutions, the general library collection originally was housed in a single room of a larger, multipurpose building. From the latter part of the nineteenth century the Lemonnier Library occupied the entire front projection of the third floor of the Main Building. In 1895 it was described as:

a magnificent gothic apartment...The arrangement of the shelving is such that every book is in reach of the visitor without the use of a ladder...the upper tiers are made accessible by a gallery around the entire hall.[1]

Campus pride in the facility was obvious. The *Notre Dame Scholastic* declares: "The room is decidedly the finest in the College"[2] and asserts that it "can be shown with pride to the visitor."[3] In 1895 the grand, undocumented claim is made that "We now have the largest college library in the West."[4]

The desire for a separate building to house the growing collection is documented as early as 1887. Father John Zahm was an enthusiastic supporter of the concept, and worked with the architect A.O. Von Herbulis to develop plans for a library. When the Rev. Paul Foik assumed the directorship of the library in 1912, he intensified the effort to convince the University administration of the urgent need for new quarters. His first annual report closed with the entreaty "There is nothing now for me to add other than to keep before you our supreme need—a new library building."[5] In another report he documents the need:

The library is being taxed far beyond its capacity...recent accessions of books to the library are being piled upon tables and almost every other place for lack of accommodation...There is a constant danger I may add, of overweighting the library, in fact my opinion is that we have just about gone the limit in this direction.[6]

Foik and Francis W. Kervick of the Architecture Department reviewed the building plans Von Herbulis had prepared earlier and sought critical feedback from a number of prominent librarians. A number of serious weaknesses were pointed out, and Theodore W. Koch of the University of Michigan library suggested that "The sooner the Von Herbulis plan is thrown in the wastebasket the better."[7] When the University administration determined to pursue a separate library building, a faculty committee was appointed with Foik as chair. This group held an architectural competition and reviewed five different plans in September 1914, but could not arrive at a consensus.[8] In May 1915 Foik wrote to the prominent architect, Edward L. Tilton, to inquire about his fees for drawing up a suitable library building. He included a lithograph of the structures composing the University group so that Tilton would have an idea of the architectural context within which his plan would function.[9]

Tilton was well-known as a library architect. He had been educated in New York City schools and trained with the prominent architectural firm of McKim, Mead & White. After attending the École des Beaux Arts in Paris, he opened an architectural practice in New York in 1890. Tilton published in library periodicals and, when contacted by Foik, had recently completed a widely admired public library for the city of Springfield, Massachusetts.

The exterior of the Springfield structure clearly derived from the single most influential library building of the era, McKim, Mead & White's Boston Public of 1894. Boston's signature facade was perhaps the key monument of the newly burgeoning Italian Renaissance style, a style whose widespread application at the turn of the century established the firm under which Tilton had trained as the nation's premier architects. While the beaux-arts classicism of that main facade was much copied, its interior layout was reviled by many librarians. The plan was devised by its architects without the consultation of working librarians, and it emphasized beauty of materials and such artful and dramatic effects as an elaborately conceived and decorated staircase well. The Boston Public Library became a showplace, but the overall plan was highly inefficient for staff operations. The books were stored in closed stacks at a great distance from the public area, resulting in long delays and wasted steps in retrieval of materials. The ornamentation of the reading rooms attracted hordes of casual viewers, making quiet study all but impossible.

Boston Public clearly had been designed with little regard for its function, and librarians reacted very strongly to what were considered the excesses of its plan. The term "monumental" in libraries became pejorative, referring to any building element that exceeded in size or cost what was necessitated by its function. While clearly influenced by the elegance and refinement of Boston's neo-Renaissance exterior, Tilton shared librarians' opinion of its interior. In 1912 he spoke of the waste and the cost of recently constructed "monumental" buildings in which less than one-half of the outlay went to library purposes with the remainder spent on dramatic effects, often to the detriment of library operations. He observed that:

Aesthetic effort expended upon ceilings and walls is naturally intended to attract admiration and to make the rooms become a magnet for visitors, whereas the primary intent of a reading room is to give tranquillity and a feeling of quiet sequestration from curious crowds. It is as illogical to adorn a reading room with beautiful frescoes as it would be to install in it a picture gallery and expect the readers to be undisturbed by those surging through to view the paintings...Extra enrichment and decoration might better be confined to delivery room, vestibules and stairways, where motion and commotion are to be expected. This does not exclude from the rest of the building handsome proportions and beautiful tints...[10]

Tilton advocated plans that were economical and well laid out, with a minimum of space devoted to corridors and stairways. He believed that if a plan was conceived along strict functional lines, the elevation would develop readily and the building's construction would be cost-efficient. He suggested that "The building's dress should be graceful but expressive of its functions and explanatory of its *raison d'être* not concealing its biblio muscles and arteries by too much overskirt."[11]

Foik was extremely impressed with the plans Tilton prepared for Notre Dame, and considered the previous competitors for the commission to be completely outclassed. One of them, A.F. Wickes from Gary, Indiana, complained in response to a missive from Foik that "The general tone of your letter gives me the impression, if you will pardon me for being frank, of your desire to be hero-worshippers."[12] Von Herbulis wrote plaintively that "inasmuch as I have spent so much time and labor and expense on the plans for your Library building, I certainly would like to see those plans carried out."[13] However, the other members of the library building committee agreed with Foik in his enthusiasm for Tilton's design.

A late entry into the competition for the library commission was a relative of a member of the building committee, Father Quinlan. He threw his support to the plans submitted by his brothers-in-law William and Joseph Kelly, and a protracted dispute ensued between him and Foik which the librarian was not at all sure of winning. He wrote to a friend that "I have had many a heartache over this situation since Mr. Kelley [sic] came into competition with the plan that had already been approved...I have been double crossed on this proposition several times,"[14] and confided "My position is exceedingly difficult on account of the wire pulling that has been done and is being done regarding this library."[15] He eventually triumphed with the University administration, and Foik proclaimed the announcement of the decision favoring Tilton "one of the happiest days of my life."[16]

Foik was able to persuade "every one from the Superior General down" on the grounds that it was worth the higher fee commanded by Tilton for the design of "a building such as shall be the pride of the University. I can say without exaggeration that Notre Dame will possess the finest library in the whole state of Indiana, and the finest Catholic library in the whole United States."[17]

The site selected for the new building was behind Walsh and Sorin Halls, near the Log Chapel and Old College, overlooking St. Mary's Lake. This location was somewhat problematic, since the original campus plan had called for all academic buildings, including the library, to be grouped along the avenue headed by the Main Building. The site was selected, however, to initiate a quadrangle of dormitories, with the library as the central structure;[18] but it was the first major departure from the campus plan of zoning by function. Foik originally had hoped to be on the avenue, but resigned himself to the new location: "The disagreeable sight of the barns and St. Joe Hall, etc., will have to be endured..."[19]

Ground was broken for the new structure on November 14, 1915. Father Foik was given the honor of turning the first spade of dirt, and "photographers and newspaper men were there in abundance."[20] While Foik won the battle with Quinlan over the choice of architect, the dispute seems to have cost him some capital politically, and he tried to adopt a low profile on the decisions regarding contracting. In reference to the University administration, he wrote to Tilton "My advice to you on this matter is to leave the matter of contracting much to their desire...You realize my position as librarian is not one of authority and while I am working in my own quiet way to get what I want in this building I do not wish to give the impression that I am suggesting anything."[21]

The Bedford Stone and Construction Company of Indianapolis was awarded the contract for the new building. The Kirkham Company of Niles, Michigan won the bid to install the plumbing, heating and vacuum systems, although "as this system is to contain many of the very latest ideas and inventions...it was only after much debating that it was finally decided to give the contract to the Michiganders."[22]

Brother Irenaeus, the Notre Dame engineer, was charged with the installation of the electrical apparatus, and the bookstacks were to be manufactured by the Snead Iron Company of Jersey City, N.J. Construction cost was estimated at $250,000.

The cornerstone of the library was laid at a formal ceremony on June 11, 1916. An academic procession was headed by the University band and included seniors, professors, and officiating clergy including Bishop Peter J. Muldoon of Rockford, Illinois. The account in the *Notre Dame Scholastic* declares:

> The Library has always been and always will be the center of the intellectual life of the University. It was indeed fitting that the construction of the new building should be solemnly begun by the blessing and laying of the cornerstone...Following the ceremony, Bishop Muldoon spoke briefly, referring to this occasion as another grand triumph of Catholic ideals, another refutation of the old charge that one of the first cares of the Church had never been education.[23]

For the library's exterior Tilton chose the Italian Renaissance idiom that McKim, Mead & White had been so instrumental in popularizing, and which he himself had utilized for the public libraries of Springfield, Massachusetts and of Manchester, New Hampshire. This vocabulary had become so integral to Tilton's approach that he used it at Notre Dame even though no other campus structure previously (or later) employed it. Constructed of white Indiana limestone, also called Bedford stone, the building measures 152 feet frontage by 108 feet depth. Tilton's facade features three registers of windows beneath a low-pitched roof of green tile. Its monumental entranceway is approached by a wide staircase and is topped by a triumphal arch reaching the full height of the building. The shape of the entrance is echoed in the arches of the reading room windows of the main story.

The library was planned to house nearly 618,000 volumes, and since the University's collection at that time numbered about 100,000, space for collection growth was considered ample. Seating was provided for 360 readers, or about one-third of the enrollment of the time. Room layout in the building reflected the latest ideas of proper library arrangement. A contemporary article declared:

Greatest attention has been given to the interior and no care nor expense has been spared to provide the latest and most approved ideas in library construction. Convenience and serviceability have been the keynotes in the interior plans, and the entire library is as nearly fire-proof, noise-proof and dust-proof as modern architectural skill can make it.[24]

The entryway, main stairway and delivery hall were finished in marble. One large reading room, intended for reference materials with an adjoining area for bibliography, was located along the south side of the building. The other, along the north, was planned to house newspapers and periodicals. Such a room was unusual in university libraries of the day, but was necessary because of Notre Dame's new and growing School of Journalism. Both reading rooms measured 108 by 32 feet and could seat 150. Tables were arranged so that all readers faced one way, a system adopted from the John Hay Library of Brown University.

The delivery hall of the 1917 library as pictured in **Public Libraries** *23 (April 1918): 174.*

The skylit delivery hall was located between the two reading rooms, and was situated so that the noise and commotion attending the requesting and delivering of books would not disturb serious study. The catalog room was placed behind it, with the staff working quarters just beyond. This location was praised for its economy, since it allowed both the public and the staff to share one catalog, thereby eliminating the common practice of maintaining a duplicate working catalog used only by the staff. The room was also located in the midst of the stacks, making for ready retrieval of requested materials.

Multitiered stack floors had come into vogue a few decades earlier, when they became recognized as the most efficient means of storing a large number of books in a relatively compact space. Five decks of closed stacks were planned to rise above the catalog room on the first floor and two more tiers were to be located in the basement below. The use of electrical illumination was still relatively new, and library planners had come to realize that this allowed the book collection to be moved to an interior location. Another modern innovation was the inclusion of 60 carrels in the stacks; this was a feature pioneered only in 1914, at the Widener Library of Harvard University.

Staff quarters were arranged along the back of the building, with three rooms on the ground floor, three more on the main level, and three in the mezzanine. Parts of the basement were designed for archives and lecture halls, and the top story was meant to house special collections, the historical museum, and the art collection. This sharing of quarters was a pragmatic move on Foik's part. In a letter he described it as "the only means to hasten the erection of this building" and asserted that "it has not been in the minds of the Committee nor of the executives of the University to place the museum with the library perpetually."[25] Still, Foik took pride in declaring "Notre Dame is the only Catholic University in the country that can boast of a library distinct from all other activities."[26]

Difficulties abounded in the erection of the library, and Foik may have regretted the low profile he had adopted when contracting decisions were being made. Numerous problems arose with the building's mechanical systems, with most of the blame directed at the University's engineer. Tilton complained that "I found it impossible always as you know to control Br. Iranaeus [sic] in any way...I was kept in such a state of worry and uncertainty that I was never able to obtain a smooth running building operation."[27] The construction clerk referred to Irenaeus as "very obstinate concerning the electrical work,"[28] and he comes in for particularly harsh criticism from Foik regarding the inadequate heating system in the library: "I hope not to be tortured in the fall as I was in the spring by disagreeably cold rooms...";[29] Brother Irenaeus "is a thorn in my side...Only after I used the strongest of duress and threatened to resign my librarianship with the Provincial, Father Morrissey, did I succeed in getting a sufficient supply of heat to keep the place comfortable."[30]

On June 3, 1917, the library was dedicated as a highlight of the University's Diamond Jubilee Celebration. Again there was an imposing procession, viewed by a crowd of 4,000 people. Bishop Thomas J. Shahan, rector of Catholic University, officiated in the blessing of the library. The Honorable Bourke Cockran then "delivered a powerful address, holding an open-air audience for over two hours..."[31]

Reaction to the library was favorable, both on campus and within the profession. Foik wrote to Tilton that "I think everyone is convinced by this time that the Library is our chief adornment."[32] The Indiana Library Association met at Notre Dame in 1919, and "the consensus of opinion was that it was the best and most efficient library they had ever seen."[33] After a subsequent meeting of that group, Foik wrote to Tilton:

> I owe to you quite a bit of the prestige that has come to me as an Indiana librarian. Had your building been a failure, I am sure that I should not have been noticed. As matters turned out, I was featured as the big gun of the first day of the convention. Consequently you see that a well-planned library is the Librarians [sic] best asset, for I am told by visitors who come from a distance that they knew the Notre Dame Library before they knew me.[34]

The library was featured in an illustrated article in the journal *Public Libraries* in April 1918. And, in Frank K. Walter's comprehensive 1920 survey of the library, he referred to it as "a building which is at once architecturally ornamental and well-adapted to its special purpose."[35] While the name "Lemonnier Library" was applied sporadically to the new building over the next decade, the newer term "University Library" became its preferred name.

Both Notre Dame as an institution and library plan theory changed dramatically over the next few decades. Student enrollment and the book collection alike experienced rapid growth, and the capacity of the University Library's reading rooms and stacks became woefully inadequate. New concepts of library use advocated open access to the stacks, and it was recognized that large open spaces held many distractions and were not necessarily the preferred study environment of all individuals. High-ceilinged reading rooms had been practical necessities in earlier libraries, both because of the need for large windows to light the rooms and also to help dissipate heat. However, refinements in electrical illumination and advances in air conditioning served to free libraries from conformity to the time-honored reading room dimensions.

The University Library was an example of a fixed-function plan, in which each space was designed to be as efficient as possible in the light of its one intended use. However, ceiling proportions in the tall reading rooms and the low stacks alike limited those areas' flexibility for conversion to different purposes. In the 1940s it became popular to subdivide main libraries into broad subject categories in an attempt at compromise between centralized general and specialized branch collections. The University Library tried to adapt by instituting first a social science, then a humanities, reading room on its main floor, and later a business and economics section in its basement.

A major survey of the library took place between 1950 and 1952. The resulting report, prepared by consultants Louis R. Wilson and Frank A. Lundy, recommended numerous internal rearrangements in an effort to eke out more reader space and to add stack capacity.[36] The third-floor art gallery finally was moved out and its space renovated for library purposes. However, it became increasingly apparent that construction of a new building was inevitable. The changing philosophy of library service that emphasized the juxtaposition of readers and books had created a conflict between form and function that could not be resolved within the confines of the 1917 structure.

The concept of "modular" libraries was pioneered by Angus Snead Macdonald of the same Snead Iron Company that had manufactured the University Library's stacks. In a series of publications beginning in 1933, he criticized monumentalism and beaux-arts planning and advocated a new type of library interior. Readers would work in homey, low-ceilinged alcoves or clusters of carrels located adjacent to the book collections. Most interior walls would be eliminated and a system of regularly spaced columns would support the ceilings. Dimensions of the columnar spacing were calculated to accommodate standard library shelving, though since interior walls were few, these "modules" could be transformed readily into reader or staff areas. Ralph Ellsworth and Keyes Metcalf, both of whom were noted library building consultants, advocated many of Macdonald's theories.[37]

Most major libraries designed after 1950 were based on this modular concept and stressed functionalism in their design. A single key element of library use, access to the card catalog, became the dominant factor in floor planning, since both library users and staff needed to have the ever-growing catalog close at hand. This led to large main floors, with both public and technical services operations grouped near the catalog. Another significant trend in university library design of the period was the separation of undergraduates from "research" space. Harvard pioneered this in 1949 with its Lamont Library which was planned for lower-level students, and the University of Michigan built a major undergraduate facility in 1958.

The desire to incorporate such recent trends as the modular interior, subject divisional arrangements, and separation of undergraduates from the research collections was keenly felt at Notre Dame. Father Theodore M. Hesburgh assumed the presidency of the University in 1952, at the time of the publication of Wilson and Lundy's report on the library. The inadequacies of Tilton's structure in the light of modern theory were apparent, and Hesburgh noted the need for an improved facility soon after his assumption of the presidency. 1952 also saw the hiring of a new library director, Victor A. Schaefer, who previously had been assistant director at the University of Michigan.

In 1958 Hesburgh announced "The Program for the Future" which was a ten-year, $66.6 million dollar fundraising target. While a number of construction projects were named in that program, student sentiment favored building a library first, since the largest of the campus' constituencies would be served by providing all with the quality study space so conspicuously lacking in the University Library.[38] There also had long been dissatisfaction with the system of closed stacks at the old library; a *Scholastic* editorial noted that "Most students ordering books from the card catalogue have often wondered if that index was a list of books the University had or wanted to buy...with open stacks we will no longer have that lingering doubt that maybe it really was there."[39]

An active planning effort for a new library was underway in 1959. Victor Schaefer solicited faculty opinion and prepared a digest of the ideas submitted. Among them were suggestions that the edifice be "modern and functional. No lost space or wasted money in details of the old Gothic School" and that its designer "be carefully chosen from among architects who have designed one or more of the recent university libraries." A "dual library," with separate areas for undergraduates and research work, was proposed by several.[40] In a memo to an assistant to the President, Schaefer supported the dual library concept and also expressed his hope that the new building would be a sensible workshop, rather than a great architectural monument.[41]

The President, however, had an expanded vision of the structure. Notre Dame was more widely known for its football team than its academics, and Hesburgh saw the new library building as an opportunity to make a highly visible statement to the outside world about the importance attached to scholarly achievement by the institution. A spectacular design could not fail to call attention to the place of learning and academic ambition in the University's priorities. In a 1963 symposium on recent library facilities, Schaefer observed that: "There was a very simple factor that influenced what kind of a building we would have...The President wanted to have a building which would be the dominating building on the campus, and I think we have that."[42]

There was some precedent on other campuses for high-rise academic library structures, and the University of Texas' Cret Library of the 1930s may have been particularly influential in the design of Memorial Library. It was 28 stories tall including its penthouse, with the lower 14 of its stack tiers devoted to book storage and the upper ones to faculty offices. The building's exterior was embellished with symbols and emblems, and the shape of its main floor plan resembles that of Memorial Library.[43] Huge stack towers were little liked by key library professionals, however. The Ohio State University intended to construct a building twenty stories tall in the late 1940s, with undergraduates on the lower two floors and research and graduate study above, but the tower was sharply criticized by experts and the plan was not utilized.[44]

The type of modular, utilitarian structure favored by librarians in the 1950s tended to have stark and unadorned exteriors. However, some felt that the emphasis on strict functionality, carried through to a no-nonsense facade, limited those libraries' visual appeal. There were two conflicting schools of thought regarding the use of windows on such buildings. One held that they were essential to relieve the monotony of the boxlike exteriors, and thus glass was used liberally, sometimes to excess. The opposing camp held that windows led to changeable and uneven light conditions, unpleasant glare at some times of the day, inconsistency of temperature control, and distraction for readers. It is within this second school of thought that the Memorial Library was conceived.

The first public announcement of the University's intentions came in December 1959, when Hesburgh revealed the plans for a library to a group of Indianapolis-area alumni. He announced that one of the sites under consideration was the historic Cartier Field on which Knute Rockne's teams played. Other locations had been actively considered, one of which would have razed the Main Building and replaced it with a combined administration-library structure. Architects found it impossible to design such a building and still retain the gold dome, and the plan was abandoned.[45] The Cartier Field site eventually was chosen, and the Navy Drill Hall and several Vetville structures were removed to make way for the new building.

The library was planned as part of a major expansion program to the east of the older section of campus; it was to be the focal point of a new mall that would include academic buildings to the south and residence halls to the north. The Ellerbe Company of St. Paul, Minnesota, which had designed a number of other buildings on campus, was selected as architects for the new library. They had an established track record at Notre Dame, having designed the O'Shaughnessy Hall of Liberal and Fine Arts, the Art Gallery and the Sculpture Studio, and Keenan and Stanford Halls during the 1950s. Ellerbe was the architectural firm of choice for the Rev. Edmund P. Joyce, Hesburgh's executive vice president and right-hand man, who masterminded the substantial number of building projects undertaken during Hesburgh's presidency. The firm has been described as "more engineers than artists, who gave the university good value for the cost."[46] When asked

for a description of the new library, an Ellerbe representative stated
somewhat vaguely that:

> One cannot really relate this as a known historical style, but rather
> allows it to conform with the traditional functional buildings prevail-
> ing in campus today, therefore the building belongs. Perhaps this is
> its style—to belong in harmony with the total campus—past—present
> and future![47]

A spectacularly successful fundraising campaign was mounted
under the direction of Father John H. Wilson, director of the Notre
Dame Foundation and Mr. J. Peter Grace, national chairman of the
campaign. The major coup was the Ford Foundation's award of
$6,000,000 to Notre Dame as part of a matching grant program also
awarded to Johns Hopkins, Stanford, Vanderbilt, Denver, and Brown
universities. A recent writer observed that:

> The choice of Notre Dame in such good academic company was itself
> a ringing affirmation of what Hesburgh had come to stand for in his
> eight years as president. Gone were the humiliating days of only a
> few years ago, when his press conferences were attended largely by
> sports writers.[48]

Hesburgh was a charismatic and enthusiastic leader of the fundraising effort. In a series of articles appearing in *Notre Dame* magazine
during 1961, he spoke eloquently of the urgent need for a new library,
for a place for students to find a quiet and calm atmosphere with a
pervading spirit of study. "We could build a library that was much less
ambitious...but this would be looking backwards instead of forward."[49]
He made it clear that generous contributions from alumni were essential:

> Because we need this, we have begun to build it—not with the money
> in hand, no more than Father Sorin had, but with the same faith in
> you and in Notre Dame's future. Whether this spells folly or vision
> is the substance of our moment of truth this Fall. Either the funds
> mount as the building mounts, or we are in trouble.[50]

And: "When you tighten your belts and give a sacrificial gift to the
new Library, you should understand that what will happen in this

Library will in some small measure affect the world and all of its problems...Tighten the belt, but do it happily..."[51]

Hesburgh had set a three-year goal of $18 million, with the construction of the library estimated at $8 million for the building and another $4 million for associated costs of physical plant upgrades; the remainder of the money would be earmarked for other campus purposes. Fundraising literature proclaimed that it was impossible for a university to achieve eminence unless it had a truly great library, and suggested numerous opportunities to establish "living memorials" in the new structure. The price tags for these ranged from $500,000 for a major reading area down through book stacks at $500 apiece.

There was an immediate response to the nationwide telephone kickoff campaign in 1961. Major gifts included $1 million from I.A. O'Shaughnessy of St. Paul, Minnesota and $500,000 from both Frank M. Freiman of Fort Wayne, Indiana and Mr. and Mrs. Carlos Tavares of La Jolla, California. The Women's Advisory Council, an organization of wives of the Lay Board of Trustees, selected the library as their special project and organized the Notre Dame Library Association to help raise funds. Five thousand volunteers were recruited to personally solicit funds from 27,000 alumni and friends. Although Notre Dame alumni had in the past proved consistently generous to their alma mater, a truly remarkable 87 percent of them made donations to this particular campaign. In February 1963 Joyce was able to announce that the drive had surpassed its target, having collected $18,004,500 from 21,156 donors.[52]

Major contractors for the building were the H.G. Christman Construction Company of South Bend and the O.W. Burke Company of Detroit. The steel fabrication was supplied by the American Bridge Division of the U.S. Steel Corporation in Gary, Indiana. Ceremony abounded at every stage of the project. A formal blessing of the library took place in August 1961, performed by Joseph Cardinal Ritter of St. Louis after an academic convocation. Publicity at the time noted that this was the largest construction project in Notre Dame's history and one of the largest structures in the state of Indiana. Hesburgh contributed to a colorful "topping out" ceremony in April 1962 to mark the hoisting into place of the highest structural beam. He added a Latin inscription to that beam, along with an American flag, before it was lifted into place.

New constructions: The 1917 library (above); the Memorial Library (below).

The University planned to open the new building at the start of the fall semester in 1963. A carpenter's strike in May delayed the construction but the goal was met. The library staff rose to the challenge of transporting 475,000 volumes across campus and inserting them in the correct locations in the new building. The books were packed in sturdy Carling Black Label beer cartons, providing predictable headlines for many a news story: "Many Beer Cases, Very Little Foam"; "Beer Cases Give Literature a Lift"; and "A Canny Way to Cart Books" are examples.[53]

The library opened its doors on September 18, 1963, at the start of Notre Dame's 122nd academic year. It was a massive structure, 210 feet tall on a site 315 feet square. The interior was fully 429,780 square feet gross, with two large lower floors capped by a narrower, nearly windowless tower of 13 stories with a smaller penthouse at the top. The two lower floors featured a more liberal use of glass along with brick and tweed granite, and the upper stories were finished in Mankato stone. The building faces south and its main concourse can be entered from three directions.

The main and second floors were called the College Library and were intended for use by undergraduates. A subject divisional arrangement was employed, with the first floor devoted to humanities and the second to social sciences and general science. Together, these two floors had a shelf capacity of 200,000 volumes and could seat over 2,400. Book stacks, service desks, and reader areas were scattered to disguise the huge expanse of these floors. The card catalog was centrally located on the main level, and technical services staff occupied 12,000 square foot quarters immediately to its east. The upper stories, called the Research Tower, were devoted to graduate and research purposes. Both closed and open carrels added to the total library seating, offering the potential to accommodate nearly half of the student body which numbered 7,723.

When the building opened, its most distinctive exterior feature, the "mural," had not yet been installed. The artist Millard Sheets, who had worked with Ellerbe architects on a previous project, was commissioned to create a work large enough to cover the southern face of the tower, visible from the football stadium. Its theme was to be saints and scholars throughout the ages, and was suggested by Hesburgh who found the mosaic on the University of Mexico library "paganistic" and thought there should be something in the United States to counteract it.[54] In an interview, Sheets explained that:

> What they asked me to do was to suggest in a great processional the idea of a never-ending line of great scholars, thinkers, and teachers—saints that represented the best that man has recorded, and which are found represented in a library. The thought was that the various periods that are suggested in the theme have unfolded in the continuous process of one generation giving to the next. I put Christ at the top with the disciples to suggest that He is the great teacher—that is really the thematic idea.[55]

As the composition evolved, the figure of Christ the Teacher was developed with arms raised in what has become known as the "touchdown" gesture. The $200,000 mural was a gift of Mr. and Mrs. Howard V. Phalin of Winnetka, Illinois. By strict definition it qualifies as neither mural nor mosaic; the process is a unique one in which 6,700 separate pieces of granite were used to create the composition.[56] By virtue of its sheer size (134 feet high and 68 feet wide) and highly visible location, it continues to attract attention as both a technical tour de force and a popular icon.

The mural was installed during the spring of 1964, but was kept covered until the day of the library's formal dedication. That ceremony was held on May 7, 1964 and included a mass and an academic convocation. Many eminent prelates and distinguished educators were in attendance, including Eugene Cardinal Tisserant, Dean of the Sacred College of Cardinals and Prefect of the Vatican Library. The event was televised live on WNDU.

The interior of the new library was praised for the obvious improvements in lighting it offered over the 1917 structure. Some innovations in carrel design and shelving were incorporated, and the color scheme of the chairs ("vermillion splendor, marigold, and citron chromate") caused comment. The vast, unbroken expanse of the lower two floors resulted in a significant problem with noise, however.

Reaction to the library's exterior was varied and not all complimentary. Many considered its scale inappropriate for its site, and students referred to it by such epithets as "Ted's Mahal," "The Brain Silo," and "Mt. Excellence." A recent writer stated that:

Rather than being dictated by library functional factors, this building's height was determined by the university's desire for a symbol of its academic excellence that would outshine its reputation for football prowess. The library fulfilled that symbolic purpose admirably, with its mosaic-bedecked facade visible from 60 percent of the seats in the stadium.[57]

A few more high-rise library buildings were constructed soon afterward, including a 14-story science library topped by a penthouse at Brown University in 1966. A year later the Bowling Green State University opened a structure that not only was similar in shape to Memorial Library but included large murals on two sides. The tallest academic library in the country was constructed at the University of Massachusetts, where a 28-story edifice opened in 1972.

Whatever the criticisms of its external features, Memorial Library quickly became a showplace, and for 30 years has been among the most familiar of the campus landmarks. With its size, prominent location and eye-catching mural it attracts the attention of even the most casual visitor, and asserts itself as a dramatic symbol of Notre Dame's aspirations to academic excellence. The building thus functions within a time-honored tradition in which respect for learning is made tangible by the special place accorded to library architecture in the overall context of a campus.

---

1. *A Brief History of the University of Notre Dame du Lac, Indiana, from 1842 to 1892, Prepared for the Golden Jubilee to be Celebrated June 11, 12, and 13, 1895* (Chicago, IL: The Werner Company, 1895), 200–201.

2. *Notre Dame Scholastic* 17 (August 16, 1883): 12.

3. *Notre Dame Scholastic* 17 (January 5, 1884): 265.

4. *Notre Dame Scholastic* 29 (November 16, 1895): 174.

5. AR, 1911–12, 11.

6. "Report of Library Conditions," undated (1914?), UNDA-UODL 2.

7. Letter from Theodore W. Koch to Paul J. Foik, June 4, 1915, UNDA-UODL 2.

8. Letter from Paul J. Foik to his sister, Mrs. W.H. Bullard, September 23, 1914, UNDA-UODL 2.

9. Letter from Paul J. Foik to Edward L. Tilton, May 22, 1915, UNDA-UODL 2.

10. Edward L. Tilton, "Scientific Library Planning," *Library Journal* 37 (September 1912): 499.

11. E.L. Tilton, "Architecture of Small Libraries," *Public Libraries* 17 (February 1912): 40.

12. Letter from A.F. Wickes to Paul J. Foik, June 1, 1915, UNDA-UODL 2.

13. Letter from A.O. Von Herbulis to the Rev. P.J. Franciscus, July 31, 1915, UNDA-UODL 2.

14. Letter from Paul J. Foik to Earl Dickens, November 18, 1915, UNDA-UODL 2.

15. Letter from Paul J. Foik to M. E. Ahern, November 4, 1915, UNDA-UODL 2.

16. Letter from Paul J. Foik to Louis J. Bailey, November 9, 1915, UNDA-UODL 2.

17. Letter from Paul J. Foik to Earl Dickens, November 18, 1915, UNDA-UODL 2.

18. Ibid.

19. Letter from Paul J. Foik to Paul R. Byrne, November 23, 1915, UNDA-UODL 2.

20. *Notre Dame Scholastic* 49 (November 20, 1915): 169.

21. Letter from Paul J. Foik to Edward L. Tilton, January 3, 1916, UNDA.

22. *South Bend News-Times*, February 18, 1916, UNDA-UDIS 18/09.

23. *Notre Dame Scholastic* 49 (June 24, 1916): 619.

24. "Notre Dame University Will Have Greatest Catholic Library Building in the U.S.," *Catholic Columbian-Record*, Indianapolis, IN, June 30, 1916, UNDA-PNDP 10-Le-1.

25. Letter from Paul J. Foik to Paul Byrne, November 23, 1915, UNDA-UODL 2.

26. Letter from Paul J. Foik to Paul Byrne, January 12, 1917, UNDA-UODL 2.

27. Letter from Edward L. Tilton to Paul J. Foik, October 24, 1918, UNDA-UNDL 2.

28. Report of Clerk, March 16–22 (1917), UNDA-UNDR 30/10.

29. Letter from Paul J. Foik to Edward L. Tilton, May 20, 1918, UNDA-UODL 2.

30. Letter from Paul J. Foik to Edward L. Tilton, December 7, 1918, UNDA-UODL 2.

31. Paul R. Martin, comp. and ed., *The Diamond Jubilee Celebration of Notre Dame University* (Indianapolis, IN: The Indiana Catholic and Record, 1917), 16.

32. Letter from Paul J. Foik to Edward L. Tilton, October 1, 1920, UNDA-UODL 2.

33. "University Host to Librarians: Indiana Library Association Opens Session in New Building at Notre Dame," *South Bend News-Times*, February 27, 1919, UNDA-PNDP 30-Li-01.

34. Letter from Paul J. Foik to Edward L. Tilton, November 11, 1919, UNDA-UODL 2.

35. Walter, 2.

36. Wilson/Lundy, 171–74.

37. *Encyclopedia of Architecture: Design, Engineering & Construction*, vol. 3, s.v. "Libraries."

38. Jim Rose, "A New Library?" *The Scholastic* 101 (October 10, 1958): 18–19.

39. *Notre Dame Scholastic* 101 (December 11, 1959): 13.

40. "New Library Building: Digest of Faculty Suggestions as of October 1, 1959," UNDA-UDIS 18/10.

41. Memorandum from Victor A. Schaefer to the Rev. Philip S. Moore, academic assistant to the President, May 6, 1959, UNDA-PNDP 30-Li-02.

42. William A. Katz and Roderick G. Swartz, eds., *Problems in Planning Library Facilities: Consultants, Architects, Plans, and Critiques*, Proceedings of the Library Buildings Institute Conducted at Chicago, July 12–13, 1963, Sponsored by the Library Administration Division, American Library Association (Chicago: American Library Association, 1964), 99.

43. *The Second Princeton Conference: A Meeting of the Cooperative Committee on Library Building Plans*, held at Princeton University, Princeton, New Jersey, June 12–14, 1946 (Philadelphia, PA: Printed by Stephenson-Brothers, 1947), 72–73.

44. *The North Carolina Conference: A Meeting of the Cooperative Committee on Library Building Plans*, held at Chapel Hill and Durham, North Carolina, March 18–19, 1947, 5–6; also, *The Chicago Conference: A Meeting of the Cooperative Committee on Library Building Plans*, held at The International House of the University of Chicago, Chicago, Illinois, January 27–28, 1948 (Madison, WI: Printed by Democrat Printing Company, 1948), 1.

45. Wade Clarke, "Cartier Field Under Consideration as Possible Site of New Library," *Notre Dame Scholastic* 101 (December 11, 1959): 13.

46. Thomas Stritch, *My Notre Dame: Memories and Reflections of Sixty Years* (Notre Dame, IN: University of Notre Dame Press, 1991), 226.

47. Letter from Tom Van Housen of Ellerbe Company to James E. Murphy, director of public relations at Notre Dame, August 11, 1960, UNDA-UDIS 18/10B.

48. Stritch, 225.

49. *Notre Dame* 14 (Spring 1961): The President's Page (5).

50. *Notre Dame* 14 (Fall 1961): The President's Page (6).

51. *Notre Dame* 14 (Winter 1961): The President's Page (6).

52. *South Bend Tribune*, February 17, 1963, UNDA-UDIS 018/10A.

53. News clippings from the University of Notre Dame Archives, UDIS 018/11.

54. Jack Rowe, "Behind the Mural," *The Scholastic* 105 (May 8, 1964): 31.

55. Ibid., 21.

56. Frederic Whitaker, "Millard Sheets: The Story of a GIANT," *American Artist* 28 (December 1964): 33–35.

57. David Kaser, "Twenty-Five Years of Academic Library Building Planning," *College and Research Libraries* 45 (July 1984): 276.

The Medieval Institute Library:
A Brief History

MARINA SMYTH

T he holdings of the Medieval Institute reflect its role as a center for research and instruction in the Christian civilization of the Middle Ages. Some 70,000 volumes, 16,000 microforms and numerous other materials devoted to the study of the intellectual life of the Middle Ages are now housed on the seventh floor of the Hesburgh Library. This is a far cry from the original situation in 1946, when the first director of the Institute, the Reverend Gerald B. Phelan, had to share his office on the top floor of what was then the University Library (now the Architecture Building), with a minimal core of books, while the bulk of the necessary research materials was scattered throughout the library's collection of almost 250,000 volumes.

The Beginnings of Medieval Studies at Notre Dame

Already in the early 1930s, when Philip Moore, C.S.C., was studying at the École des Chartes in Paris, the University administration made the conscious decision to emphasize medieval studies at Notre Dame. As one might expect of a Catholic institution of higher learning, basic resources such as the *Patrologia Latina* were acquired early in the history of the University. But library records from the early 1930s onward show that a marked bent toward the study of the Middle Ages was already influencing the choice of research materials in a University that was slowly developing graduate courses. Even before Father

Moore returned from Paris, he was selecting materials for the Notre Dame Library, as recorded in the *Notre Dame Alumnus*:[1]

> William J. Corbett, Chicago, Ill., by the gift of one thousand dollars, has created a foundation at Notre Dame to be known as the William J. Corbett Research Library of Philosophy. The work of collecting material for the Library has already begun by Reverend Philip Moore, C.S.C., '24, now taking advanced studies in Paris. Mr. Corbett is the father of William J. Corbett, Jr., '27.[2]

The Scholastic of December 9, 1932, explained further (on p. 11):

> The majority of the works will pertain to Medieval Scholastic Philosophy. They are intended for use in graduate work. At present, Notre Dame offers no doctorate in the field of Philosophy proper, although work is offered leading to the master's degree. According to plans already maturing, the Department of Philosophy will offer doctoral work within the next few years. Father Philip Moore, C.S.C., who is an Enfield Scholar to Paris from the Catholic University in Washington, is now purchasing the books. He has already presented lists of the foremost works of the ages and from these lists several titles have been selected.

The General Accounting Office at Notre Dame reports that a Corbett fund was set up in 1933, for the library "to purchase books and manuscripts." On June 15, 1934, financial reports of the University enter under the heading of *Fellowships and Foundations* a "James Corbitt Foundation"[sic] for a "Medieval-Philosophy Library." Since it was not mentioned in the previous cumulative quarterly report of March 15, we might assume that the fund was officially reported to the administration in the intervening period.[3] Within a year, this same fund had been renamed "Medieval Studies Foundation," and was still designated for a "Medieval-Philosophy Library." It eventually was ascribed to "miscellaneous donors" in the financial reports, a phrase which might simply mean that the donor(s) wished to remain anonymous. William J. Corbett, a Chicago businessman with an interest in the Middle Ages, was a trustee of the University from 1941 until his death in May 1948; he and his wife Laura continued their generous benefactions to the University and in particular to the program of medieval studies, as acknowledged by the Reverend Philip Moore,

C.S.C., in the Memorial Booklet printed at Notre Dame at the time of Mrs. Corbett's death in 1961.[4]

In 1933, a program of research, publication and instruction in medieval studies was initiated by Father Moore, just recently graduated from the École des Chartes, and "in the fall of 1933, the University of Notre Dame offered for the first time graduate courses in medieval studies. This new academic venture was undertaken with the assistance of M. Étienne Gilson, professor at the College de France and member of the faculty of philosophy of the Sorbonne, who was an annual visitor at Notre Dame since 1931."[5] A total of eight such graduate courses were offered in 1934–35, including two courses in English by James H. McDonald, C.S.C., who had just finished his Oxford dissertation.

The library's 1933–34 Annual Report mentions that since three courses in medieval English were planned for the fall, "it will be necessary to make some rather extensive purchases in this field as the library is not well equipped" (p.12). Indeed the list of full sets of basic reference materials—or at least as much as was published at the time—that were acquired that year is quite remarkable and included: *Patrologia Latina* (now complete), *Recueil des Historiens des Gaules et de la France*, *Monumenta Germaniae Historica*, *Gallia Christiana*, *Gallia Christiana Novissima*, *Études de Philosophie médiévale*, *Archives d'Histoire doctrinale et littéraire du Moyen Age*, *Bibliothèque Thomiste*, and Manitius' *Geschichte der lateinischen Literatur*.

On October 4, 1934, when the Reverend John O'Hara, C.S.C., President of the University of Notre Dame, composed a list of "Certain Needs of the University of Notre Dame" for "the consideration of the officers and trustees of the Carnegie Corporation of New York," the Great Depression had been devastating the country for some years. Yet he affirmed that "in these times of distress, the University of Notre Dame has not curtailed its budget in any important particular." Indeed, it appears that the University had stood by its commitment to medieval studies, since he reported (speaking somewhat loosely) that the University had just "inaugurated the first Institute of Medieval Studies in the United States." After listing the qualifications of the five scholars associated with this program, three of whom were members of the Congregation of the Holy Cross (C.S.C.) who had recently been granted the doctorate, he went on: "At its own cost, the University is preparing six priests for professorships in this Institute: one at St.

213

Michael's College [in Toronto], one at Oxford and Louvain, and four at Notre Dame."[6] It is fully consistent with this goal that the director of the Notre Dame Library reported that despite the shortage of funds during 1934–35, "we have been able to add some really valuable research materials during the year," namely, the following full sets: *Mansi, Thesaurus Linguae Latinae,* Alexander of Hales' *Summa,* and St. Bonaventure's *Opera.* The trend continued in 1936–37, with some very substantial additions (including all back-issues, as usual): the complete *Rolls Series, Bibliothèque de l'École des Chartes,* sets of catalogs of the British Museum and the Bibliothèque Nationale. The following year the library budget mentions for the first time a specific— and substantial—fund for the acquisition of reference materials, a number of them of immediate relevance to medieval studies. These new acquisitions included: *Dictionnaire de Théologie Catholique, Dictionnaire d'Histoire et de Géographie Ecclésiastiques, Dictionnaire de Droit Canonique, Publications* of the Early English Text Society and of the Société de l'Histoire de France, *Fontes rerum austriacarum,* and an outstanding list of new journal subscriptions (often with back-issues). In addition to the growing number of regular paid subscriptions, the annual report of the Periodicals Department for 1938–39 records that the Department of Medieval Studies held four periodical subscriptions received in exchange for Notre Dame publications sent to other institutions. During the following few years these exchanges dwindled at times to one title only, due no doubt to difficulties in obtaining materials from Europe, the home of most medieval scholarship. Wartime conditions also affected other types of acquisitions, and in fact, no substantial additions are recorded for the Institute during World War II.

The Corbett endowment extended the financial resources available for collection building. Most materials obtained through this fund were intended for the use of the Department of Medieval Studies and were shelved with the general collection. Some, however, were kept in the Treasure Room, a rare book collection which contained a total of 990 volumes in 1938.[7] Use of the fund appears to have been somewhat erratic, with nothing spent some years, and overspending in others.[8] Byrne commented in his annual report for 1943–44, that "important graduate material" was obtained through the generosity of the Reverend Moore, who "allowed a number of French works dealing with medieval drama and poetry to be charged against the Corbett Fund," so we can assume that Moore, who became dean of the Graduate School in 1944, controlled that fund. To this day, the Corbett Fund remains a very important book-buying endowment for the Medieval Institute, supplemented in recent years by the generous Margaret Conway Fund.

In 1944–45, the following major acquisitions are recorded for the Medieval Department: a complete set of the publications of the Camden Society (which was seen to be useful also to the history and classics departments), a complete set (less two volumes) of the *Publications* of the British Society of Franciscan Studies, and "a nice run" of the yearbooks of the Aristotelian Society. It is clear that the pattern of substantial buying had resumed.

The Medieval Institute

Fall 1946 brought large numbers of students back to the campus, students who were older than usual, taking advantage of their veterans' benefits. With Father Moore as dean of the Graduate School, the Department of Medieval Studies was formally constituted as a "Medieval Institute," much to the dismay of Byrne, who had for several years been requesting more space in the library building: in his 1945–46 Annual Report, he wryly noted that a Medieval Institute was to be established in September 1946, and its "headquarters are announced for the library. This will probably mean that more space will be withdrawn from library use." The Reverend Gerald B. Phelan, former president of the Pontifical Institute of Medieval Studies in Toronto, was appointed director of the Institute, a position he filled until 1952.

A memorandum outlining plans for the Medieval Institute mentions "that a fitting locale is to be provided, for the present, on the second floor of the University Library Building"[9] and indeed Room 202 was originally assigned for this purpose. However, the peculiar layout of the building (now the Architecture Building), which involved at that time five different levels, meant that Room 202 was generally viewed as being on the fifth floor! As Professor Astrik L. Gabriel, director of the Institute from 1952 until 1975, put it in a recent conversation: "Never mind the room numbers, it was all on the fifth floor!" However one counts, the Medieval Institute was on the top floor, in the southwest corner of the building, and terribly hot in summer. Professor Gabriel mentions a particularly scorching evening when he and Leslie S. Domonkos (then his student assistant) were so hot working in the Medieval Institute that they stripped to their underwear, and he recalls with glee the consternation of the nun who had to seek their help after being locked in the building at closing time.

From the library's point of view, the simultaneous creation of the Institute and the renewed access to European materials meant a great deal of additional work. During the year 1945–46, the four periodical exchanges mentioned earlier seem to have been reactivated and while "efforts to secure complete files of German magazines for the use of the Medieval Institute have not been too successful yet,"[10] "the periodical files are bulging because of the many new subscriptions which have been placed for the Medieval Institute."[11] Medievalists were also active in the library-at-large: Father Beichner, C.S.C., a specialist in medieval English literature, was the arts and letters representative on the Library Committee which was reactivated in 1946–47. Moreover, faculty members associated with medieval studies were regularly recorded as donors to the library, and for some of them at least this remained a pattern, publicly acknowledged in the case of Gabriel by conferral upon him in 1984 of the University Libraries' first Honored Life Patron Award.

When the Medieval Institute was created in 1946, an annual allocation was specifically set up for building its research collection. Funding for acquisitions was deemed to be fully satisfactory throughout the 1950s. Financial difficulties in purchasing desired materials began to be noted in the 1960s, leading eventually to gradual modest increases in funding, followed by substantial increases in the late 1980s.

The University Library's annual report for 1948–49 recorded as follows the arrival of the first librarian for the Medieval Institute collection:

In February, Miss Eva Jung arrived from Rome, Italy. She was assigned to the Medieval Institute Library. She checks and collates bibliographies and prepares the purchase orders for books for the Institute. This has lessened considerably the research carried on heretofore by the Acquisitions Department. Because of the growth of the collection, Room 202 has been completely reorganized and part of the books have been moved into Room 203.

In fact, 383 new monograph volumes were added to the collection that year, representing 198 new titles. There was also an increase of at least 71 bound volumes of periodicals. Another 200 volumes of periodicals were added the following year, as well as 953 monograph volumes. The collection was growing rapidly, creating backlogs in the processing section of the University Library. In July 1950, Miss Helen Cheadle, a cataloger, was transferred to the Medieval Institute to take the place of Miss Jung. The following May, she began cataloging all books received for that collection, which improved the cataloging situation considerably (over 1,000 volumes were added that year).

In 1950, the University administration requested the American Library Association to make a survey of the University Library to determine its effectiveness and to make recommendations for change. The survey was conducted by Louis Wilson, dean emeritus of the Library School at the University of Chicago, and Frank Lundy, director of libraries at the University of Nebraska. Wilson and Lundy's recommendation pertaining to the Medieval Institute Library led to a temporary reversal of the policy of special treatment which had benefitted both the library and the Medieval Institute collection:

> The Medieval Institute Library is located on an upper floor corner of the central library building. It is supervised by a full-time professionally trained librarian. In effect this library is a separate branch library, housed in the central library building. The librarian in charge gives reference assistance to [patrons] and devotes a substantial amount of time to cataloging and indexing the collection. It is the opinion of the surveyors that the limited size of the Institute Library and the relatively small number of individuals served do not justify the assignment of a full-time librarian whose services could be used to much greater advantage in the general reading rooms in the humanities and social sciences downstairs. The Medieval Institute Library could be adequately supervised by suitable student or clerical assistants. The surveyors recommend that the Medieval Institute Library be managed as an enlarged seminar library (which functionally speaking, it really is) and that its Librarian be reassigned to services in the central Library.[12]

Victor A. Schaefer, who became director of the Notre Dame Library in 1953, followed this recommendation and assigned a non-professional to the Medieval Institute Library.[13] However, the previous practice was restored on September 1, 1955, when Dr. Francis D. Lazenby, also of the Classics Department, was appointed as "Graduate-Research Librarian, Medieval Institute Librarian and Curator of the Treasure Room." According to Gabriel this was the first time the Medieval Institute had a librarian with the specialized scholarly qualifications necessary to the job.

In 1954–55, in the wake of the Wilson-Lundy study, there came an evaluation of the quality of the collections in the Notre Dame Library. In particular the adequacy of the medieval holdings had been checked against the bibliography in Bulletin no.16 of *Progress of Medieval and Renaissance Studies in the U.S. and Canada* as part of the Wilson-Lundy study and were re-checked in 1954–55 by the Reference Department: "Of 45 sets of major publications in the field of Medieval and Renaissance Studies in the U.S. and Canada held by 61 American libraries, the Notre Dame library held 23 and one half. It was outranked by 22 other institutions. The results of re-checking: we now have 27 out of the 45, or 60 percent."[14] Clearly, while the medieval collection had come a long way and was fairly well provided with standard basic source materials, the director and the librarian of the Institute had their work cut out to build it into a top-rate collection.

From the mid-1950s on, the yearly lists of important acquisitions for the library included an impressive array of early printed books and substantial source materials for medieval research. The Medieval Institute was extremely well-financed at that time, with a regular purchasing budget that was larger than those of physics, biology and mathematics combined. It was the third largest acquisitions budget, reflecting the importance attached to this new endeavor by the University administration: the general fund was only about five times larger, and the law budget not quite three times larger. Toward the end of the 1950s, it is clear that the sciences were catching up and even overtaking the Medieval Institute budget, but with the strong U.S. currency, acquisitions in medieval studies remained generally satisfactory; rare printed books and even an occasional manuscript were regularly bought for the collection and for the Treasure Room.

The first annual report from the Medieval Institute Library was written in 1956. It is clear from perusal of Lazenby's annual reports that thanks to his understanding of the needs of students and scholars alike, he set the pattern for the activities which were to become expected as a matter of course from all librarians associated with the Medieval Institute. He studied new and antiquarian catalogs with a view to making recommendations for purchase (in consultation with the Medieval Institute director), typing the order requests and, if necessary, checking that they were correctly processed and cataloged before displaying the new acquisitions for browsing. Not only books, but numerous photographic reproductions and microfilms were regularly acquired for the Institute. Journals and monographic series were checked for lacunae, and items were sent to be bound as necessary.[15]

Lazenby believed strongly in instructing students on effective use of the library, and provided specialized reference services involving numerous languages:

> I have given much time and service to users of the Medieval Institute Library with research problems, bibliographies, and above all, translation of Greek, Latin, French, German, and Italian texts and reference materials... One of my major services to undergraduate users has been assistance in selection of pertinent source and ancillary material for use in writing term papers and theses.[16]

He also dealt extensively with requests for information or materials from scholars at other institutions.

In addition to his own scholarly research, lectures and publications, he developed the public relations component of the job: tours to visitors of all types, exhibits throughout the library of materials dealing with aspects of the Middle Ages, seizing the occasional opportunity for visibility through various news media.

During the summer of 1956, Lazenby supervised a major reorganization of the medieval collection. While the original plan to create a "Medieval Library" on the fifth floor by pulling together all the books in the general library stacks dealing with the Middle Ages had to be abandoned for lack of space,[17] a workable alternative was devised which is remarkably similar in concept to the present organization of the collection. Three rooms and a stack area were devoted to the Institute and its collection. The main reading room housed approximately 2,110 volumes, chiefly of a non-circulating reference nature. Another room contained 1,141 volumes of catalogs, early French texts, miniatures, and paleography, and was also used as a classroom. The third room, with 953 volumes, mainly constituting the History of the

Universities collection but soon to include the Stokes Collection,[18] also housed the microfilms, photostats and the new Kodagraph,[19] and was the office of the director of the Medieval Institute. Finally, 5,293 volumes were shelved in the stack area.[20] Thus, in the mid-1950s the Medieval Institute collection contained some 9,500 volumes. Since then some 60,000 volumes have been added. These figures give some sense of the phenomenal expansion in the last 40 years of the "Jewel of the Notre Dame Library system."[21] Another measure of this growth is the increase in the number of yearly acquisitions from 345 volumes a year[22] to well over 2,000 volumes at the time of this writing.

In 1958–59, there was an unexplained cut of about a fifth of the Medieval Institute acquisitions budget, and a distinction was made between the book fund and the periodical fund. The moneys were apparently restored to the Medieval Institute's "earmarked fund" in 1959–60, although in his annual report for that year, John J. Philippsen, head of the Acquisitions Department, complained of the library's general financial struggle to fulfill its role. The following year saw not only a modest increase in the Medieval Institute's acquisitions funding, but a marked increase in expenditure in all the branches of the sciences, whose funds would soon outstrip the Medieval Institute and leave it trailing far behind. By the mid-1960s, the Medieval Institute was overspending its allocated funds and Bogdan Deresiewicz—the Medieval Institute librarian after Lazenby became assistant director for the Humanities Department—mentioned several times that the Corbett Fund had fortunately come to the rescue in making important orders possible. It is noteworthy that even through this difficult period there was a steady increase in subscriptions to periodicals for the Medieval Institute, which was consciously building up its strength.

In particular, an outstanding collection on the history of universities in the Middle Ages was developed at Notre Dame. In this connection, Gabriel still speaks with admiration of Lazenby's monumental achievement in securing every single item listed in the bibliography of the survey article by Sven Stelling-Michaud, "L'histoire des universités au moyen âge et à la renaissance au cours des vingt-cinq dernières années."[23] Over the years, more than 2,000 microfilms of original documents and out-of-print books, as well as files of photographs and other related materials were added to this important specialized collection which, in 1983, was aptly named the Astrik L. Gabriel Universities Collection.

The other outstanding addition to the Medieval Institute Library during Gabriel's directorship was what is commonly known as the Ambrosiana Collection—more correctly, the Frank M. Folsom Microfilm and Photographic Collection. This is the extensive collection of microfilms of the medieval and Renaissance manuscripts in the Biblioteca Ambrosiana in Milan and in the Monza Archives. The project of microfilming this collection was conceived in 1960, when Giovanni Battista Cardinal Montini (later Pope Paul VI) came to the University to receive an honorary doctorate. Microfilming began in 1962 with support from the National Science Foundation, and under the direction of Gabriel and Monsignor Angelo Paredi, Prefect of the Ambrosiana. Over the next decade, "the Institute acquired both negative and positive 35mm microfilms of over 10,000 manuscripts."[24] When, in August 1963, the Medieval Institute moved into its "not only adequate but luxurious"[25] quarters on the seventh floor of the new Memorial Library, a special room adjacent to the Reading Room was provided for housing this precious collection of microfilms as well as the books and equipment which would facilitate research in that collection. In the early part of 1966, these quarters were extended to the east in order to accommodate the "slides and photographs of the most valuable paintings, drawings and miniatures from the collection of the Biblioteca Ambrosiana" obtained thanks to a grant from the Samuel H. Kress Foundation.[26]

In June 1967, the Reverend James W. Simonson, C.S.C., was director of libraries and Gail Marti was acting librarian of the Medieval Institute. Her successor after February 1, 1968 (whose name I could not determine) reports on a healthy flow of acquisitions of books (800) and microfilms associated with the history of universities (400), as well as the new red carpet in the reading room. By June 1969, there were over 20,000 volumes in the collection. In May 1973, the Medieval Institute Library assistant, Linda L. Genda, submitted a very detailed account of her duties to Dr. George Sereiko, assistant director for public services. It is clear that she was involved in the processing of the photographs and slides from the Ambrosiana Project as they reached the Institute, that the available book shelves were no longer sufficient, and also that she was kept very busy and felt cut off from the rest of the library.[27]

In his annual report for 1971–72 (pp. 15–16), David Sparks, the director of libraries, mentioned:

...the purchase of the private library of Canon Eugene Jarry, Professor of Medieval Studies at the Institut Catholique in Paris. Through the good offices of Professor Pierre [sic] Laporte and the energetic efforts of Dr. Astrik Gabriel, the Director of the Medieval Institute at Notre Dame, this collection of more than 13,000 volumes of French monographs, journals and pamphlets was acquired at the modest price of $10,500.00 exclusive of shipping and insurance charges. The work of unpacking and processing this collection is now proceeding and will continue for another twelve months or more.

This was felt to be a particularly good buy in view of rising book prices and the low value of the dollar. Of course there were duplicates, which were eventually sold, but the Medieval Institute benefitted greatly from this purchase.

Carl Berkhout, a young medievalist working on his doctoral dissertation (which he completed in the English Department in 1975), was put in charge of the Medieval Institute Library in the Fall of 1973, and immediately responded to the obvious need for specialized reference service.[28] He also perceived the urgent need for an inventory of the collection, which he carried out with the help of student assistants and the Cataloging Department, tidying up many problems along the way[29] and revamping the circulation system which was inadequate to handle the increasing use of the collection. Medieval Institute books would now be charged out at the libraries' main circulation desk. In 1974, Berkhout recorded "116 regularly received non-monographic serial titles";[30] there are now over 300 such titles, reflecting the explosion in serial publications in recent years. He also advocated rationalization both within the existing library collections (mostly by transferring to the Institute materials in the general collection which he felt were logically related to the current holdings) and by coordinating acquisitions with other departments—a need all the more imperative since "it has become painfully clear that we cannot possibly keep up with even half of what is being published each year in medieval studies."[31]

Early in 1975, the year in which Gabriel retired as director and the Ambrosiana Collection was formally separated from the Institute, an interesting new group of microfilms began to arrive in the Institute

Library, the product of earlier arrangements by Gabriel to reproduce medieval and Renaissance manuscripts in several Yugoslavian libraries.[32] The current civil war in that area, and the ensuing destruction, may well make these microfilms a particularly valuable asset of the Notre Dame Libraries.

New Directions

Only two of the Medieval Institute's three graduate students were in residence during 1974–75,[33] but activity increased substantially when Jeffrey Russell became director of the Institute. Open carrels were installed at the south end of the reading room, where students now tended to stay and study. A statue of Dante (with a broken shoe, unfortunately) was "rescued from his wretchedness on the fourth floor and provided a happier home in the reading room,"[34] where it has remained ever since. The collection was estimated at 40,000 volumes in 1976, and for a while, despite the shortage of funds, it benefitted from the excellent collaboration between the new director and the librarian in planning acquisitions for the Institute. An undergraduate sequence of courses in medieval studies was inaugurated in fall 1976, and while it did not really take off for about ten years, this addition to the Institute programs eventually affected the Medieval Institute Library. As predicted,[35] it produced a sharp increase in the reference service required, although it was not yet realized at the early stages that it would also impact upon the selection of materials for the Institute; for example, large numbers of translations of primary sources were first acquired in the 1980s. The brief period of expansion came to an end with Russell's departure in August 1977, and for a whole year, Berkhout (who had recently acquired faculty status within the library structure) found his duties expanded in matters related to the operation of the Medieval Institute when he became deputy to Acting Director Robert Burns, associate dean of the College of Arts and Letters.

That year also saw the beginning of two major changes affecting the collection:

The year's most notable development was the purchase of the Milton V. Anastos Library in Los Angeles. Apart from the Harvard/Dumbarton Oaks Collection, the Anastos Library is unquestionably the richest Byzantine collection in the United States, currently amounting to over 30,000 volumes...Its accession during the next decade or so will add a wholly new dimension to our medieval strengths at Notre Dame.[36]

This collection has not yet come to Notre Dame, although there is close cooperation with Mr. Anastos who is still enriching it, and the records of newly acquired materials are entered into Notre Dame's online public catalog.

The other major achievement was the successful application for a large grant from the Mellon Foundation to begin cataloging the western manuscripts in the Ambrosiana Collection. There were additional funds from the National Endowment for the Humanities and in the 1980s, the Samuel S. Kress Foundation was supporting the cataloging of the Renaissance drawings in the Ambrosiana Collection. These projects brought new staff to the Medieval Institute, with new demands on the collection and the physical layout of the Institute. There were already many resource materials associated with the Ambrosiana, but such acquisitions were drastically boosted to support both cataloging projects. Thus the collection has become very strong in materials dealing with developments in northern Italy in the Middle Ages and the Renaissance, and with Renaissance drawings in general. In 1982–83, Louis Jordan was coordinating both projects for the Ambrosiana materials and together with Robert Coleman, now a member of the Art Department, he organized a travelling exhibit of master drawings from the Ambrosiana in Milan.[37] Three volumes of the catalog of western manuscripts have appeared to date, and there is a substantial computerized database of information available for the Renaissance drawings.

The year 1978–79 saw many changes for the Medieval Institute. Robert C. Miller was the new director of libraries, Ralph M. McInerny the new director of the Institute and George Sereiko, assistant director for public services, became acting librarian for the Institute in March 1979. The position of professional librarian within the Institute was put on hold until its new organization could be clarified, although David Sparks, the former director of libraries, did serve as librarian for a brief period.

The report of the director for public services for 1979–80 records the following structural changes:

The Library Administration entered into a new relationship with the Medieval Institute with regard to providing for its needs for library services and materials. During the past year, the Library gradually turned over to a member of the Institute's staff [Dr. Christine Eder] the primary responsibility for collection building and the provision of information to its unique clientele. The Library retained for itself the responsibility to acquire and to process library materials for the use of the Institute and the ownership of all materials purchased with funds assigned to the Library.

This was an unusual set-up, presumably prompted by particular circumstances, and it ended when Dr. Louis Jordan, who had been associated closely with the Ambrosiana Collection when he was a graduate student in the Institute, assumed the duties of institute librarian in the Fall of 1980.

Jordan promptly set out to repair the damage created by several years of confusion, in particular to reinstate a number of vital journal and monograph subscriptions which had been inadvertently canceled in the early 1970s, including the Leonine edition of the works of Thomas Aquinas and the *Monumenta Germaniae Historica* set.[38] The Institute received a major transfer of materials, from the general collection, associated with medieval philosophy and theology, involving some 4,000 volumes, a shift which was not completed until October 31, 1986.[39]

The preservation of Medieval Institute materials became a matter of concern. Worrisome "brown spots" on some of the negative microfilms prompted careful chemical investigation which led in turn to the meticulous cleaning of the film, which was then stored in protective, acid-free boxes. (In 1985, the negative films of the Ambrosiana Collection were finally brought down to the more stable climatic conditions of the Rare Book Room.) The Ambrosiana photographic materials were similarly provided with protective sleeves in 1981–82. There was a conscious effort to have the damaged spines and covers of books replaced or repaired, especially for important reference materials, such as the *Acta Sanctorum*. Custom-made acid-free boxes were provided for the large folders of paleography materials and other valuable damaged items which could not safely be repaired. Wider shelves were installed to better support the large quantities of oversize books in several areas of the stacks. By this date, the Medieval Institute

Library included the Maritain Center collection, and these materials also needed archival protection.[40] In 1991, recognizing the importance internationally of the Medieval Institute collection as a resource for research, the National Endowment for the Humanities awarded the University Libraries a three-year grant of more than $629,000 to begin preserving the content of embrittled scholarly volumes in that collection by microfilming those printed before 1950.

The collections continued to expand in a variety of ways. A concerted effort was made to contact hundreds of European publishers in order to secure their relevant catalogs thus facilitating and improving book selection. In 1982, a project to trade duplicates with the library of the Universita Cattolica del Sacro Cuore, Milan, was initiated by Professor Billanovich of that university. This proved to be a worthwhile enterprise, securing for the Institute several hundred out-of-print volumes by European publishers.

In the fall of 1983, "the library's collections were further enriched by the generosity of Dr. Astrik L. Gabriel who donated a collection on medieval universities which consists of microfilms of manuscripts, his notes and papers on the subject, photographs, and plaster impressions of medieval seals. The librarian compiled a 20-page bibliography which was added to the dedicatory pamphlet that marked the occasion of the receipt of this gift."[41] This bibliography was in fact a listing of the microfilms in the Medieval Universities collection, thus providing this useful information in readily available format.[42]

Approval plans set up in the 1980s by the Collection Development Division of the University Libraries, in particular the Harrasowitz Plan for books published in Germany, have regularly provided materials for the Medieval Institute collection. The collections have also benefitted from a change in the handling of income from restricted endowments instituted by Collection Development. The goal of this action was to "[utilize] these endowments to acquire retrospective and expensive materials in the subjects that are beyond the capacity of the current allocation."[43] Thus, Jordan, the Medieval Institute bibliographer, was made responsible for the Corbett fund, as well as the Conway endowment when it was received some years later. In recent years, the faculty of the Medieval Institute, however, has been very active in planning the use of these financial resources.

During the 1980s, several conferences and summer institutes held at Notre Dame made the Institute even better known in the wider scholarly community, so that the number of visitors increased steadily, some scholars even electing to spend extended periods here in order to avail themselves of the superior library resources.

The summer of 1985 saw a new director in the Institute, John Van Engen, of the History Department. He soon instituted a special Medieval Institute Library Committee to promote greater faculty interest in the well-being of this important research collection.

The latter part of the 1980s witnessed the wholesale introduction of technology into the Medieval Institute Library. Microfilm and microfiche readers had long been familiar equipment, and the Ambrosiana cataloging projects made effective use of personal computers at a very early stage in their development, but this was different: all patrons were affected when public access to the libraries' UNLOC system was made available on August 24, 1987. For the Medieval Institute this was soon followed by another remarkable development in technology: the capability for full-text searching on CD-ROM using the IBYCUS system, which gave ready access to the *Thesaurus Linguae Graecae*, i.e., to the texts written by most Greek authors into the medieval period (another CD-ROM searchable by this system contains classical Latin texts and the Vulgate version of the Bible). During the winter 1992–93, this was supplemented by the installation of new equipment to allow the searching of the database of the *Cetedoc Library of Christian Latin Texts*, soon to be followed no doubt by many such specialized aids to scholarship.

Thus, through the support of generous donors and the hard work of the staff throughout the libraries, the Medieval Institute collection continues to grow in both its traditional and new formats. Better ways to serve the faculty and students at Notre Dame and the wider community of medieval scholars are constantly being sought. The sum total of the diverse efforts of the librarians and scholars directly associated with the Institute has yielded an outstanding and well-maintained collection which is admired and envied by its many visitors.

---

1. *Notre Dame Alumnus* 11 (Dec. 1932): 76.

2. And the grandfather of William J. Corbett, III, currently the University pilot at Notre Dame.

3. Notre Dame Financial, Budget, Cost & Statistical Reports, Quarterly Report of March 15, 1934 and Annual Report of June 15, 1934, URPT, UNDA. I wish to thank the staff of the Archives of the University of Notre Dame, especially Peter Lysy, for invaluable expert assistance in researching the origins of the Institute.

4. "William J. Corbett Jr.," folder, UDEV (development), UNDA.

5. "Syllabus of Graduate Courses in Medieval Studies offered by the University of Notre Dame," 1934–35, PNDP 40-ME-01, UNDA.

6. "Certain Needs of the UND...Recommended to the Carnegie Corp.," Oct. 4, 1934, UPOH, 67, UNDA.

7. AR, 1937–38, 5.

8. UPHO, 87/18, UNDA.

9. "Memorandum on a Medieval Institute," 3, UODL, 24/47, UNDA.

10. AR, 1945–46, 4.

11. Ibid., 3.

12. Wilson/Lundy, 108.

13. Brother John Federowicz, C.S.C., "Forces Affecting the Deveopment of Libraries at the University of Notre Dame, 1843–1968" (Master's thesis, Kent State University, 1968), 116.

14. AR, Reference Department, 6.

15. Lazenby also had to supervise the proper shelving of books and, when necessary, he searched high and low for apparently missing items. Such a "missing" item was even once found in the "Grill," that is, the locked cage in which books on the *Index of Forbidden Books* were safely preserved from inquiring minds (until Vatican II rendered the concept obsolete).

16. AR, Medieval Institute, 1955–56, 1–2.

17. Ibid., 7.

18. Recently acquired from Yale University.

19. A gift of the Grace Fund: AR, Medieval Institute, 1955–56, 6.

20. Ibid., 7–8.

21. As the Medieval Institute collection is called on page 4 of the pamphlet, published in 1990, describing the Medieval Institute.

22. AR, Medieval Institute, 1956–57, 9.

23. Published in *Rapports I: Méthodologie, Histoire des universités, Histoire des prix avant 1750*, XIe Congrès International des Sciences Historiques, Stockholm, 21–29 août 1960 (Uppsala: Almqvist & Wiksell, 1960), 97–143; see AR, Medieval Institute, 1960–61, 1–2.

24. Louis Jordan and Susan Wool, eds., *Inventory of Western Manuscripts in the Biblioteca Ambrosiana. Part one: A-B Superior* (Notre Dame, Ind., University of Notre Dame Press, 1984), xi.

25. AR, Medieval Institute, 1963–64, 4.

26. AR, Medieval Institute, 1965–66, 3; see the floor plan of the seventh floor in the 1970 *Guide to the University of Notre Dame Libraries*, which shows also the sequence of four offices right next to the reading room, as well as what was called the Medieval Institute Annex, i.e., the open stacks where circulating books were shelved. The second office from the north, facing the main entrance to the reading room, was and still is for the librarian.

27. AR, Medieval Institute, 1972–73, 4, 9, 10.

28. AR, Medieval Institute, 1973–74, 3.

29. Ibid., 5–7.

30. AR, Medieval Institute, 1973–74, 8.

31. AR, Medieval Institute, 1974–75, 4.

32. Ibid., 5–6.

33. Ibid., 2.

34. AR, Medieval Institute, 1975–76, 2–3.

35. Ibid., 5–6.

36. AR, Medieval Institute, 1977–78, 6–7.

37. AR, Medieval Institute, 1982–83, 3.

38. AR, Medieval Institute, 1980–81, 1.

39. Ibid., 2, and the appendix on the *Medieval Institute Project Statistics*, to AR, Circulation/Stacks Services Department, 86–87.

40. AR, Medieval Institute, 1981–82, 4–5.

41. AR, Special Services and Collections Division, 1983–84, 9.

42. Astrik L. Gabriel, *History of Universities Collection* (Medieval Institute, University of Notre Dame, 1983). Pamphlet.

43. AR, Collection Development Division, 1983–84, 4–5.

The Reverend Edmund P. Joyce, C.S.C., Sports Research Collection

ROBERT C. MILLER

Origins and Early Collecting

While university special collections commonly reflect the influence of individual faculty members, the Edmund P. Joyce, C.S.C., Sports Research Collection at the University of Notre Dame is distinctive in that its origins were totally separate from the curricular and research interests of faculty at the University. Over the years, only a few courses dealing specifically with sports matters have been offered, and few faculty or graduate students have done research in sports-related areas. The collection's support of these courses and researchers has been largely unplanned. In fact, the collection was established and developed because of the interest and influence of a few individuals with no academic credentials or experience, and in some cases with no formal affiliation with the University. Thus, although it is formally a "library" collection, its development has been strongly influenced by forces outside the library. Until recently, with one notable exception, it was built largely through gifts and had no regular funding base. In its early history, it tended to have an independent existence within the library, lacking both administrative direction and control. Thus, collections were acquired and services offered outside normal library channels. In addition, for many years there was strong interest in

230

including much that is more commonly found in museums than in libraries or archives; for example, uniforms and sports equipment.

The concept of a sports collection at Notre Dame was first formally proposed in the mid-1960s by the director of the library, Victor Schaefer, at the urging of the Library Advisory Council, an external group of business and professional people appointed by the President. Upon approval by the vice president of academic affairs, the Rev. Philip S. Moore, C.S.C., a "Central Committee" chaired by Francis Wallace of the Library Advisory Council was established, with D.C. "Chet" Grant as secretary. Grant, a 1922 Notre Dame graduate and football player under Knute Rockne, later served as an assistant coach and was an enthusiast of Notre Dame, football, and sports throughout his life.

Planning proceeded for the newly established International Sports and Games Research Collection and an office was provided for its secretary in the library's administrative offices. Shortly thereafter, Schaefer resigned as library director and, in June 1966, began a leave of absence. He returned to Notre Dame in the fall of 1968 to assume the newly created position of director of special collections. At that point the office for the sports collection was moved out of the administrative offices to the Department of Special Collections.

The program was publicly announced in a brochure issued in March 1968.[1] The scope of the new collection was extremely broad: "Memorabilia of Sports and Games, amateur and professional, athletic and non-athletic, going back at least to the early Olympics..." and would include "Books, manuscripts, letters, notes, magazine articles, news stories, photographs, drawings, records, tapes, microtexts, programs, brochures... ." This comprehensive concept was emphasized some ten years later by the then curator, Herb Juliano, in an address to the North American Society for Sport History in which he described the collection as "...unlimited in scope...either geographically or categorically."[2] In addition to the Central Committee, the brochure listed separate committees which had been established regionally and also committees for individual sports. The initial mailing of the brochure was accompanied by a memo from the Central Committee and included suggestions on how individuals might help in building the collection.[3] Membership in the regional committees included politicians, coaches, Religious, sports writers, journalists, attorneys, judges, businessmen and athletic administrators. Among the more prominent members were George Romney, governor of Michigan, Jerome Cavanaugh, mayor of Detroit, Irv Kupcinet, newspaper columnist, and the bishop of Steubenville, John King Mussio. In this initial stage, there were committees for at least 25 states and the District of Columbia.

In actual fact, this structure existed primarily on paper. Only the Chicago committee, chaired by Harvey Foster—a Notre Dame alumnus and executive with American Airlines—appears to have been active. Contacts were made with several major league teams in Chicago about depositing team archives at Notre Dame. Especially promising were the arrangements made with Avery Brundage, chair of the U.S. Olympic Committee, for the microfilming of his papers relating to the Committee. Frank Clark, the University's microfilmer, began work on the project in 1969. Subsequently the death of Brundage's secretary and Brundage's later personal health problems necessitated a halt to the filming in late 1970. Before the work could be resumed, Brundage had a change of heart and in 1974 turned the collection over to the University of Illinois where the materials were rearranged.[4] The negative films of Clark's efforts are available in the Joyce Collection.

By 1975, Chet Grant, the real driving force behind what he had designated the International Sports and Games Research Collection, ISGRC, was 70 and had for some time expressed a desire to step down from his active role in managing the collection. His written reports suggested an academic replacement, but this was apparently never acted upon.[5] Eventually, he encouraged the hiring of Herbert Juliano which was in fact done in the spring of 1975 by Anton Masin as head of the Department of Special Collections.

Prior to this changing of the guard, the provost, the Rev. James Burtchaell, C.S.C., initiated discussions regarding the possible purchase of the stock of a California collector and sports book dealer, Goodwin Goldfadden. In June of that year the director of libraries, David Sparks, along with the newly hired Herb Juliano and Frank Clark, spent two days in Los Angeles reviewing the collection which was housed in six separate locations, including the ADCO Sports Book Exchange. The report of the reviewers indicated that more than 500,000 pieces were involved, including 30,000 hard-cover books. They estimated that 90 percent of the latter might be usefully incorporated into the collections at Notre Dame, and that overall perhaps 25 percent of the total collection might be retained.[6] Based on this, the provost completed the negotiations and Juliano returned to Los Angeles to supervise the shipment to Notre Dame in three semi-trailer trucks. There was no space immediately available in the Memorial Library for the more than 500,000 items purchased, so space was obtained off-site at the Holy Cross Hall Annex.

It was clear even before the collection was purchased that there would be considerable duplication, both within the collection and to a lesser extent with existing library holdings. It was decided to sell the duplicates directly and individually rather than as a block to a dealer. When the collection arrived, a secretary was hired to prepare lists for distribution to prospective buyers and handle the paperwork involved. The operation continued until 1979 and after considerable discussion and negotiation, the remaining volumes were sold to a local dealer in 1983.[7]

Despite the large volume of these sales, there is no doubt that the libraries' collections were greatly enriched by the Goldfadden collection. As many as 20,000 volumes of books and journals were added to the permanent collection, along with many thousands of pieces of ephemeral printed materials, including programs, press guides, etc.

Other than the Goldfadden purchase, most of the collection's growth has depended on gifts. Among the more significant of these have been the Jack Pfiffer wrestling collection, the Jack Level golf collection, the Joe Wilman collection on bowling, the Sutton billiards collection and the Einhorn collection on boxing and wrestling. Even special capital needs have tended to be met with gift funds, as was the film cleaning equipment which was purchased in 1986 with funds from Edward "Bucky" O'Conner.

In 1980 the collection received a large gift of historic Notre Dame football film. Unfortunately, the film was silver nitrate and hence unstable, indeed dangerous to house. With special funding support from the executive vice president, Father Joyce, the film was shipped to New York, stored in special quarters and over the next two-and-a-half years converted to 16 mm. safety film which was incorporated into the collection.[8]

Administration and Later Collecting

For many years, there was no regular budgetary support for the collection, other than for the curator's position. On a number of occasions interns from other institutions and student assistants from Notre Dame's Monogram Club provided limited assistance, but there was none on a regular basis. The first regular acquisitions funding came with the establishment of the John Campbell endowment in 1977.

Throughout its history, the sports collection has tended to operate on a highly personal basis, subject to the collecting and service interests of its curators. Indeed, on a number of occasions over the years proposals were made by individuals connected with the collection to move it out of the library and establish it as a freestanding unit within the University, although this never apparently received a sympathetic hearing in administrative quarters. This independent approach created service, administrative and legal problems on a number of occasions. Until the late 1970s personnel in the department operated on the assumption that all sports material in the libraries should be located in and serviced through the unit. There was in fact no significant funding for purchases, no control on the acceptance of gifts, no coordination with the University Archives on Notre Dame–related materials, and no bibliographic control or information outside the unit as to the resources held. As early as 1979 the newly appointed director of libraries raised concerns about the collection and its operations and directions.[9] Steps were taken in the ensuing years to rationalize the sports collections and services and bring them into conformity with normal library practice, though these were frequently resisted by the curator. The first effort at a disciplined definition of the collection occurred in 1980 with the issuance of a formal collection development policy.[10] This document, initiated by the director of libraries, limited collecting to reference materials, works on the theoretical, historical, sociological and cultural aspects of sports, the Olympic Games, treatments of major U.S. sports including biographies, and sports at Notre Dame.

The divergence in philosophies on collections, services and management between the director and Juliano culminated in the latter's rather acrimonious resignation in 1982.[11] He was replaced by Jethrow Kyles. While not trained in librarianship or archives, Kyles was eager to learn and devoted considerable attention, under the direction of the new head of Special Collections, David Sparks, to a detailed analysis and description of the holdings. He also worked hard with the media, a major category of users of the collection, and with various athletic department personnel.

In the 1980s the athletic department began the regular transfer of film to the sports collection for storage and servicing. This eventually created serious space problems. Fortunately, a change in the University's phone system (housed in the basement of the library) in 1982 permitted significant expansion space for the Department of Special Collections. This area of some 1,600 square feet became the new home for the sports collection. In part because of the increased involvement with and work for the athletic department, including servicing of its film collections, the director of libraries began to regularly request special financial assistance. In response, in September of 1987 the libraries received word of the establishment of a major endowment for the Edmund P. Joyce, C.S.C., Sports Research Collection, in honor of the retiring executive vice president.[12] For the first time regular funding supported both personnel and acquisitions. Regular part-time staff assistance was obtained and the acquisitions program expanded to provide for current publications not covered by the libraries' approval program. It also enabled the libraries to take advantage of special opportunities such as the acquisition, in 1989, of a major collection on the Pete Rose trial and the filling in of gaps in the collections, especially in scholarly journals and non-athletic aspects of sports, such as baseball in literature.

A major event in the development of the sports collection occurred in 1987 with the acquisition of the personal collection of the sports journalist, Walter W. "Red" Smith. Smith, a 1927 Notre Dame graduate and recipient of an honorary doctor of laws degree in 1968, was the dean of American sports journalists and recipient of a Pulitzer Prize in 1976. Formally dedicated in March 1988 as a major University event, the collection includes clippings and drafts of his columns from the *New York Times* and other papers as well as almost 1,000 volumes of books along with photographs, audio tapes, awards and memorabilia. Its acquisition represented a major new thrust in collecting interest: sports journalism.[13]

Two persistent sources of controversy through the years have been the location within the libraries of monographic and journal literature on sports, and the relationship between the sports collection and University Archives. A survey of the collection in the late 1970s revealed many volumes of uncataloged monographs and journals that might appropriately be located in the general collection. The following years saw several largely abortive attempts to catalog this material and transfer it to the general collections, but much remains to be done.[14] The current operating philosophy calls for all but truly rare and/or ephemeral materials of research value to be located in the general collections.

The effort to rationalize the relationship between library and archives responsibilities in collecting has been going on for a number of years. In 1991, the libraries' holdings of manuscripts and archives relating to Knute Rockne were moved to the archives,[15] and in 1993 all remaining archival film and non-print materials relating to Notre Dame sports were relocated to the archives. Henceforth, the libraries' sports collection will deal only with non-Notre Dame sports, while the University Archives will collect all material and handle all enquiries related to Notre Dame.[16] Because of the changed nature of the collection that resulted from this shift, Kyles chose to resign to seek other opportunities.

At this juncture the libraries' sports collection remains very strong, with fully cataloged materials in the general collections exceeding 8,300 volumes in addition to an estimated 300,000 pieces within the Department of Special Collections. The latter group consists of programs, pamphlets, press guides, photographs (including glass negatives), clipping files, magazines, realia (including balls, bats, gloves, uniforms, etc.), personal papers, diaries, business papers and posters. Also still within Special Collections are several thousand monographs and journal runs awaiting cataloging and transfer to the general collections. While virtually all sports have coverage within the collection, especially strong holdings exist in collegiate sports, boxing and wrestling, golf, billiards, baseball and the Olympic games. Despite an early interest in sports from throughout the world and from all periods, most holdings deal with the American scene.

In light of the diversity of these holdings and the lack of a strong local academic interest in sports, the libraries have decided to seek the services of an academic consultant to advise on the strengths and weaknesses of the current collections relating to sports, and to recom-

236

mend appropriate directions for collecting in the future. This effort is designed to provide a more structured, rational and academically oriented basis to what is believed to be among the largest and finest general sports research collections in the United States.

---

1. "Announcing the Establishment of an International Sports and Games Research Collection," Memorial Library, University of Notre Dame, 1968, [5]. Brochure.

2. Herb T. Juliano, "Sports Research: the Insport Input." Paper presented at the North American Society for Sport History, University of Maryland, May 26, 1978. In Sports Collection files of Director of Libraries, Hesburgh Library, University of Notre Dame, (hereafter cited as SC/DOL).

3. D.C. Grant to Members of Collection Committee, March, 1968, SC/DOL.

4. David E. Sparks to Harvey G. Foster, March 19, 1975, SC/DOL.

5. Grant to Sparks, April 11, 1983 [sic, 1973], SC/DOL.

6. "Report on Inspection of Goodwin Goldfadden Sports Collection, Los Angeles, California, Monday, June 30, 1975," SC/DOL.

7. George E. Sereiko to William Farmer, June 22, 1983, SC/DOL.

8. Summarized in letter from Robert C. Miller to the Rev. Edmund P. Joyce, C.S.C., July 22, 1983, with attached data on the project, SC/DOL.

9. Miller to Timothy O'Meara, April 9, 1979, SC/DOL.

10. "Collection Development Policy for Sports," in "Library Policies and Procedures, (LPP80:09)," Dec. 30, 1980, ULND, Administrative Offices, Hesburgh Library.

11. "Update," *Sports Illustrated* 56 (June 28, 1982): 12.

12. "Joyce Collection Set Up," *Notre Dame Report* Issue 17 (1987): 203.

13. "The Red Smith Collection," ULND, 1988. Pamphlet.

14. See, for example, memos from Miller to Tillie O'Bryant, January 29, 1981, and from Sereiko to Miller, March 24, 1983, SC/DOL.

15. Miller to Wendy Schlereth, September 30, 1991, SC/DOL.

16. Miller to Kyles, January 10, 1993, SC/DOL.

Automation in the Libraries:
An Unfinished Story

MAUREEN GLEASON AND ROBERT J. HAVLIK

If we define automation as the application of a mechanical process to an operation, the very first automation in the Notre Dame Library may well have occurred in 1938. In that year, direct action was taken to solve a problem; namely, losses incurred due to the use of fictitious names by patrons charging out books. An electric charging machine was purchased which allowed a metal plate with an ID imprinted on it to substitute for a handwritten charge slip. It was successful; fictitious charges numbering as many as fifteen per year had been eliminated according to the annual report two years later.[1] Simple, but effective; fifty-five years later, that is still an ideal for automation in the libraries, but for a long time after the 1938 improvement, very little happened.

Preparing the Ground—1958–1968

By 1958, the strains of an expanding library in a growing University were beginning to be felt, as witness the Circulation Department statement: "When daily circulation reaches 300 a day, and stays there the present system breaks down."[2] The solution was not yet clear, but some sort of punched card system was seen as a possibility. The assistant director for technical services, Robert Ennen, by the early 1960s was touting automation as a means of handling large amounts of data, offering "greater efficiency," "reduction of errors," and "rapidity." He looked into a random filing, automatic retrieval unit marketed under the name Electrofile, but found the card stock it used too expensive. In the fall of 1963 Ennen's investigations culminated in an experimental computerization of the circulation file which produced printouts which were displayed for several weeks at the service desks.

At about the same time, Ennen traveled to inspect an automated card reproduction system at the University of Missouri,[3] and he later spoke hopefully of being able to load tapes produced by Library of Congress in the new standardized, machine-readable (MARC) format onto the mainframe computer.[4] None of these possibilities came to fruition, and one can guess the reasons. Cost is mentioned more than once. Ennen complained of the need to rely on part-time programming help from the Computer Center, and a remark from the Computer Center's liaison to the library, Norman Viss, quoted in Ennen's 1963–64 Annual Report may also be revealing as a clue to obstacles faced. Viss said: "Success in future work will not be likely unless the librarians feel that the improvements are of and for the librarians,"[5] and the Circulation Department head's failure to mention the experimental computerization in 1963–64 in his annual report may suggest the absence of such feeling.

Changes were taking place, however, which were the remote precursors of things to come. In 1964 discussions with the Office of Student Affairs and others resulted in new card imprinters using student IDs at Circulation. Cataloging card photocopying began in 1966, and was soon enhanced by the use of a Polaroid camera to transfer *National Union Catalog* records to local catalog cards. Ennen preached "a total systems approach,"[6] and initiated flow charting and a revision of the serials check-in files, moves intended as preparations for automation.

The next step forward was in a different area, when, in the spring of 1968, the computerization of the book budget was undertaken "on a modest scale," using punched cards. The system was apparently developed by the University Accounting Department to keep track of expenditures, and presumably did that adequately. However, in 1972, a new director was to lament a "disturbing failure" on the part of the library to use these fiscal tools, referring to acquisitions printouts piled in a cupboard.[7] By that time, the University Comptroller's Office was working with the library to incorporate the Acquisition Department's vendor file into an improved system using an IBM computer and key punch combination.

A Giant Step Forward with OCLC

The external library environment had begun to change by the late 1960s. Cataloging and information transmission standards that would be compatible with the use of new electronic equipment were being developed, and interlibrary networks using new communications technology for the interchange of information were forming. The first steps at the national level were taken by the Library of Congress' Information Systems Office (ISO) MARC Pilot Project. The result of this project was the publication of the MARC II (Machine-readable cataloging) format. This format set the standard for the exchange of bibliographic information both nationally and internationally.

This same period saw the formation of interlibrary cooperative networks such as the New England Library Information Network (NELINET), the Washington Library Network (WLN), and the Ohio College Library Center (OCLC). In addition to providing the mechanism for the exchange of cataloging information through the development of a database and software to access it, these networks also linked their members together through the new electronic communications technology. By 1969, the Library of Congress was distributing to selected libraries magnetic tapes containing records of currently cataloged monographs in MARC format. OCLC among others began to develop systems to make this cataloging information, plus other cataloging records contributed by its member libraries, available to cooperating libraries via long-distance telephone lines and computer terminals. Systems were also developed to print catalog cards on demand via a terminal interface.

Several state consortia were also formed during this period to promote intrastate library cooperation and the utilization of new services such as those offered by OCLC. For Notre Dame, the most significant of these was the Indiana Cooperative Library Services Authority (INCOLSA) through which OCLC services were made available to Indiana libraries. A glimpse of the motives pushing the Notre Dame Libraries in this direction can be found in the February 1974 interim statement of the Task Force for the Improvement of Technical Services.[8] It urged: "greater use of available library technology, specifically the computer and its capabilities in the area of serials, serials management, and cataloging," and by the time of the Task

Force's final report in June 1974, the assertion "Notre Dame's use of bibliographical processing techniques such as the Ohio College Library Center... is only a matter of time," could safely be made.[9] In fact, Notre Dame had become a charter member of INCOLSA in May of 1974, and had already embarked on plans to adopt OCLC as its means of cataloging.

The process by which the library planned and implemented its first major automation effort can be sketched briefly by means of a chronology:

May 1974 —Video tapes describing OCLC were shown to library faculty and staff.

March 1975—Committee visited OCLC headquarters and Ohio University to see the system in operation.

June 1975—Library asked the University for $88,200 from Endowment C to finance the project.

September 1975—University grants $39,213.

September 1975—Coordinating Committee for Machine Assisted Processes appointed, with assistant director for technical services, technical services department heads, and the personnel assistant as members.

October 1975—OCLC coordinator appointed.

October-December 1975—Training in the MARC format for books takes place.

December 1975—Notre Dame hosts a state-wide workshop on the MARC serials format.

January 1976—Two OCLC terminals installed.

April 1976—OCLC terminals used to search for bibliographic records.

July 1976—Full cataloging production on OCLC begins.[10]

Full cataloging production meant that when a record for a book Notre Dame was cataloging was found in OCLC, Notre Dame holdings could be added, and cards ordered or, alternatively, if no record was found, Notre Dame catalogers could input a record and then order cards. The card catalog with all its features was retained, but the process of creating it was automated.

The desire expressed by Assistant Director Ennen in 1967 to make use of LC tapes had now been realized, but, as is often the case with the introduction of new technology, in a manner different from what was anticipated earlier. What the library hoped to achieve by these new processes is summed up in the letter of Robert Havlik, assistant director for technical services, in his final report on the project:

> 1. reduction of the inflationary cost of acquiring, cataloging and processing books in the University Libraries [as a result of a cost study earlier, Havlik had projected a savings of $188,000 in additional costs over a three-year period];
> 2. creation of new and improved procedures seeking further savings in library operations;
> 3. provision of more accurate and prompt library information;
> 4. faster, more efficient processing of all library materials;
> 5. expansion of the resources available to the library through interlibrary cooperation.[11]

Continuing changes in circumstances make the degree to which these expectations were met hard to document. Certainly, the productivity of the Cataloging Department increased almost immediately: in 1974–75, 13,415 titles were cataloged; in 1975–76, 19,669 were cataloged, 16,716 of them on OCLC, with no increase in staff. Of course, OCLC was not free; libraries paid for the use of records, and there were telecommunications charges, although some financial assistance was available through INCOLSA. At the start, although OCLC records provided by LC were accepted, catalogers were somewhat suspicious of the quality of those submitted by other libraries. By June 1976, acceptance of such records had begun to be discussed,[12] and eventually this barrier was breached, although not without objections. And the ready availability of cataloging records on OCLC meant some internal work adjustments. More rapid verification of orders submitted created a bottleneck at the point of placing those orders, and the reconciliation of other libraries' cataloging with Notre Dame's long-established practices meant more work for the editors of the catalog. Despite the adjustments, however, few, if any, wanted to turn back, and the adoption of OCLC launched the libraries on the wave of the future.

The cooperative rationale that was the basis of OCLC was reinforced in April 1979, when interlibrary loan operations began to use the system. The effects appeared almost immediately: response and receipt time were shortened, and there was a 25 percent increase in interlibrary loan activity, one more sign that the library world was changing.[13]

242

Successes and Failures, Starts and False Starts

By the mid-1970s, proposals to automate processes were becoming more and more common. In December 1975, the libraries decided to give their bindery contract to a firm that could offer a computer preprinted binding ticket system.[14] At the time, many thought that further automation would come through OCLC, particularly serials control and acquisitions. The bibliographic and fiscal control of serials had long been a problem for the libraries. In 1973–74, a derivative magnetic tape from the Indiana Union List of Serials had been used to create a serials review list to assist in effecting cancellations and controlling future costs. Relying on OCLC to develop an acquisitions system was also being discussed, but in the meantime, the breakdown of the equipment in use in the Acquisitions Department encouraged the development of a local system, ACQUIS, in 1978. That was probably the most significant automation development in the libraries between OCLC in 1976, and the integrated system, NOTIS, in 1987.

ACQUIS was a combined effort of the assistant head of the Acquisitions Department, the libraries' systems analyst (a position that had been created in 1974 in anticipation of events to come) and Computer Center personnel. Order information was input to the IBM mainframe through Acquisition's terminals, orders were printed, encumbrances and expenditures recorded through an interface with the University's accounting system, and an in-process file was printed out which listed items from the time of order until three weeks after cards had arrived from OCLC, or six weeks after cancellation. It was a widely appreciated improvement on the paper, manually maintained, in-process file, and upgrading of its contents and functioning continued to be made until it was replaced by the NOTIS acquisitions module in 1992. However, it had a substantial drawback which doomed it as a system of the future: it was not integrated with the bibliographic database, and therefore required separate inputting and, in addition, its data were not available in the online catalog.

The library world was full of projects to ease the path toward full automation, and Notre Dame participated in some of them. "Project Circ" was to explore ways in which INCOLSA libraries might cooperate in developing specifications and plans for mini-computer-based circulation systems, including the possibility of obtaining vendor systems cooperatively through OCLC. This did not happen, and individual libraries chose their own automated systems. Ultimately, cooperative automation efforts among Indiana libraries were to take another, more circuitous route. Another cooperative effort in which the Notre Dame Libraries participated was CONDOC, a consortium to develop specifications for an online system that would meet the needs of university libraries. The hope was to encourage vendors to create such systems, and there is some evidence that it was indeed used as a guide in developing systems for libraries.

An occurrence which did not involve automation but is of interest because of its relationship to events leading up to automation of the card catalog, was Notre Dame's implementation of the second edition of the *Anglo-American Cataloging Rules* (AACR-2) on October 18, 1980. Because the rule changes pertaining to the form and choice of headings used in the bibliographic record were significant, they made integration of new cataloging into the old catalog a very difficult operation. Implementing the new version potentially implied a choice between an enormous revision and refiling operation on the one hand, or widespread confusion for catalog users on the other. A report entitled "Bibliographic Control and Access in the University of Notre Dame Libraries" by James Neal, head of the Collection Management Department, detailed the problem of large card files: difficulty and high cost of maintaining; poor editorial condition; finding qualified staff to carry out repetitive tasks; physical condition; and security. His view that "any library that does not have its bibliographic database in machine readable form by the 1990s may be inoperable," was certainly a reasonable prediction. However, the Notre Dame Libraries' database reached the desired state by an unanticipated path rather than that envisioned by Neal, who recommended that: "planning for the utilization of our OCLC archive tapes in the production of a COM [computer output microfilm] catalog to replace the card catalog should begin immediately."[15]

To that end, an AACR-2 Implementation Team was formed, and its composition represents a trend which was followed in future planning leading to an online catalog; that is, it included personnel from outside the Cataloging Department and involved public service staff. The trend had begun in 1978, when the assistant director of technical services reported that a recently appointed serials task force was "notable in that its chair and a majority of its members were from outside Technical Services."[16] The significance of this development is reinforced by the statement in Neal's report that successful catalog planning would require "blurring of traditional administrative and functional structures," and is one more way in which the discussions surrounding the AACR-2 adoption prepared the way for future automation.

In the end, there was no COM catalog, and extensive cross references in the existing catalog accommodated the rule changes. No official explanation was given, but it appears likely that by the fall of 1980 some positive financial portents made a fully automated library system seem much more imminent than was the case a year earlier.

Preparing for the Great Event

August 19, 1987 was the day on which an online public access catalog was first available to the Notre Dame community. That happy occasion was preceded by years of planning, controversy and hard work which probably began with the first "University Libraries' Five Year Development Program 1980–84," written by Director of Libraries Robert C. Miller, in 1980. Two of the goals in that plan are relevant here:

> We must develop an accurate, machine readable data base of holdings, accessible through COM and/or an online catalog.
>
> We must automate our circulation system.[17]

By the time of the 1983–88 "Five Year Development Plan," the decision for the online catalog had been made, and the director was able to add the following recommendation:

> The University Libraries need to convert to machine readable form records for all monographic and serial titles not in that form.[18]

The crucial event that allowed these goals to be realized was former trustee of the University John T. Ryan's gift in excess of $1.7 million to be used to automate the libraries, a donation which was announced in December 1982. In anticipation of this enabling act, an assistant director for automated systems/coordinator of technical services, Larry

Woods, was appointed in April 1982, and in August, an Automation Advisory Committee was appointed. Chaired by the new assistant director, it followed the by now accepted practice of including members from departments devoted to collection building, collection access, and collection use. By December 1982, the libraries had a needs assessment which laid out future directions. The integration of functions such as the public catalog, circulation, and ordering based on a single database was regarded as crucial. Improvements through remote access to the database (so that students and faculty could search the catalog from their desks), as well as greater flexibility within it (to make changes easier) were to be sought. An automated circulation system was seen as essential, as was a serials system. More effective maintenance of the database, and the production of information and statistics leading to better collection management were expected results from automation. And most important: "in order to successfully implement an integrated system we must retrospectively convert all of the libraries' holdings to machine readable form."[19] An order of priority was established: retrospective conversion, online catalog, circulation control, serials control, acquisitions, online authority control, resource sharing, and a backup system.

A "SPEC Kit" issued by the Association of Research Libraries' Office of Management Studies in January 1983 reported on a survey of automation plans of 31 member libraries, and the situation it reflected can be compared to that of Notre Dame at the time. Virtually all of the libraries were planning to automate, although such planning was in various stages. Priorities differed from those of Notre Dame with the latter ranking the online catalog and retrospective conversion more highly. Factors inhibiting automation progress were overwhelmingly financial, with most of the surveyed libraries depending on regular library budget and special appropriations from their respective universities. Only four percent of these libraries expected to receive funds from private donations, whereas such a donation made all the difference for Notre Dame.[20]

The needs assessment which established the goals of an automated system also established a timetable. The tasks identified in that timetable provide a useful overview of what had to be done to create a working system. The deadlines established for the completion of the tasks reveal the optimism that prevailed at the start, an optimism that came to be tempered by experience. Conversion of both monographic and serial records to machine readable form was to be completed by July 1987. Although the conversion of serials, done locally, even today is not quite complete, conversion of monographic records moved quickly. The libraries already had approximately 200,000 records on OCLC tapes, and contracted with Carrollton Press to convert other monographic records as part of the REMARC project. In his 1983–84 Annual Report, the assistant director for automated systems calls REMARC a "model for other libraries," completed ahead of schedule and under budget. By the end of 1983–84, the libraries had roughly 500,000 records ready to go into the system.[21]

Piece conversion (barcoding), database processing, database loading, and database correction were all to be done during 1984. Site preparation had two parts—construction of the machine room in the Hesburgh Library basement to accommodate the system's computer, and the preparation of terminal sites in the libraries and on campus. Most of this was also to be done in 1984, and in fact, the machine room was finished in spring 1984. Unfortunately, the decision was made later to mount the system on the University's mainframe, and so the facility (now the home of the original cataloging section) was never used for its intended purpose—another example of the shifts and turns which are inevitably part of automation planning.

According to the timetable, the system was to be selected by September, 1983 and the online catalog, the first step in implementation, available by July 1, 1984. Actually, the request for proposal which had been developed by the Automation Advisory Committee, was sent out in August 1983. A consultant was hired to review the responses, and the libraries' selection of the BLIS system, offered by Biblio-Techniques took place in December 1983, only a few months behind schedule. That marked the beginning of an extended period of delay that was a cause of considerable frustration within the libraries.

The contract for the system naturally had to be approved by the University administration which wanted further investigation of two matters: "the corporate strength of the company"; and "the definition of the required interfaces with existing systems on campus." Resolution of the latter required re-examination by the libraries of the VTLS system which had been rejected earlier, since it operated with the Hewlett Packard hardware preferred at the time by Administrative Computing.

This was particularly demoralizing to those involved in the choice of BLIS, and the assistant director said: "The caution shown by the [University's] Executive Committee for Computing Policy is a source of frustration, but it is understandable considering the size of the investment and our accountability to the donor."[22]

As it turned out, questioning the financial viability of Biblio-Techniques proved warranted, since the company went out of business in 1986, causing trouble for a number of university libraries which had chosen BLIS. The system itself was very attractive to university libraries desiring flexible and sophisticated capabilities. However, the company's demise, according to one who analyzed its history, took place not only because it lacked capital, but because it was "based on an innovative and promising, but complex and incomplete product."[23]

The Great Event: An Online Catalog

Notre Dame had to begin again, and by the beginning of 1986, had chosen the NOTIS system. The assistant director left to take another position, and a library systems manager, Robert Wittorf (who became assistant director for systems and administrative services in 1988), was hired. Rebuilding enthusiasm among library faculty and staff was important and led to a Library Automation Day in September 1986 and a "name the catalog" contest which produced the name UNLOC, for University of Notre Dame Libraries' Online Catalog. Following the August inauguration of UNLOC, in September 1987, keyword-Boolean searching was introduced and by December, fully 90 percent of the monographs were represented in UNLOC. By the end of the following year, bibliographic records for all currently received serials (one-quarter of them with holdings recorded) were there too. Users took to the new catalog immediately, and a survey taken at about that time shows that they wanted more—automated circulation and article indexes, for instance.[24] The card catalog was being allowed to "freeze-shrink" (with nothing added except for main entries, and misleading records removed) as of October 1987, and faculty who had not noticed earlier attempts to inform them on the progress of automation were concerned that they had no voice in such a momentous decision. Of course problems, such as difficulties in searching names of classical and early Church authors, did surface. Some faculty became increasingly skeptical; a presentation by the director to the Faculty Senate was made in an attempt to reassure them. A giant stride forward had been made, however, and movement has been continuous ever since.

The NOTIS circulation system was the next major achievement, and its coming was heralded by one of those all too rare occasions when an entire organization pulls together to accomplish a widely recognized goal. For two weeks in August 1988, after much careful planning, most of the faculty and staff worked in shifts to barcode over 600,000 volumes to make possible the implementation of the circulation system. The employees who contributed were rewarded with T-shirts, a group picture in the *South Bend Tribune*, and a lot of camaraderie. If the rejection of BLIS was the organizational pits, this was the high point. A graduate student in the Life Sciences Library charged out the first book by computer on January 25, 1989, and by July 1989 the system was up in Hesburgh Library as well.

Planning for the NOTIS acquisitions module was complicated by the need to coordinate its operation with that of the University accounting system, but difficulties were successfully overcome, and an integrated automated system became a reality in September 1992. Whether or not to implement the NOTIS serials module was still being debated in September 1993.

Consequences of Automation

A number of generalizations can be drawn from the history of library automation. One is that a persistent justification for automation efforts from OCLC onward, was its support in providing for cooperation among libraries. Another is that progress is speeded by grants and gifts to finance projects. These conditions came together in 1990 when Notre Dame received $375,000 from Lilly Endowment, Inc. to expand the State University Library Automation Network (SULAN) by including Saint Mary's College, Bethel College, and Holy Cross Junior College in the local NOTIS system, with their catalogs appearing as menu items on the UNLOC screen. The Lilly grant also financed an upgrading of the Notre Dame system, the addition of systems staff, the upgrading of local hardware, the completion of the final stage of monographic conversion, and the addition of documents (not yet achieved) and microform collection records to the database.[25] The development of

PACLINK software to provide additional links and borrowing opportunities among Indiana libraries has been fraught with technical difficulties and is still not fully operational, but the principle of using automation to further cooperation is well established.

To say that automation is accepted and welcomed is not to deny problems. When new systems or upgrades do not work as expected, or when new versions mean major adjustments, the sense of competence of the staff who depend on them is threatened. The NOTIS circulation system, particularly, was beset with difficulties that were overcome after much stress.

The demands on programmers for system maintenance have been greater than anticipated, which has necessitated establishing priorities. The lack of system-produced management reports and statistics has been disillusioning, and has led to still more calls on programmers' time to extract these from the database. In August of 1991 the NOTIS Implementation and Policy Committee (NIPCOM) was established to, as the assistant director for systems and administrative services put it, "help arbitrate the desperate calls on the programmers' time."[26] NIPCOM was also to manage the introduction to new systems, arrange for system testing, monitor authorizations, etc. The 1993 appointment of a product manager in the systems office was still another effort to respond to the demands of an increasingly automated library.

The assistant director for collections/technical services summarized one effect of nearly 20 years of automation in her 1990–91 Annual Report:

> Technical Services is more and more dependent on computers to carry out its work. The number of tasks that can be performed away from the terminal is shrinking. Perhaps job redesign is in order and jobs should be more broadly conceived.[27]

By this time an epidemic of cumulative trauma disorders was affecting the physical well-being of staff members and by June 1992, 20 percent of the staff had been referred to University Health Services for this reason. The libraries responded by purchasing more ergonomically satisfactory furniture, by arranging training workshops, and by some job redesign.

Libraries generally have seen the "other," non-salary, non-material portion of their budget gradually increase in the past few years, and no small part of this increase can be attributed to the cost of equipment. Automation cannot achieve its purposes without well-maintained and regularly replaced equipment, and Notre Dame has gradually begun to assimilate that reality, with "other operating expenditures" rising from 6.3 percent of total expenditures in 1979–80 to 9 percent in 1992–93.

Other effects of automation testify to its success, but nonetheless require unanticipated adjustments. Circulation increased by 21 percent during the first year after the automated system was installed, and this became painfully obvious when more books than ever were returned at semester's end only to be piled on floors and tables awaiting shelving by an overworked staff.[28] When in 1988–89 Acquisitions was able to provide brief records in UNLOC for those books in its gifts unit which previously could be identified only through searching a separate ACQUIS printout, the number requested by patrons increased from three or four a year to 337 during 1989–90. A wonderful service, but not a savings in staff.[29]

Not Just a System: Other Automated Operations

A February 15, 1983 "Library Administrative Announcement" heralded the arrival of the first microcomputer in the University Libraries, located in the Administrative Offices. By the end of 1985–86, there were 21 personal computers for library use, with four or five more on order. They were being employed in a variety of ways in addition to ordinary word processing—to keep track of serials requests, to keep interlibrary loan statistics, to compile a list of parish histories, to create bibliographies, to maintain address files, etc. In the spring of 1985, a task force on library use of microcomputers with a specific charge to plan training and to recommend software, was formed; by now this was a typical response to the advent of a new manifestation of automation. By the end of 1988–89, 70 microcomputers were distributed among all library units,[30] and in July 1989, the University initiated the Faculty Workstation Program, which was eventually to provide all library faculty members with their own computers. By March 1987, electronic mail had been introduced, and the following year, an electronic mail coordinator helped to spread use among library faculty and staff. At some point between then and 1993, e-mail evolved from the plaything of a few to an accepted mode of communication in the libraries.

In 1993, computers are ubiquitous in the libraries, and the use of common software packages is extensive. This use is also in most cases superficial, and discussions, course offerings, and users group meetings are revealing an unmet need for much more in-depth training before computers can truly transform the nature of the work.

Automation in Public Services

Not long after automation began to be applied to technical processes in the libraries, it made its appearance in the services and resources available to the libraries' public. During 1980–81, a computer-assisted information retrieval system, DIALOG, was introduced into reference service throughout the libraries. Librarians did the online searching of a variety of indexes, and to introduce the service, two free searches were provided, along with demonstrations, classroom lectures, and brochures.[31] A Database Committee was formed, and expansion of the service continued, with several new databases, and the training of two new searchers in 1981–82. For the next several years, the volume of searches conducted fluctuated, and there was a sense of disappointment at the relatively low level of use despite an active educational campaign. As a possible stimulus, the 1983–88 "Five Year Development Plan" recommended that all reference librarians be trained to conduct searches, and that costs be covered by the libraries. Cost was indeed a crucial factor in discouraging widespread use. For instance, the one type of search that steadily increased was the "ready reference" done without charge to the inquirer. More successful, too, was the CAS Online Academic Program in the Chemistry/Physics Library, which allowed *Chemical Abstracts* to be searched during limited hours at a substantial discount and was paid for jointly by the libraries and the Chemistry Department. Initiated in 1984, the 1985–86 Chemistry/Physics Library Annual Report describes some consequences of its success: "...patrons now alerted to the possibilities offered by automation are requesting related services such as document delivery and the crystallographic data tapes."[32]

But still another technological development hastened the decline of mediated online searching. In 1986 the Reference Department was trying *INFOTRAC*, an optical disk product that indexed journal articles. The database coordinator commented in her 1986–87 report:

> The extensive use of INFOTRAC by students and faculty pointed out 2 things to the reference department...that students and faculty are eager to do their own electronic searching and that INFOTRAC coverage of disciplines within humanities and social science is at best inadequate and at worst non-existent.[33]

By 1987–88 the consequences of this judgement were apparent in *INFOTRAC* 's disappearance from the Reference Department and its replacement by CD-ROM versions of four Wilson periodical indexes, the *Public Affairs Information Service* (*PAIS*), and *DISCLOSURE*, a business and financial statistical database. In that year, too, the *TLG (Thesaurus Linguae Graecae)*, which made ancient Greek texts available in electronic format, and required its own software and workstation, was purchased for the Medieval Institute. The *Cambridge Structural Database*, the libraries' first mainframe-mounted database, was acquired in 1986–87. *Wordcruncher*, a disk containing the full-text of classic works in many fields, was here. The libraries were subscribing, by 1987–88, to an online accounting database, *NAARS*. By the late 1980s, a wide range of disciplines and formats were represented in Notre Dame's comparatively small collection of electronic resources.

Not all of these resources were discrete products, however. In 1990–91, the Multiple Database Access Service (MDAS), from NOTIS, was added to the system, thereby providing access through UNLOC to three periodical indexes. A critical advantage of MDAS over CD-ROM indexes was its accessibility through computers outside Hesburgh Library, and this feature dictated the choice of databases mounted initially. Of the three, two, *General Science Index* and *Applied Science and Technology Index* were of particular interest to the branch libraries, which were not supplied with the CD-ROM products that were becoming more and more numerous in the Hesburgh Library—at that time, only *MATHSCI* in the Mathematics Library existed in the branches.

The means of access to materials not in the local collection was also changing in the automated environment, as illustrated by the libraries' subscription to *UNCOVER* in 1992. *UNCOVER* contains a comprehensive table-of-contents database of thousands of serials which could be

253

searched, with the option of ordering copies of articles and having them transmitted by fax (facsimile transmitting). Its local use was made possible by campus access to the Internet, an international communication system of linking networks containing an enormous store of data of all sorts. Vital, too, was the libraries' ownership of fax machines, the first of which had been acquired in 1986–87 as part of a state-wide program for improving interlibrary loan response time.

Networking, in fact, was becoming ever more familiar in the libraries. A local area network (LAN) using its own software had linked Reference Department CD-ROMs first in 1990–91. The catalogs of other libraries accessible through the Internet were being used to verify citations and to locate titles by 1991. In that same year, Community-Wide Information Service (CWIS) made information from the libraries, as well as other campus units searchable from individual computers. During 1992–93, the Hesburgh Library was linked to Notre Dame's campus backbone network as some branch libraries had been earlier, with full operation scheduled for fall of 1993.

What Has Been and What Will Be

All of these developments suggest the future direction of automation in the University Libraries, but difficulties and dilemmas remain. Complexity impedes decision making: a Committee on the Delivery of Electronic Information, appointed in 1993, is attempting to sort out the most cost-effective method of delivering high-demand resources from among a whole array of options.

The frustration felt as a result of inadequate equipment is captured in the 1988–89 Annual Report:

> The Libraries' capital budget is grossly underfunded to deal adequately with rising demand and rapidly changing technology.[34]

and in the 1990–91 Reference Department Annual Report:

> As of this writing, the Documents Center is holding nearly 90 disks which cannot be played due to inadequate equipment.[35]

Financing this changing technology and the proliferating resources it produces in all formats is a continual challenge for the libraries.

Initially, in order to encourage movement into new collecting areas, a separate line for electronic media was provided in the acquisitions budget, but in 1990–91 this was eliminated in favor of integrating electronic purchases into ordinary decision-making on the use of funds. The intention was to promote a focus on collection need regardless of format. Finding funding for the mix of data, equipment, software, and training necessary to realize the promise of new electronic resources is straining not only library dollars but also traditional library budgeting.

This account of automation in the University Libraries ends very much *in medias res*. What computer technology has done for Notre Dame—in facilitating operations, making more accessible the contents of collections, expanding resources, enabling the sharing of resources with other libraries—it will continue to do, in more and better ways. The questions technology poses—how to apply it effectively, how to understand its complexities, how to predict and control its effects—will continue to trouble the libraries for some time to come.

---

1. AR, Circulation Department, 1939–40. Statistics, accounts of events, etc., not otherwise attributed can be assumed to be based on the annual report of the director of libraries for the years mentioned.

2. AR, Circulation Department, 1958–59, 7.

3. AR, Assistant Director for Technical Services, 1963–64, 4–5.

4. AR, Assistant Director for Technical Services, 1966–67, 6.

5. AR, Assistant Director for Technical Services, 1963–64, 4.

6. Ibid., 5.

7. AR, 1971–72, 5.

8. "Minutes, Task Force on the Improvement of Technical Services, February 6, 1974," (ULND, 1974).

9. "Report, Task Force on the Improvement of Technical Services," (ULND [1974]), 3.

10. Robert J. Havlik, "Final Report on the Project 'Introduction of the Library Automation Program of the Indiana Cooperative Library Services Authority in the Cataloging Department of the University Libraries'," (ULND, July 6, 1977), 4–6.

11. Ibid., 1.

12. AR, Assistant Director for Technical Services, 1975–76, 2.

13. AR, Public Services Division, 1978–79, 3.

14. AR, Acquisitions Department, 1975–76, 3.

15. James G. Neal, "Bibliographic Control and Access in the University of Notre Dame Libraries; AACR-2 and the Future of the Card Catalog," (ULND, May 25, 1979), 4–15.

16. AR, Assistant Director for Technical Services, 1977–78, 3.

17. Robert C. Miller, "Five Year Development Program, 1980–84," (ULND, 1980), 2, 6.

18. Miller, "Five Year Development Plan, 1983–88," (ULND, 1983), 9.

19. "Needs Assessment Summary and Five Year Automation Plan," (ULND, [1982]), 5.

20. Association of Research Libraries, Office of Management Studies, "SPEC Kit, #90" (Washington, D.C., ARL, 1983), 81–86.

21. AR, 1983–84, 5.

22. AR, Assistant Director for Automation, 1983–84, 2.

23. Raymond DeBuse, "Biblio-Techniques, Inc.: The Promise That Was BLIS," *Library Hi Tech* Issue 19 (Fall 1987): 44.

24. Maureen Gleason, "University Libraries Surveyed," *Access* no.36 (December 1988): 1, 5.

25. AR, 1990–91, 3.

26. AR, Assistant Director for Systems and Administrative Services, 1991–92, 3.

27. AR, Assistant Director for Collections and Technical Services, 1990–91, 18.

28. AR, Access Services Department, 1989–90, 6.

29. AR, Acquisitions Department, 1989–90, [1].

30. AR, Assistant Director for Systems and Administrative Services, 1988–89, [7].

31. AR, Assistant Director for Public Services, 1980–81, 2.

32. AR, Chemistry-Physics Library, 1985–86, 3.

33. AR, Database Coordinator, 1986–87, 3.

34. AR, 1988–89, 6.

35. AR, Reference Department, 1990–91, 3.

The University Libraries and Notre Dame: A Chronology

ROBERT C. MILLER

The Collegiate Years, 1842–1916

1842

- The University of Notre Dame du Lac founded.

1865

- Instruction in science begins.

1869

- Mention of a "college library" with 7,000 volumes.
- Instruction in law begins.

1873

- A central circulating library for students established in the Main Building at the initiative of the President, the Rev. Augustus Lemonnier, C.S.C.
- Instruction in engineering begins.

1874

- Jimmie Edwards named first librarian of Notre Dame's circulating library.

1879

- (April 23)—The Great Fire! The Main Building is destroyed along with all but 500 books in the library.
- The Rebirth—the Main Building is rebuilt and a library opens in September.

1882

- The "Fathers" or College library merged with the students' circulating library.
- First formal library budget—$500.
- 16,000 volumes in the library.

1883

- William J. Hoynes appointed first dean of law.
- Library becomes a depository for U.S. government documents.

1884

- Science Hall, with a separate library, opens.

1885

- 25,000 volumes in the library.

1886
- First telephone in the library.
- First electric lights in the library.

1888
- A new library on the third floor of the Main Building opens.

1893
- Hibernian library acquired from the Columbian Exhibition.

1898
- A college of architecture established.

1900
- 52,000 volumes in the library.

1907
- First professional librarian, Florence Espy, hired to catalog the library.
- Orestes A. Brownson library purchased.

1909
- *The American Midland Naturalist* begins publication and is subsequently used as a basis for exchange programs with universities and research agencies throughout the world.

1910
- 60,000 volumes in the library.

1911
- Death of Jimmie Edwards.

1912
- Rev. Paul J. Foik, C.S.C., appointed librarian.

1913
- Instruction in business begins.

1914
- Separate law library established.

1915
- Edward L. Greene collection of historic botany acquired.

A University Library, 1917–1962

1917
- (June 10)—a new separate library building dedicated.
- Manual Labor Training School closes.

1918
- First summer school program.
- First library science courses.
- First graduate courses.

1919
- Hoynes College of Law dedicated.

1920
- 103,000 volumes in the library.
- Survey of the library conducted by Frank Walter of the University of Minnesota.

- Administrative reorganization of the University into Colleges of Arts and Letters, Science, and Engineering.

1921
- College of Foreign and Domestic Commerce established.
- John A. Zahm Dante collection acquired.
- Committee on Graduate Studies reactivated.

1924
- Rev. Lawrence V. Broughall, C.S.C., serves as librarian.
- Paul R. Byrne named librarian.

- Hiring of Marie Lawrence who would remain in active employment in the library in various capacities until her final retirement in 1984.

1928
- Lobund Laboratory for germ-free research established.
- First photocopy machine in the library.

1929
- Reclassification of collections from Dewey to Library of Congress system.
- Rev. Thomas T. McAvoy, C.S.C., appointed archivist.

1930
- New Law School building, with library, opened.
- 143,000 volumes in the library.

1932
- Graduate School established.
- Capt. Francis P. O'Neill collection of Irish music acquired.

1933
- Corbett endowment for medieval studies established.
- First separate engineering library opened in Cushing Hall.

1935
- First wind tunnel on campus opened.

1938
- First electric charging machine acquired for library circulation.
- Separate biology library opened in Wenninger-Kirsch (now Haggar) Hall.

1939
- *Review of Politics* started by Waldemar Gurian.

1940
- 195,000 volumes in the library.

1945
- First microfilm reader acquired.

1946
- Medieval Institute, with separate library, established.

1947
- Faculty Library Committee established.
- Notre Dame Foundation, the first formal and continuing University fundraising program, established.

1948
- University of Notre Dame Press established.

1950
- 263,000 volumes in the library.
- External review of the library conducted by Louis R. Wilson and Frank A. Lundy.

1952
- Paul R. Byrne retires as director of libraries.
- Victor Schaefer appointed director of libraries.

1953
- Library science program closed.
- Library joins Midwest Inter-Library Center (later, Center for Research Libraries) as a founding member.
- Nieuwland science library for chemistry, physics and mathematics opened.
- Frank Long hired as first science librarian.

1954
- Anson Phelps-Stokes collection of medieval studies acquired.

1955

- International Documentation Center established.

1957

- Administration of the Law Library transferred to the Law School.
- First installment of the Walter Trohan collection of literature and history received.

1959

- President Theodore M. Hesburgh, C.S.C., announces plans for a new library building.
- Notre Dame Library Association (later, Friends of the Library at Notre Dame) established.

1960

- First major University capital campaign, occasioned by a Ford Foundation Challenge Grant, begun.
- 550,074 volumes in the library.

1961

- Ground-breaking for the new library, designated the Memorial Library.
- First of the John Bennett Shaw collection (literature and bibliography) acquired.
- Francis Lazenby appointed first assistant director.

1962

- The Freshman Year Program, a distinctive feature of undergraduate education at Notre Dame, established.
- Mathematics and Computer Science library opened.

A Research Library, 1963–1975

1963

- Notre Dame admitted to the Association for Research Libraries.
- Radiation Laboratory established.
- Memorial Library, with subject-based services and separate undergraduate and research collections, opened.
- Radiation Laboratory library opened.
- Architecture library opens in old main library building.
- First experiments with an automated circulation system.

1964

- Frank Clark hired as library microfilmer.

- Closed Index Collection abolished.
- Jeremiah D.M. Ford collection of Romance language and literature received.

1965

- Advisory Council for University Libraries established.

1966

- Victor Schaefer takes a leave of absence as director of the library.
- Rev. James Simonson, C.S.C., appointed director of the library.

1967

- First university press approval program begun.
- Governance of the University transferred to a lay board.

1968

- International Sports and Games Research Collection established.
- Library of Jose Caparo, on history of science and engineering and Spanish-American history and geography, purchased.

1969

- Lester Olson Library on Franklin D. Roosevelt received.

1970

- Life sciences library opened in Galvin Life Science Center.
- One-millionth volume added (1,012,578 volumes reported).

1971

- Plans for proposed merger with Saint Mary's College collapse.
- Jarry Collection (theology) acquired.
- David Sparks appointed director of libraries.

1972

- Subject divisional arrangement of collections and services in Memorial Library ended.
- Hackenbruch collection of historic newspapers acquired.
- Women admitted to the undergraduate program.

1973

- Binding procedures automated.
- William Bacon Stevens collection (theology) purchased.
- Report of Committee on University Priorities (COUP) issued.

1974

- Susan Baldwin appointed first systems librarian.

1975

- Africana library of the Center for Applied Research in the Apostolate (CARA) acquired.
- Goldfadden sports collection acquired.

Technology and the Research Library, 1976–

1976

- The University Libraries join the Indiana Cooperative Library Services Authority (INCOLSA) and begin using Ohio College Library Center (OCLC) for online cataloging.
- First formal library instruction position established.

1977

- Howard and Evangeline Phalin Endowment, the first formal endowed University Library Collection, dedicated.

1978

- Locally developed processing control system (ACQUIS) introduced.
- Robert C. Miller appointed director of libraries.
- NEH challenge grant of $400,000 received for retrospective purchasing in the humanities.
- *Catalogue of Medieval and Renaissance Manuscripts of the University of Notre Dame*, edited by Prof. James Corbett, published.
- Milton Anastos library of Byzantine studies acquired.

- Douglas Woodruff collection (literature and history) purchased.
- Frank Long receives a University Presidential Citation.

1979

- Joseph Huebner appointed as first full-time bibliographer, for the fine arts.
- Map collection transferred to Memorial Library.
- A catalog of incunabula in Memorial Library, edited by Anton Masin, published.
- First general U.S. approval acquisitions program established.
- Notre Dame becomes a member of the Area Library Services Authority 2, a regional library cooperative.

1980

- Canon law library of the Rev. Thomas J. Tobin acquired.
- Database services introduced.
- Collection Development Division established.
- Materials expenditures exceed $1 million for the first time.
- Collection Analysis Project begun.
- Earth sciences library closed, with most collections transferred to Memorial Library.
- Early morning burglary of the Rare Book Room results in $20,000 theft of coins and medals.
- College Library abolished, resulting in a shift of the entire Memorial Library collection.
- First Library Development Plan issued.
- 1,310,918 volumes in the libraries.

1981

- Library acquires first personal computer.

1982

- Lawrence Woods appointed first assistant director for systems.
- New Engineering library opened.
- Helen Kellogg Center for International Studies established.
- John T. Ryan gift for library automation.

1983

- PACE (Priorities and Commitments to Excellence) Report issued.

1984

- Institute for Scholarship in the Liberal Arts established.
- Conway collection on Edward Gorey received.

1985

- First HEA IIC grant, for cataloging and preservation of the Greene Collection, received.
- Roger Jacobs appointed law librarian.
- Libraries begin collecting videos.

1986

- 1,546,048 volumes in the libraries.
- The NOTIS automated library system acquired; initial installation begins.

1987

- Final Report of the University Task Force on Computing.
- Use of electronic mail begun within the libraries.
- Memorial Library renamed for President Emeritus Theodore M. Hesburgh, C.S.C.
- The endowed Edmund P. Joyce, C.S.C., Sports Research Collection established.
- First CD-ROM product.

- Libraries' card catalog closed (no more cards filed).
- First public access to UNLOC (University of Notre Dame Libraries' Online Catalog).
- Indiana's State University Library Automation Network (SULAN) established with Notre Dame as a charter member.

1988

- External review of the University Libraries conducted under the auspices of the Graduate Council.
- The "Great Bar-Coding Project," in connection with the pending automated circulation system.
- Red Smith sports library acquired and dedicated.
- Niels Rasmussen, O.P.'s library of liturgical works acquired.
- First fax machine in the libraries.

1989

- First formal staff recognition program.
- First library preservation unit established.

1990

- Lilly grant to establish the Michiana Academic Library Consortium, providing a single automated library system for Notre Dame, Saint Mary's College, Holy Cross College and Bethel College, received.
- HEA IIC grant with University Archives, for cataloging of manuscript and archival collections on OCLC, received.
- Penguin Books Collection in honor of Laura K. and Theodore S. Weber, acquired.

1991

- Byrne Fund to support library faculty research established.
- Kellogg Center Reading Room opened.
- NOTIS Multiple Database Access System, incorporating periodical indexes into UNLOC, inaugurated.
- Herbert Marshall collection of Soviet poetry, theater and cinematography, acquired.
- NEH preservation grant, for microfilming of portions of the Medieval Institute Library, received.
- Chicago Bar Association Library acquired for the Law Library.
- Early Irish Map collections received from Thomas McGrath.
- Paul J. Foik, C.S.C., award for library faculty established, with Maureen Gleason as first recipient.

1992

- Sue Dietl receives a University Presidential Citation.

1993

- Kickoff of the Two Million and 30 Reasons to Celebrate program with a Friends of the Library dinner on April 23, including presentation of the Two-Millionth Volume by Astrik L. Gabriel and the Two-Millionth-and-First by the Friends.
- *Colloquy 2000* final report issued.
- The Astrik L. Gabriel Collection of Early Printed Books transferred to the University Libraries.
- *UNCOVER*, online contents service, introduced.
- Notre Dame sports materials transferred to the University Archives.

Bibliography

Byrne, Paul. "The Library of the University of Notre Dame." *The Catholic Bookman* I:1 (September 1937): 44–46, 50.

Federowicz, John, C.S.C. "Forces Affecting the Development of Libraries at the University of Notre Dame, 1843–1968." Master's thesis, Kent State University, 1968.

Hope, Rev. Arthur J. *Notre Dame, One Hundred Years*. South Bend: Icarus Press, 1978 (c1948).

Moore, Philip S. *Academic Development, University of Notre Dame: Past, Present and Future*. Notre Dame: University of Notre Dame, 1960.

Schlereth, Thomas. *The University of Notre Dame: A Portrait of its History and Campus*. Notre Dame: University of Notre Dame Press, 1977.

Schmuhl, Robert. *The University of Notre Dame, a Contemporary Portrait*. Notre Dame: University of Notre Dame Press, 1986.

University Libraries, University of Notre Dame. *Annual Reports*. Format varies.

Two Million
and 30
Reasons to

Theodore M.
Hesburgh
Library

C E L E B R A T E !

1963   1993